A Fantasy

by Bryan Talbot

DARK HORSE BOOKS

For Robyn

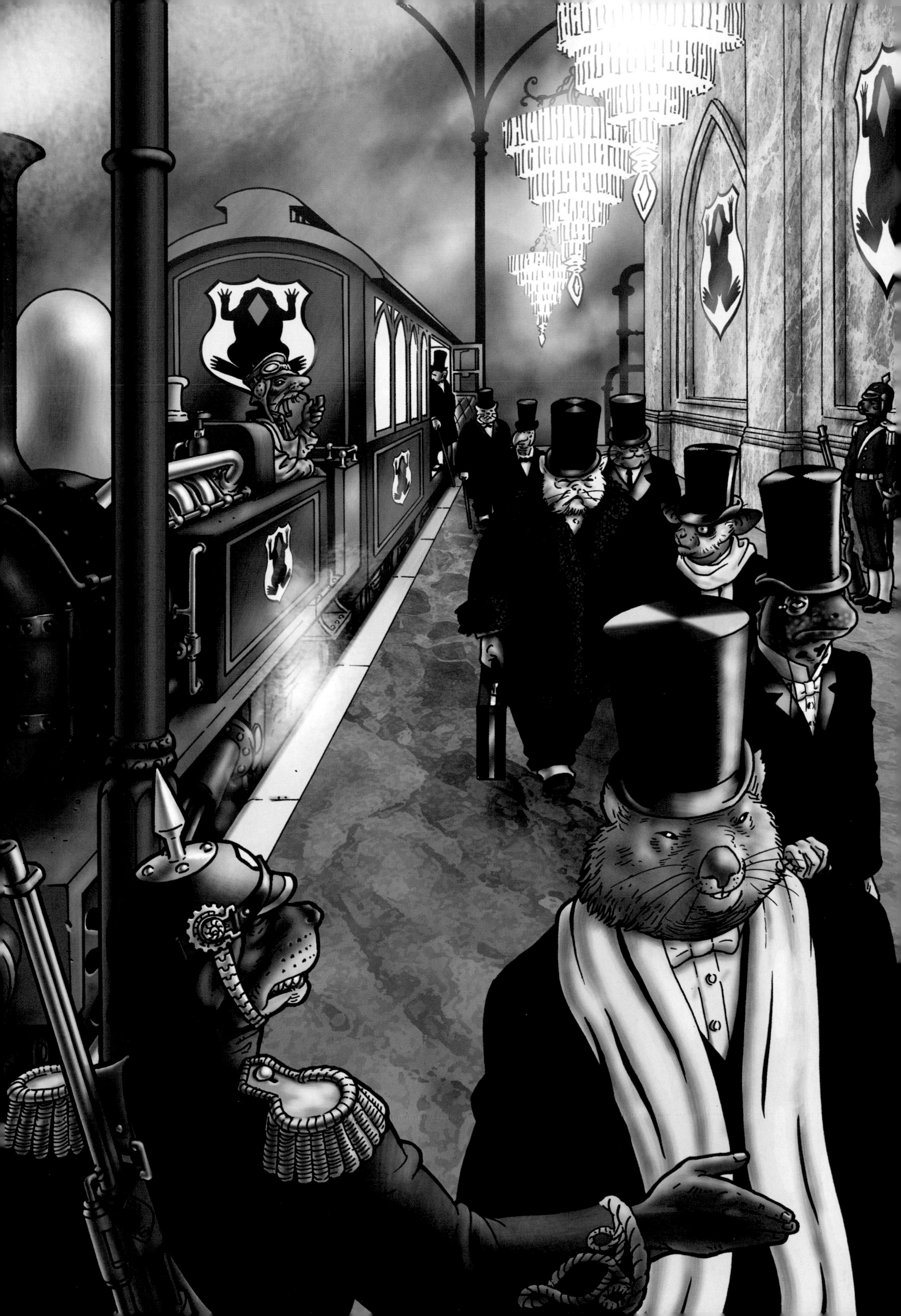

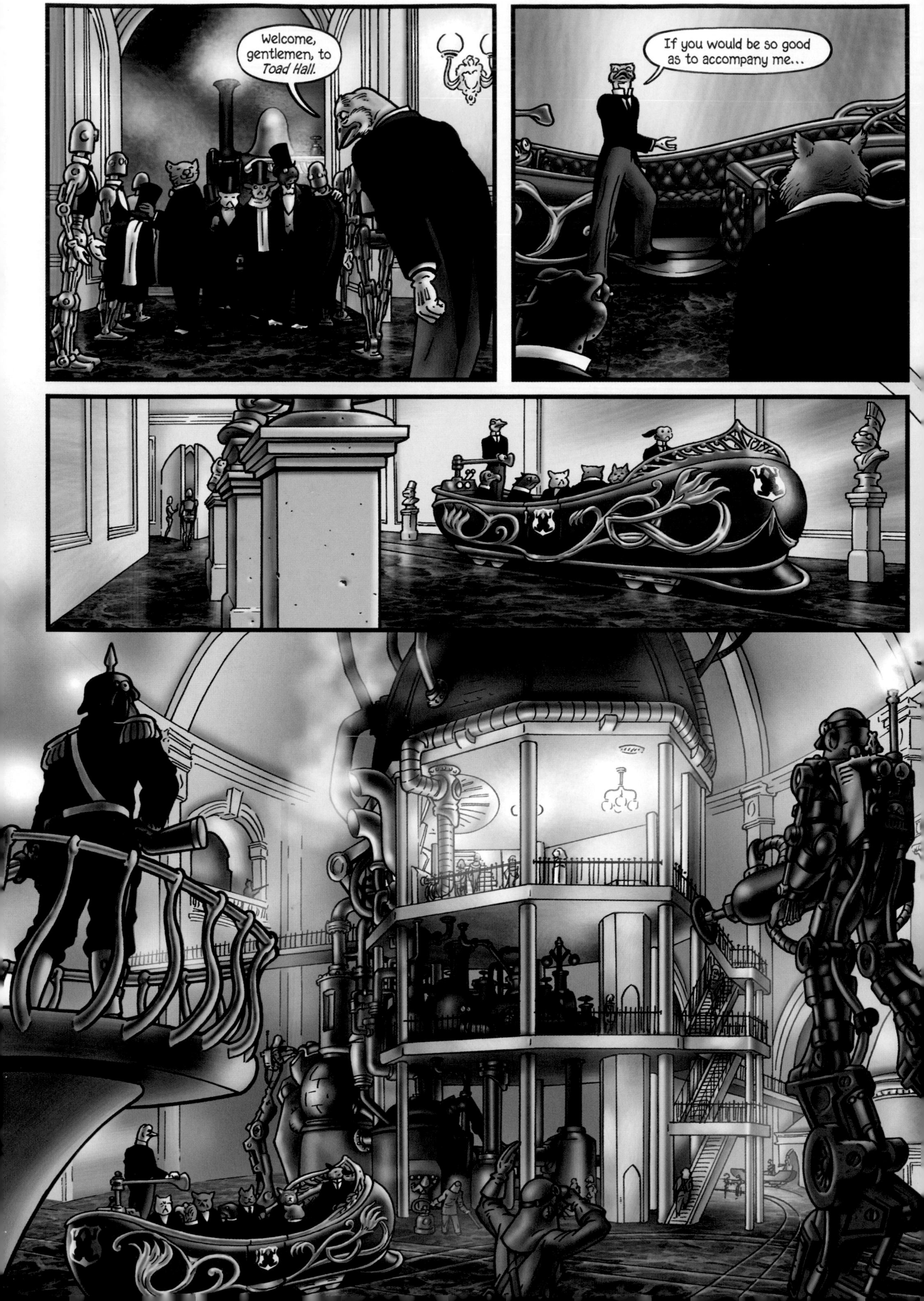
Welcome, gentlemen, to *Toad Hall.*
If you would be so good as to accompany me...

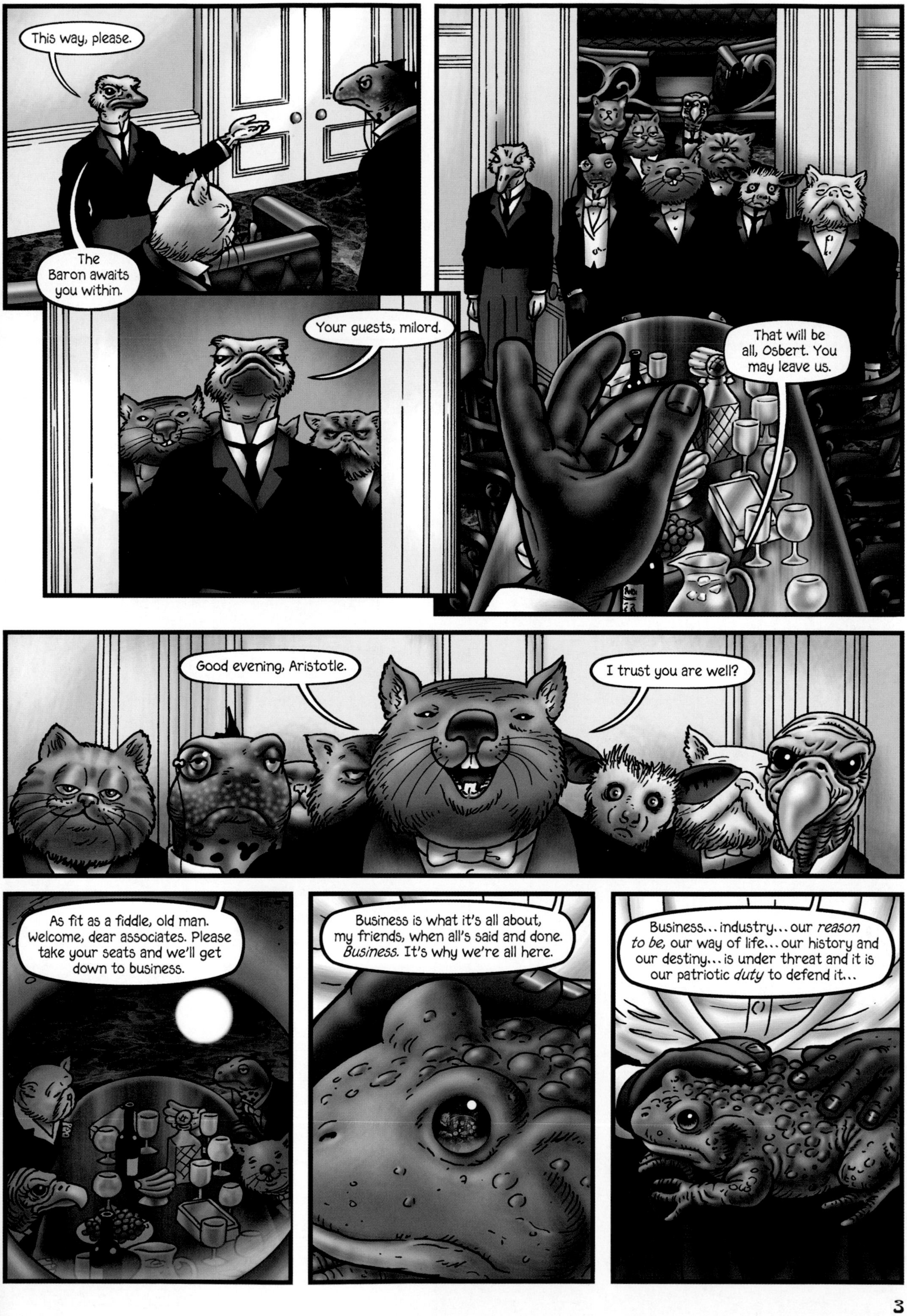
This way, please.
The Baron awaits you within.
Your guests, milord.
That will be all, Osbert. You may leave us.
Good evening, Aristotle.
I trust you are well?
As fit as a fiddle, old man. Welcome, dear associates. Please take your seats and we'll get down to business.
Business is what it's all about, my friends, when all's said and done. *Business.* It's why we're all here.
Business... industry... our *reason to be,* our way of life... our history and our destiny... is under threat and it is our patriotic *duty* to defend it...

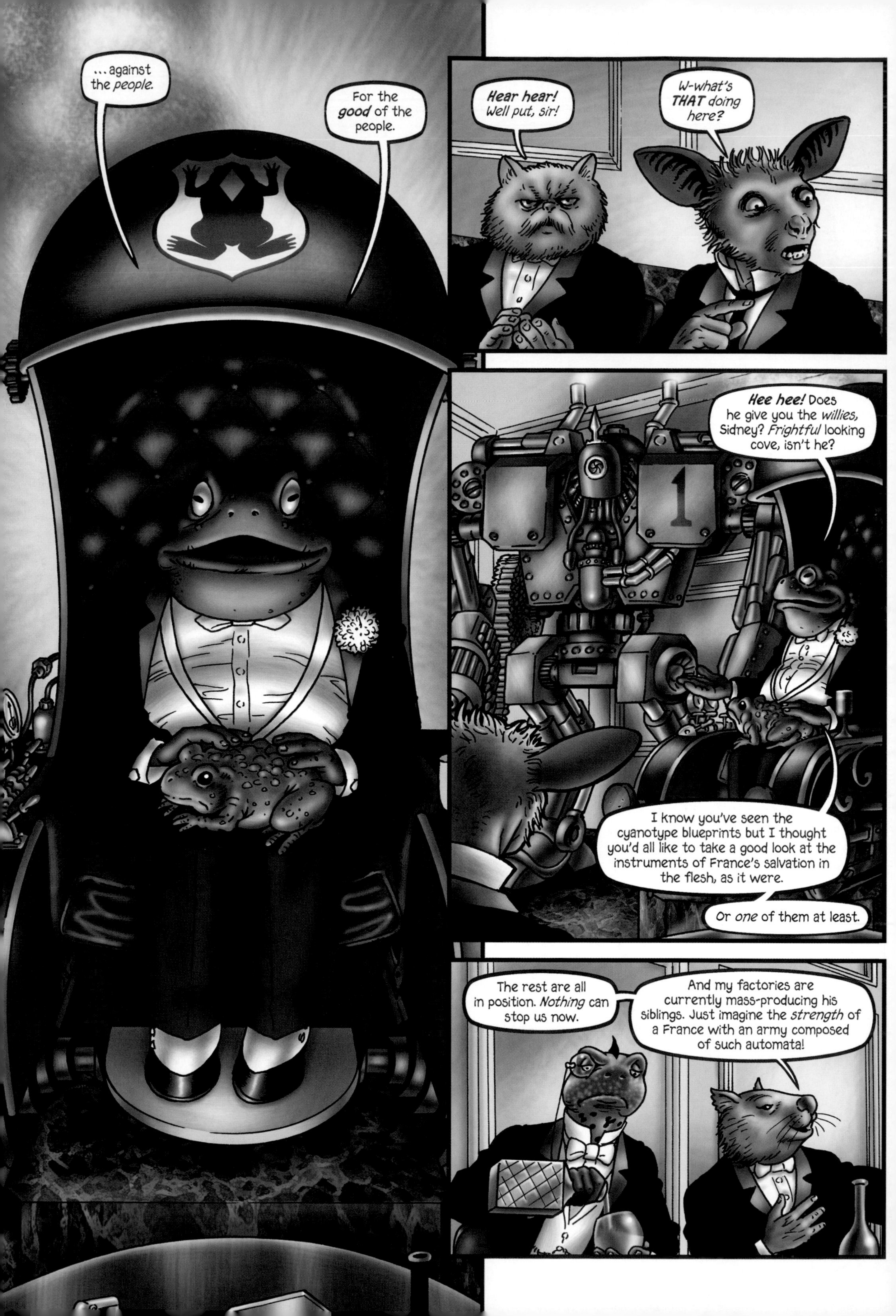

...against the *people.*
For the **good** of the people.
Hear hear! *Well put, sir!*
W-what's ***THAT*** *doing here?*
Hee hee! Does he give you the *willies,* Sidney? *Frightful* looking cove, isn't he?
1
I know you've seen the cyanotype blueprints but I thought you'd all like to take a good look at the instruments of France's salvation in the flesh, as it were.
Or *one* of them at least.
The rest are all in position. *Nothing* can stop us now.
And my factories are currently mass-producing his siblings. Just imagine the *strength* of a France with an army composed of such automata!

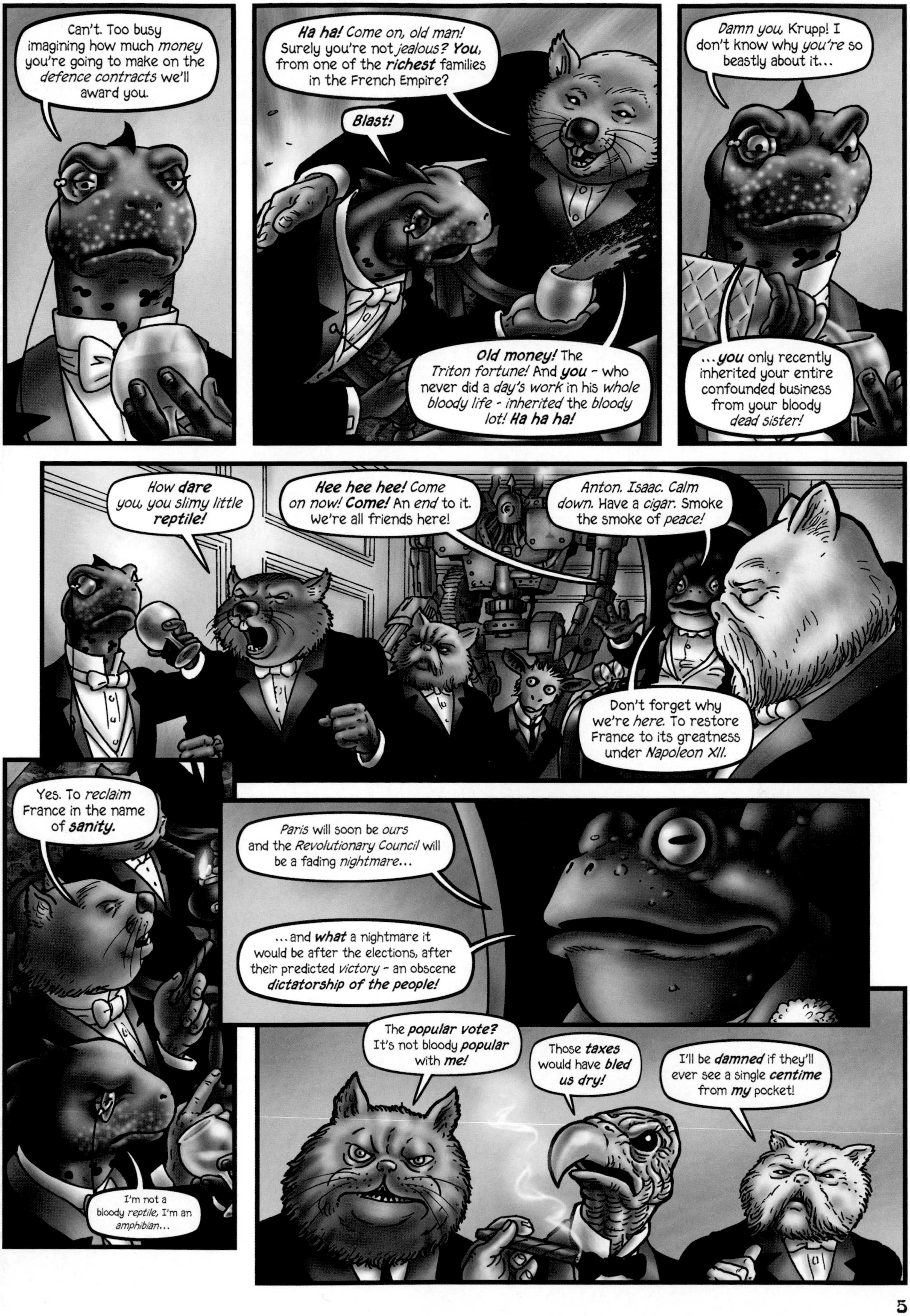
Can't. Too busy imagining how much *money* you're going to make on the *defence contracts* we'll award you.
Ha ha! *Come on, old man!* Surely you're not *jealous?* ***You,*** from one of the ***richest*** families in the French Empire?
Blast!
Old money! The *Triton fortune!* And ***you*** - who never did a *day's work* in his *whole bloody life* - *inherited* the bloody lot! ***Ha ha ha!***
Damn you, Krupp! I don't know why *you're* so beastly about it...
...***you*** only recently inherited your entire confounded business from your bloody *dead sister!*
How ***dare*** *you, you slimy little* ***reptile!***
Hee hee hee! Come on now! ***Come!*** An *end* to it. We're all friends here!
Anton. Isaac. Calm down. Have a *cigar.* Smoke the smoke of *peace!*
Don't forget why we're *here.* To restore France to its greatness under *Napoleon XII.*
Yes. To *reclaim* France in the name of ***sanity.***
I'm not a bloody *reptile,* I'm an *amphibian...*
Paris will soon be *ours* and the *Revolutionary Council* will be a fading *nightmare...*
...and ***what*** a nightmare it would be after the elections, after their predicted *victory* - an obscene ***dictatorship of the people!***
The ***popular vote?*** It's not bloody ***popular*** with ***me!***
Those ***taxes*** would have ***bled us dry!***
I'll be ***damned*** if they'll ever see a single ***centime*** from ***my*** pocket!

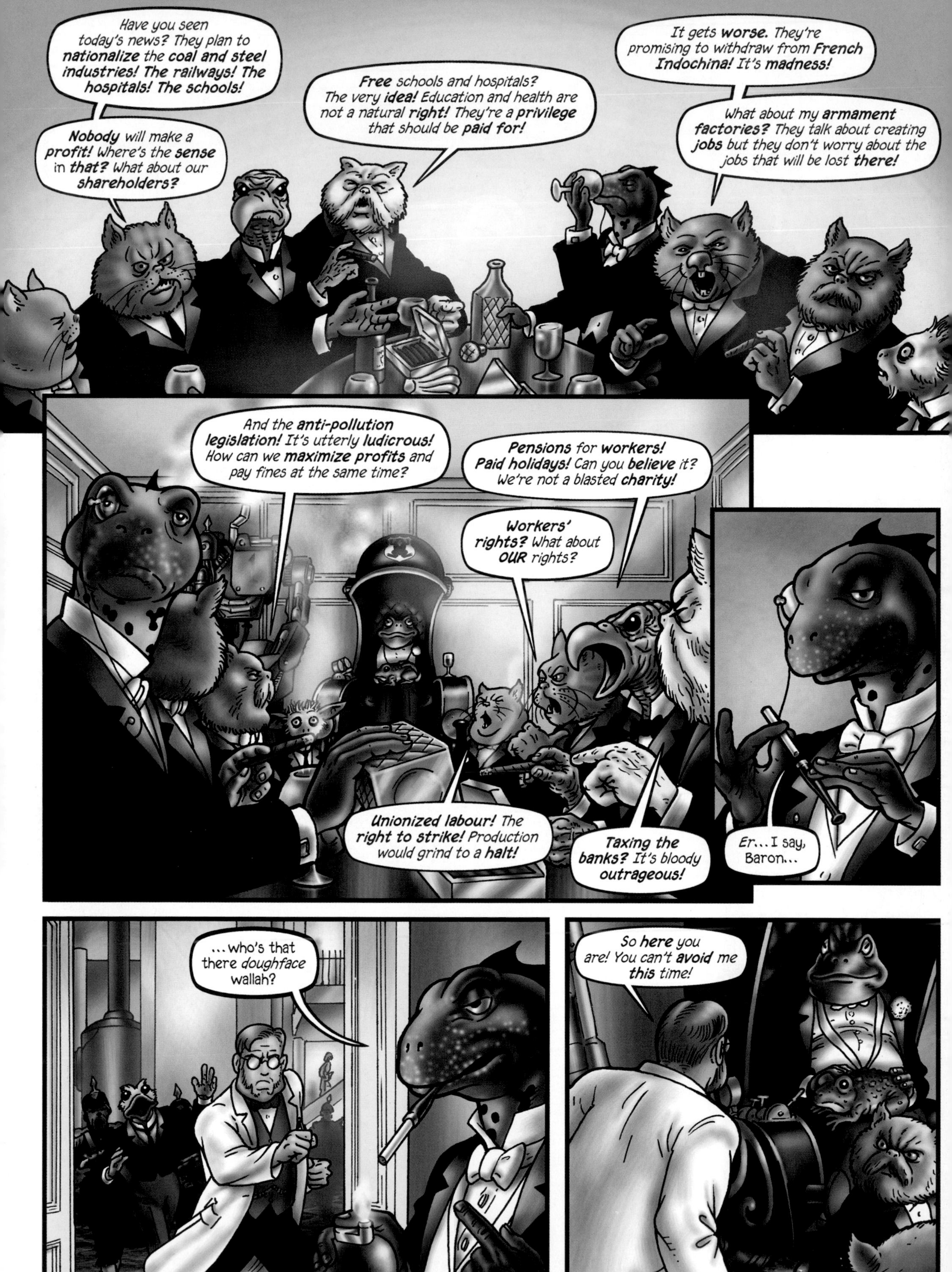
Have you seen today's news? They plan to nationalize the coal and steel industries! The railways! The hospitals! The schools!
Nobody will make a profit! Where's the sense in that? What about our shareholders?
Free schools and hospitals? The very idea! Education and health are not a natural right! They're a privilege that should be paid for!
It gets worse. They're promising to withdraw from French Indochina! It's madness!
What about my armament factories? They talk about creating jobs but they don't worry about the jobs that will be lost there!
And the anti-pollution legislation! It's utterly ludicrous! How can we maximize profits and pay fines at the same time?
Pensions for workers! Paid holidays! Can you believe it? We're not a blasted charity!
Workers' rights? What about OUR rights?
Unionized labour! The right to strike! Production would grind to a halt!
Taxing the banks? It's bloody outrageous!
Er... I say, Baron...
...who's that there doughface wallah?
So here you are! You can't avoid me this time!

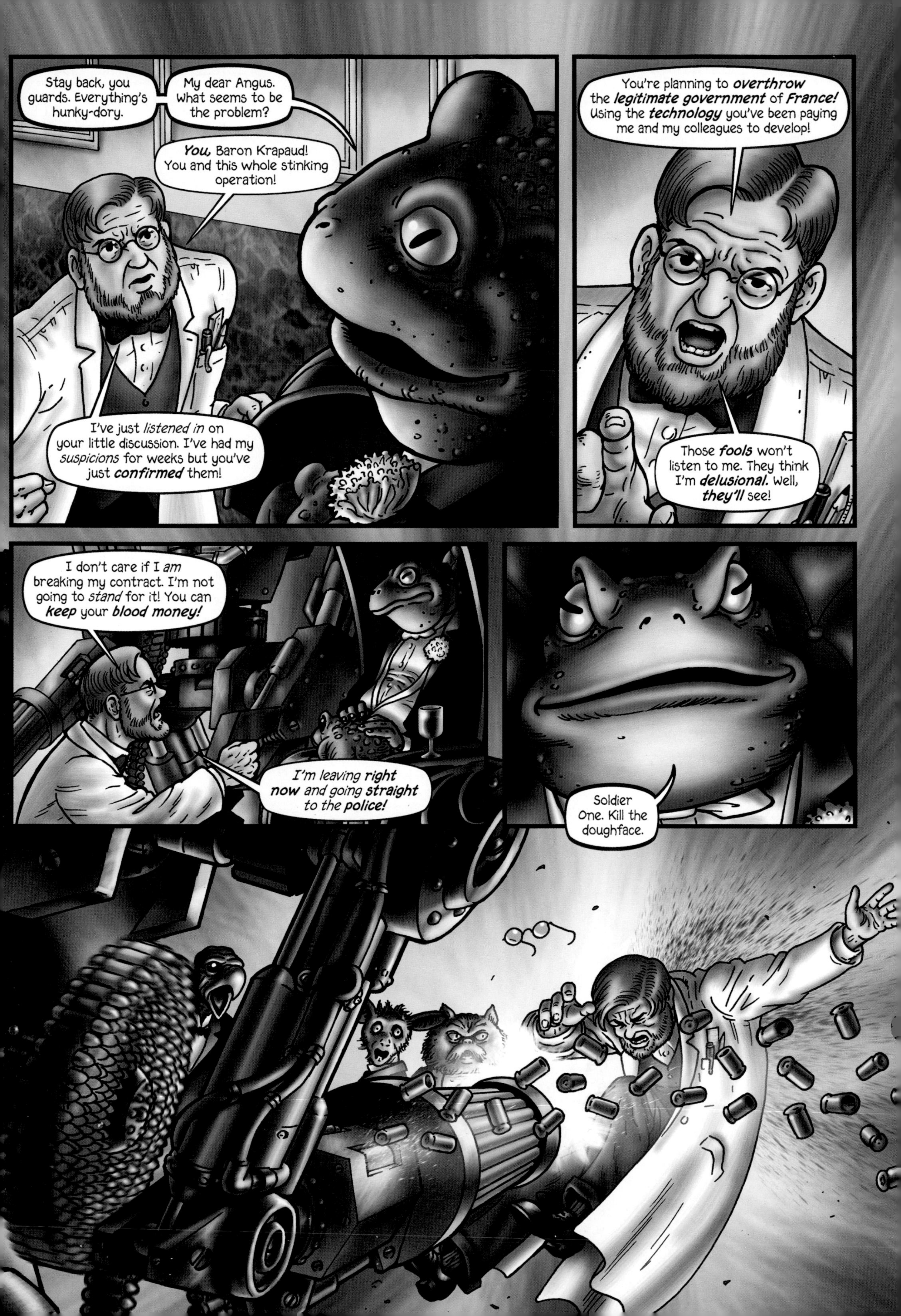
Stay back, you guards. Everything's hunky-dory.
My dear Angus. What seems to be the problem?
You, Baron Krapaud! You and this whole stinking operation!
I've just listened in on your little discussion. I've had my suspicions for weeks but you've just confirmed them!
You're planning to overthrow the legitimate government of France! Using the technology you've been paying me and my colleagues to develop!
Those fools won't listen to me. They think I'm delusional. Well, they'll see!
I don't care if I am breaking my contract. I'm not going to stand for it! You can keep your blood money!
I'm leaving right now and going straight to the police!
Soldier One. Kill the doughface.

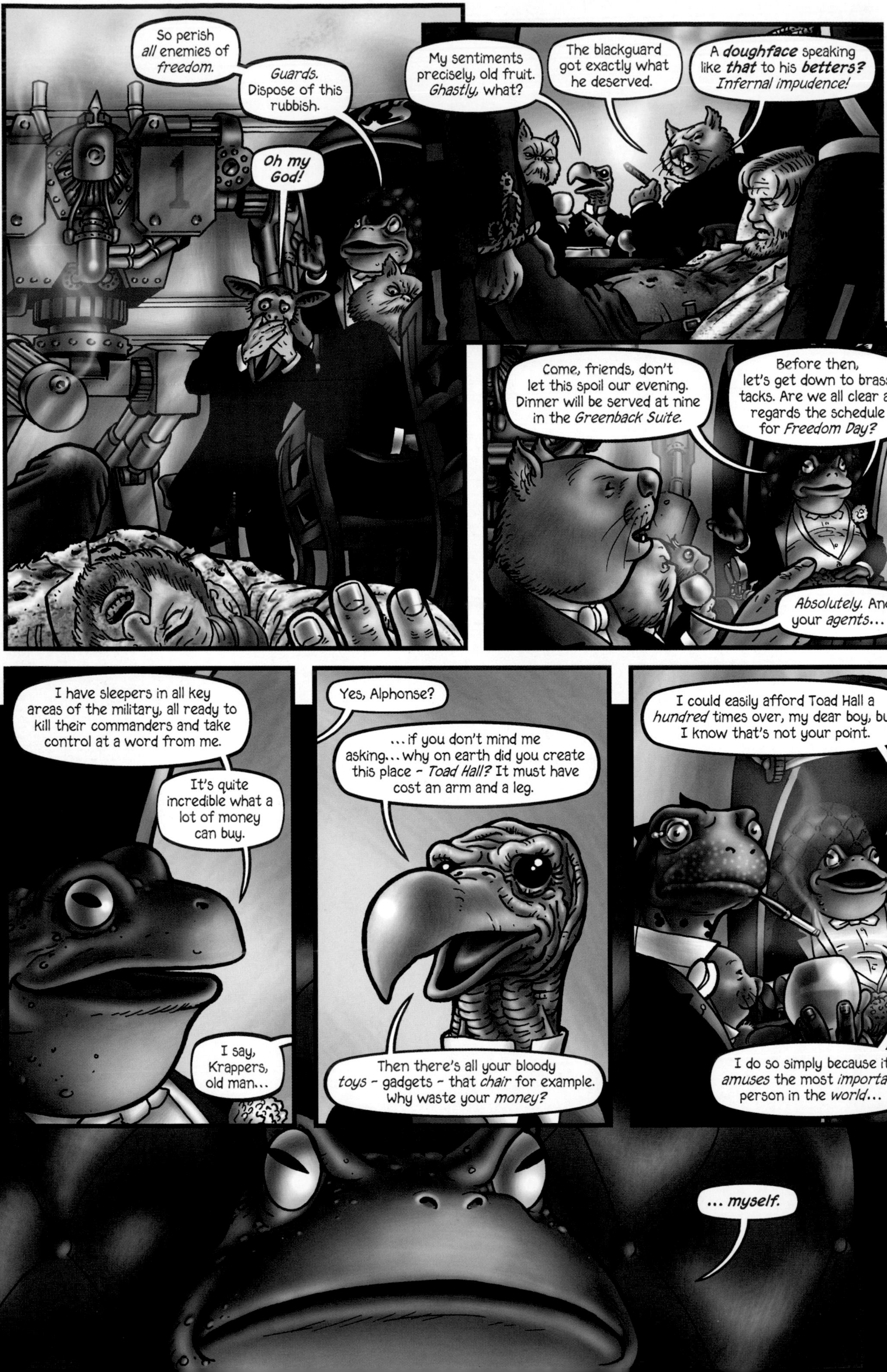

So perish *all* enemies of *freedom.*
Guards. Dispose of this rubbish.
Oh my God!
My sentiments precisely, old fruit. *Ghastly,* what?
The blackguard got exactly what he deserved.
A ***doughface*** speaking like ***that*** to his ***betters?*** *Infernal impudence!*
Come, friends, don't let this spoil our evening. Dinner will be served at nine in the *Greenback Suite.*
Before then, let's get down to brass tacks. Are we all clear as regards the schedule for *Freedom Day?*
Absolutely. And your *agents...?*
I have sleepers in all key areas of the military, all ready to kill their commanders and take control at a word from me.
It's quite incredible what a lot of money can buy.
I say, Krappers, old man...
Yes, Alphonse?
...if you don't mind me asking... why on earth did you create this place - *Toad Hall?* It must have cost an arm and a leg.
Then there's all your bloody *toys* - gadgets - that *chair* for example. Why waste your *money?*
I could easily afford Toad Hall a *hundred* times over, my dear boy, but I know that's not your point.
I do so simply because it *amuses* the most *important* person in the *world...*
...myself.

Grandville
Bête Noire

A Fantasy

by
Bryan Talbot

Script, art & book design: Bryan Talbot

Colouring on pages 11 to 21: Bryan and Alwyn Talbot
Bryan Talbot lettering font produced by Comicraft
Colour flats: Pages 2 - 8, Jesse Kindzierski, pages 11 - 96, Chrissie Harper
French Advisors: Frederic Manzano & Eric Bufkens

Art Nouveau steampunk pattern by Bryan Talbot,
based on the endpapers of "Dampf und Elektricität:
die Technik im Anfange des XX Jahrhunderts."
Berlin: W. Herlet. [c.1900]

Sincere acknowledgements for proof-reading,
comments on the work-in-progress and other important input to
Chaz Brenchley, Eric Bufkens, Dan Franklin, Annie Gullion,
Stephen Holland, Dr Mel Gibson, Lovern Kindzierski,
Dr Mary Talbot and Chris Warner

"Bugger" used by kind permission of Chaz Brenchley

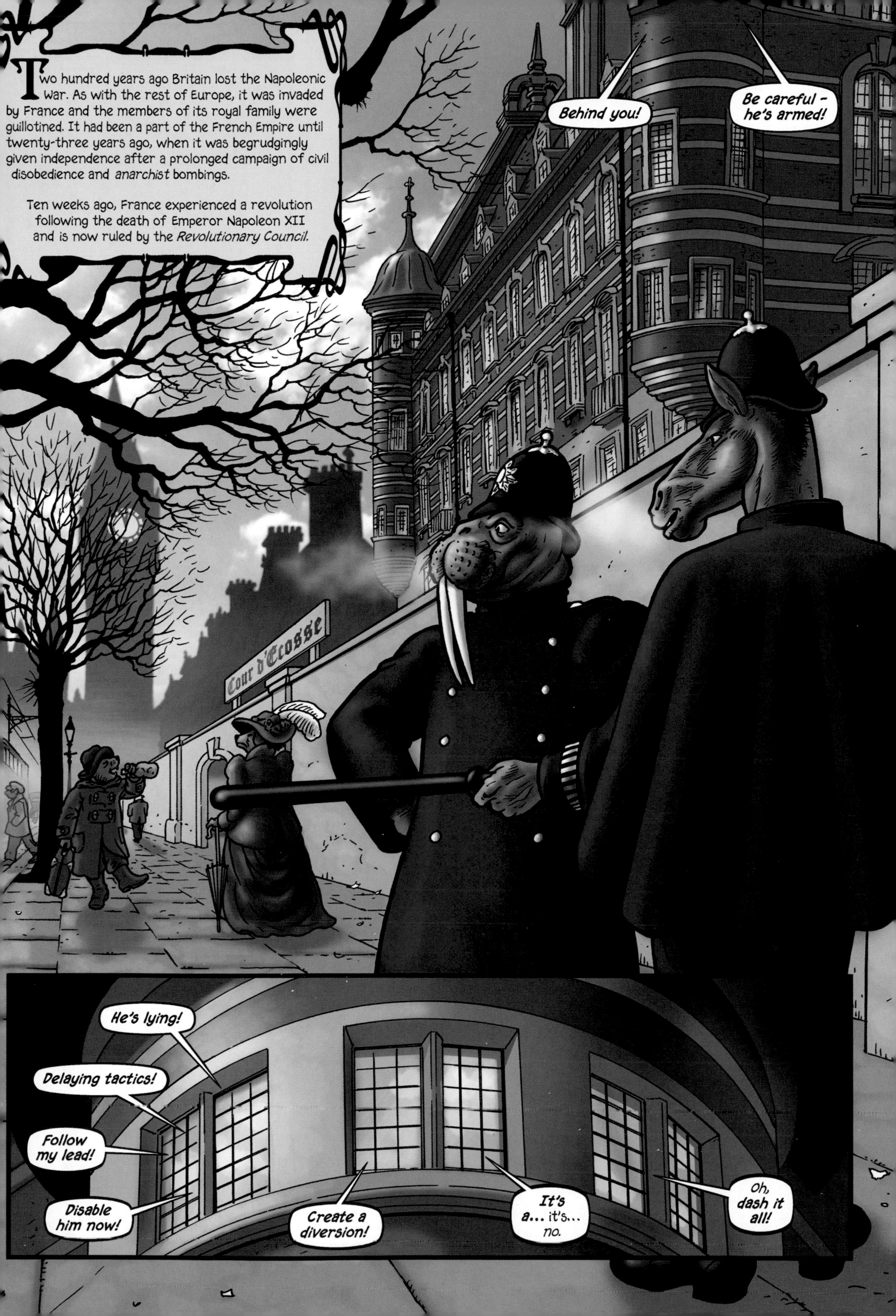
Two hundred years ago Britain lost the Napoleonic War. As with the rest of Europe, it was invaded by France and the members of its royal family were guillotined. It had been a part of the French Empire until twenty-three years ago, when it was begrudgingly given independence after a prolonged campaign of civil disobedience and *anarchist* bombings.
Ten weeks ago, France experienced a revolution following the death of Emperor Napoleon XII and is now ruled by the *Revolutionary Council*.
Behind you!
Be careful - he's armed!
Cour d'Ecosse
He's lying!
Delaying tactics!
Follow my lead!
Disable him now!
Create a diversion!
It's a... it's... no.
Oh, dash it all!

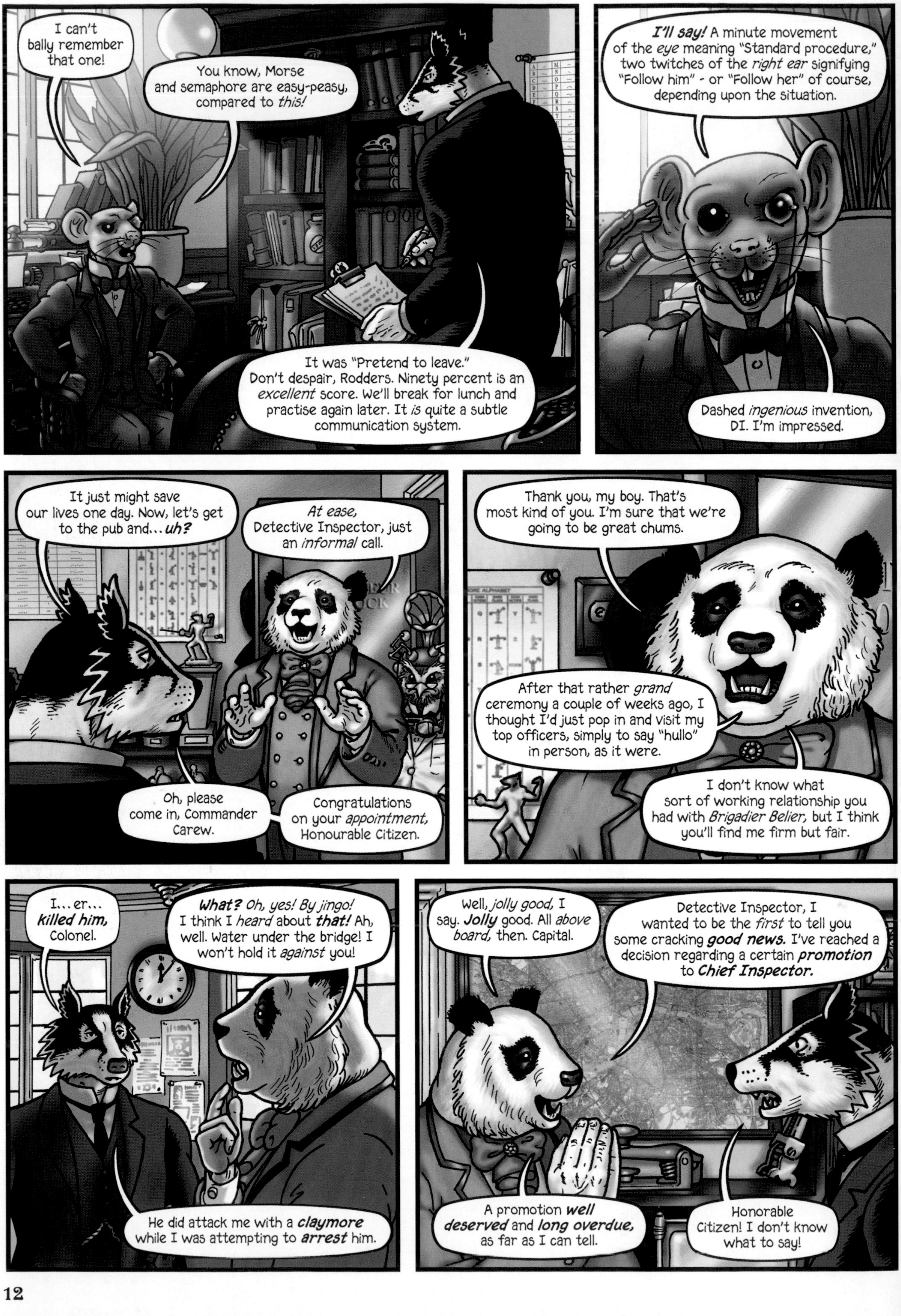

I can't bally remember that one!
You know, Morse and semaphore are easy-peasy, compared to *this!*
It was "Pretend to leave." Don't despair, Rodders. Ninety percent is an *excellent* score. We'll break for lunch and practise again later. It *is* quite a subtle communication system.
I'll say! A minute movement of the *eye* meaning "Standard procedure," two twitches of the *right ear* signifying "Follow him" - or "Follow her" of course, depending upon the situation.
Dashed *ingenious* invention, DI. I'm impressed.
It just might save our lives one day. Now, let's get to the pub and... ***uh?***
At ease, Detective Inspector, just an *informal* call.
Oh, please come in, Commander Carew.
Congratulations on your *appointment,* Honourable Citizen.
Thank you, my boy. That's most kind of you. I'm sure that we're going to be great chums.
After that rather *grand* ceremony a couple of weeks ago, I thought I'd just pop in and visit my top officers, simply to say "hullo" in person, as it were.
I don't know what sort of working relationship you had with *Brigadier Belier,* but I think you'll find me firm but fair.
I... er... ***killed him,*** Colonel.
What? *Oh, yes! By jingo!* I think I *heard* about ***that!*** Ah, well. Water under the bridge! I won't hold it *against* you!
He did attack me with a ***claymore*** while I was attempting to ***arrest*** him.
Well, *jolly good,* I say. ***Jolly*** good. All *above board,* then. Capital.
Detective Inspector, I wanted to be the *first* to tell you some cracking ***good news.*** I've reached a decision regarding a certain ***promotion*** to ***Chief Inspector.***
A promotion ***well deserved*** and ***long overdue,*** as far as I can tell.
Honorable Citizen! I don't know what to say!

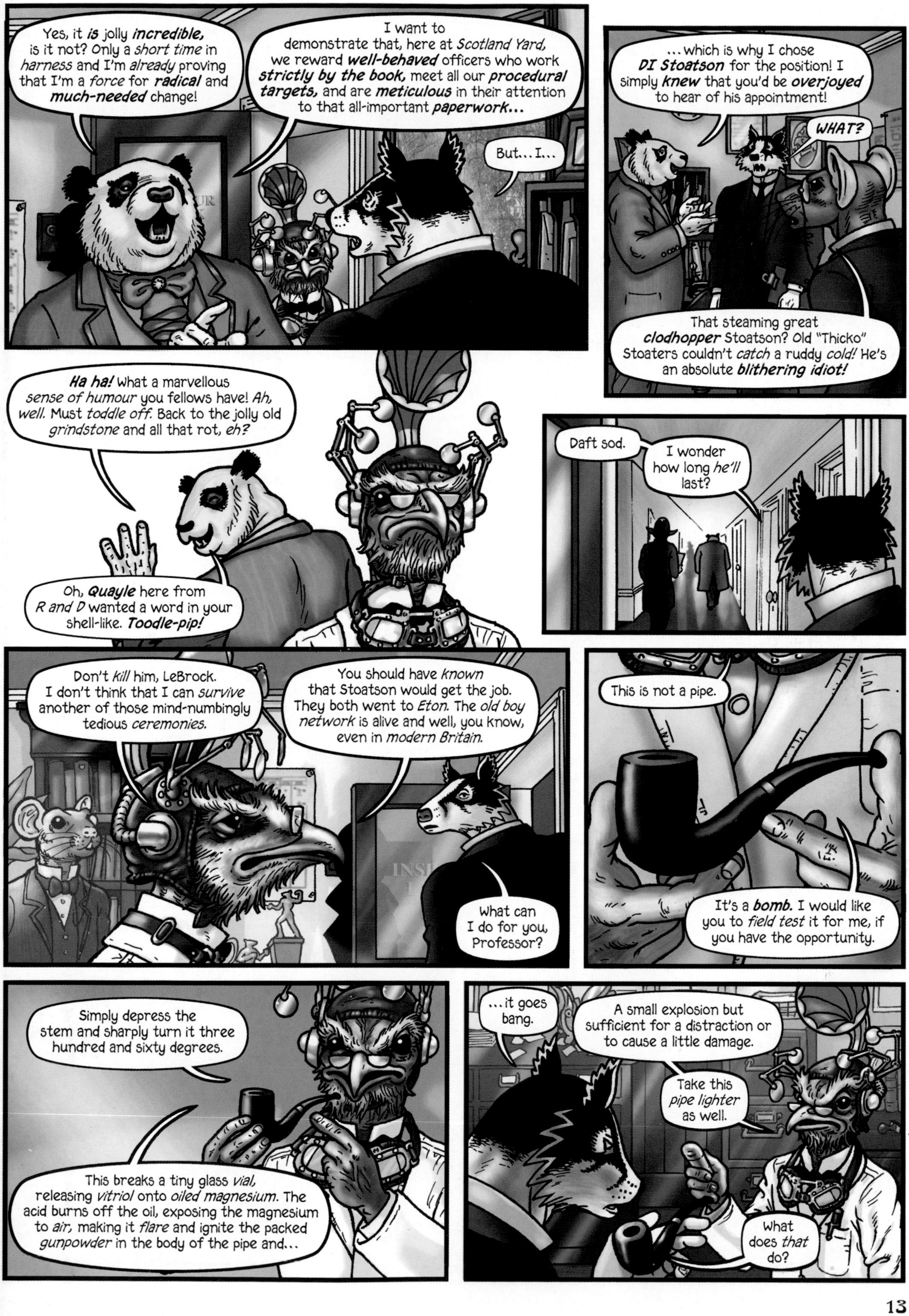
Yes, it *is* jolly *incredible,* is it not? Only a *short time* in *harness* and I'm *already* proving that I'm a *force* for *radical* and *much-needed* change!
I want to demonstrate that, here at *Scotland Yard,* we reward *well-behaved* officers who work *strictly by the book,* meet all our *procedural targets,* and are *meticulous* in their attention to that all-important *paperwork...*
But... I...
...which is why I chose *DI Stoatson* for the position! I simply *knew* that you'd be *overjoyed* to hear of his appointment!
WHAT?
That steaming great *clodhopper* Stoatson? Old "Thicko" Stoaters couldn't *catch* a ruddy *cold!* He's an absolute *blithering idiot!*
Ha ha! What a marvellous *sense of humour* you fellows have! *Ah, well.* Must *toddle off.* Back to the jolly old *grindstone* and all that rot, *eh?*
Oh, *Quayle* here from *R and D* wanted a word in your shell-like. *Toodle-pip!*
Daft sod.
I wonder how long *he'll* last?
Don't *kill* him, LeBrock. I don't think that I can *survive* another of those mind-numbingly tedious *ceremonies.*
You should have *known* that Stoatson would get the job. They both went to *Eton.* The *old boy network* is alive and well, you know, even in *modern Britain.*
What can I do for you, Professor?
This is not a pipe.
It's a *bomb.* I would like you to *field test* it for me, if you have the opportunity.
Simply depress the stem and sharply turn it three hundred and sixty degrees.
This breaks a tiny glass *vial,* releasing *vitriol* onto *oiled magnesium.* The acid burns off the oil, exposing the magnesium to *air,* making it *flare* and ignite the packed *gunpowder* in the body of the pipe and...
...it goes bang.
A small explosion but sufficient for a distraction or to cause a little damage.
Take this *pipe lighter* as well.
What does *that* do?

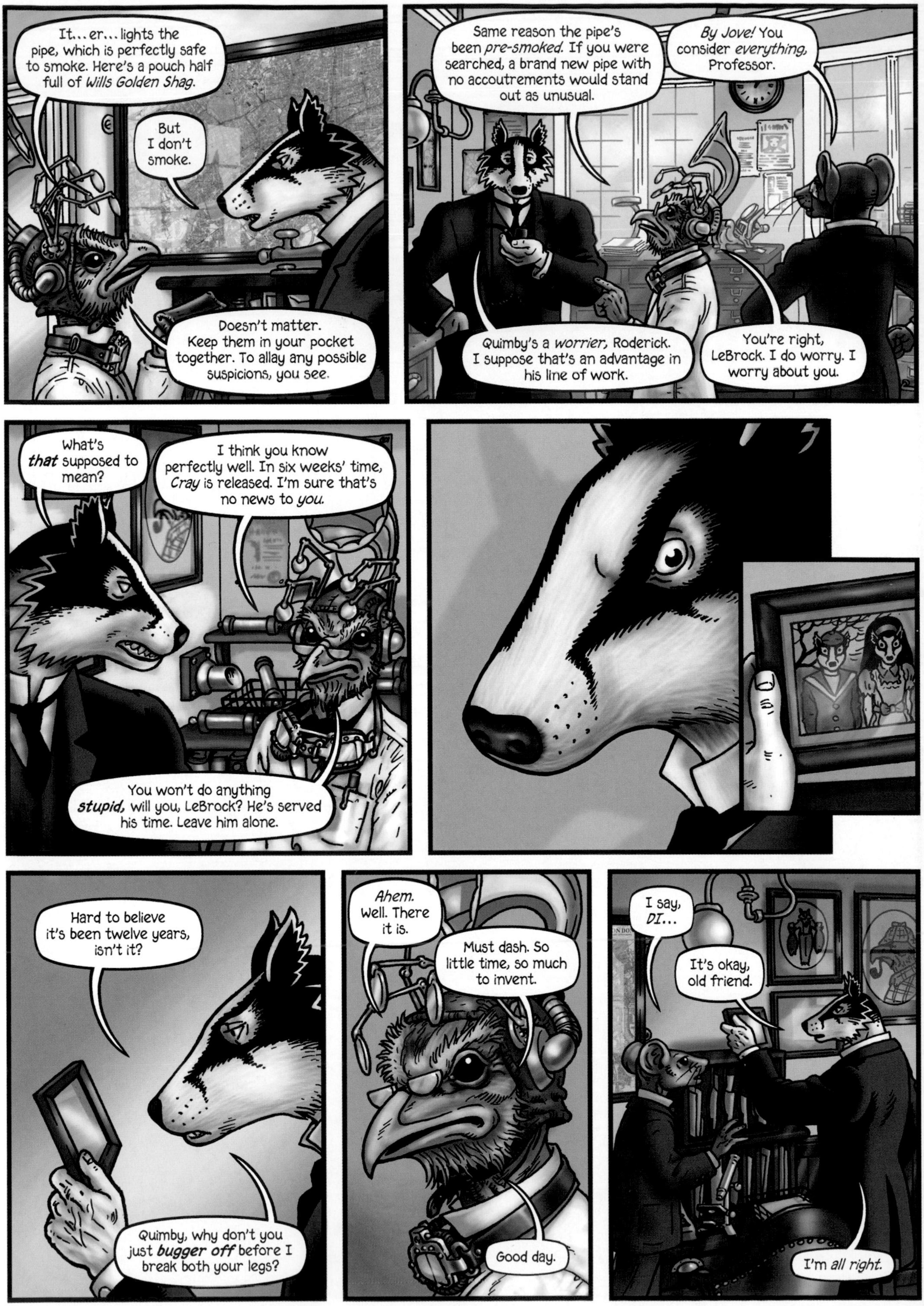
It...er...lights the pipe, which is perfectly safe to smoke. Here's a pouch half full of *Wills Golden Shag*.
But I don't smoke.
Doesn't matter. Keep them in your pocket together. To allay any possible suspicions, you see.
Same reason the pipe's been *pre-smoked*. If you were searched, a brand new pipe with no accoutrements would stand out as unusual.
By Jove! You consider *everything*, Professor.
Quimby's a *worrier*, Roderick. I suppose that's an advantage in his line of work.
You're right, LeBrock. I do worry. I worry about you.
What's ***that*** supposed to mean?
I think you know perfectly well. In six weeks' time, *Cray* is released. I'm sure that's no news to *you*.
You won't do anything ***stupid***, will you, LeBrock? He's served his time. Leave him alone.
Hard to believe it's been twelve years, isn't it?
Quimby, why don't you just ***bugger off*** before I break both your legs?
Ahem. Well. There it is.
Must dash. So little time, so much to invent.
Good day.
I say, *DI*...
It's okay, old friend.
I'm *all right*.

That bloody quail will blow us all to smithereens one day.

What do you think, Roderick? Do I suit a pipe?

I should ruddy say *not!* I don't want you *stinking up* the bally orffice!

'Scuse me, guv. Your door was open.

There's a *gentleman* as wants to see you. 'Ere's 'is callin' card.

Hm? *French,* is he?

Cripes, guv! 'Ow did you know that?

Because you pronounced "gentleman" in that peculiar *tone* you always use when mentioning *anything* to do with *France.*

Eh? I – I jus' remember the *occupation* is all, guv. I was in the *Resistance,* like.

So was I. Show him in, Bert.

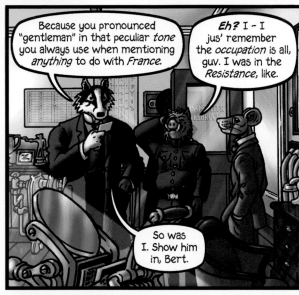

It is. My friends, I need your advice...on a *murder case.* The *Security Brigade* is completely *stumped!*

The deceased is a famous and popular *artist* – the painter and designer *Gustave Corbeau* - and the newspapers and CNN are *screaming* for justice. How can I *admit* to them that we don't have one single lead? Hence this secret visit.

Can you help me?

Give us the details.

Who the deuce is he?

Chief Inspector Rocher of the *Paris Prefecture,* unless I'm very much mistaken.

But this says *"Mister A. Procyon Esq."*

"Procyon" is the raccoon genus.

Smell the card. It's Rocher all right. That distinctive blend of John Paul Gautier cologne, "Gipsy Woman" pipe tobacco, new leather gloves and...

...*garlic!* Don't forget the garlic! Good to see you, Archie. You too, Roderick.

My dear Jules! What brings you to London?

And why the *subterfuge?* If you're travelling *incognito,* this is obviously an *unofficial* visit.

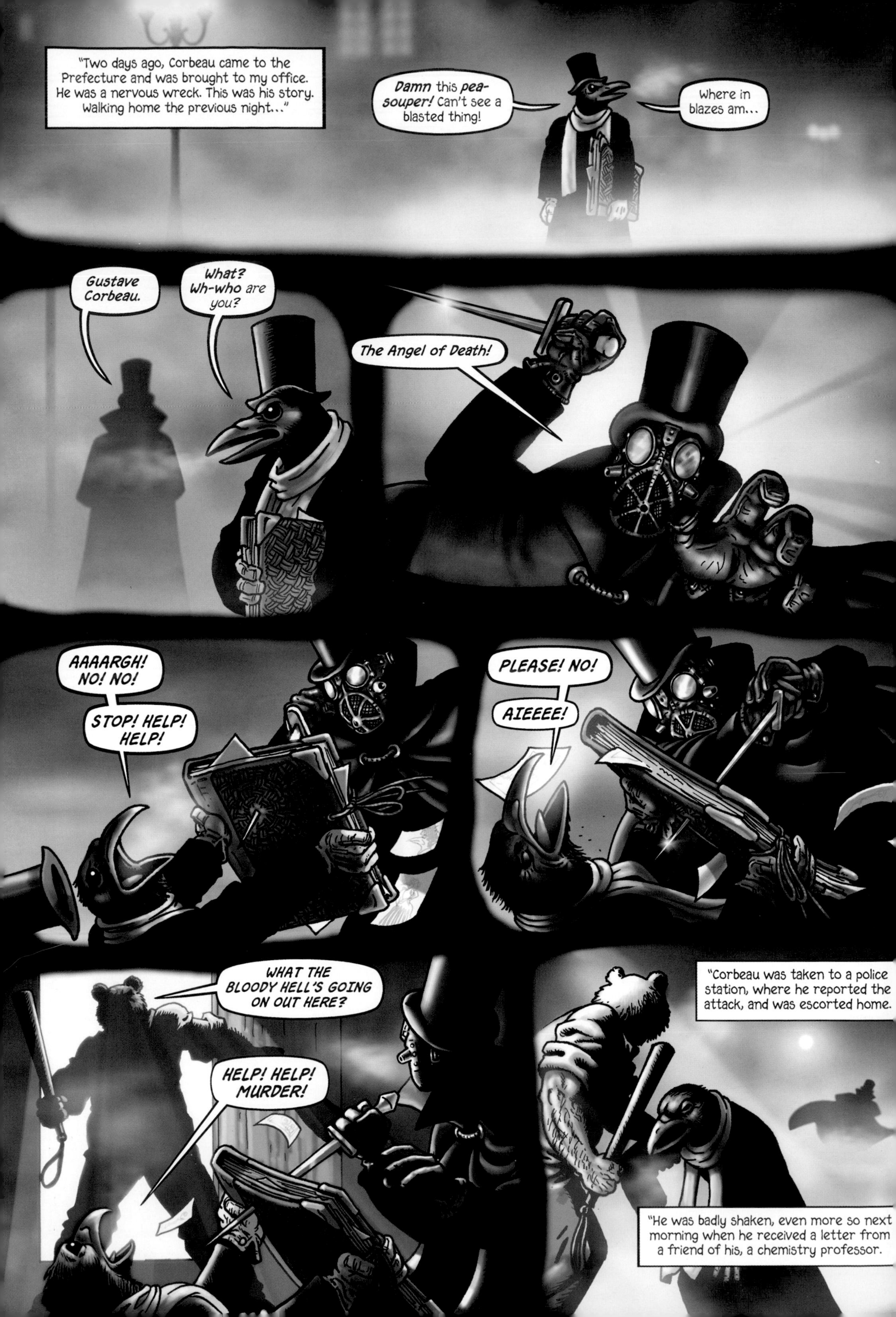

"Two days ago, Corbeau came to the Prefecture and was brought to my office. He was a nervous wreck. This was his story. Walking home the previous night..."
Damn this pea-souper! Can't see a blasted thing!
Where in blazes am...
Gustave Corbeau.
What? Wh-who are you?
The Angel of Death!
AAAARGH! NO! NO!
STOP! HELP! HELP!
PLEASE! NO!
AIEEEE!
WHAT THE BLOODY HELL'S GOING ON OUT HERE?
HELP! HELP! MURDER!
"Corbeau was taken to a police station, where he reported the attack, and was escorted home.
"He was badly shaken, even more so next morning when he received a letter from a friend of his, a chemistry professor.

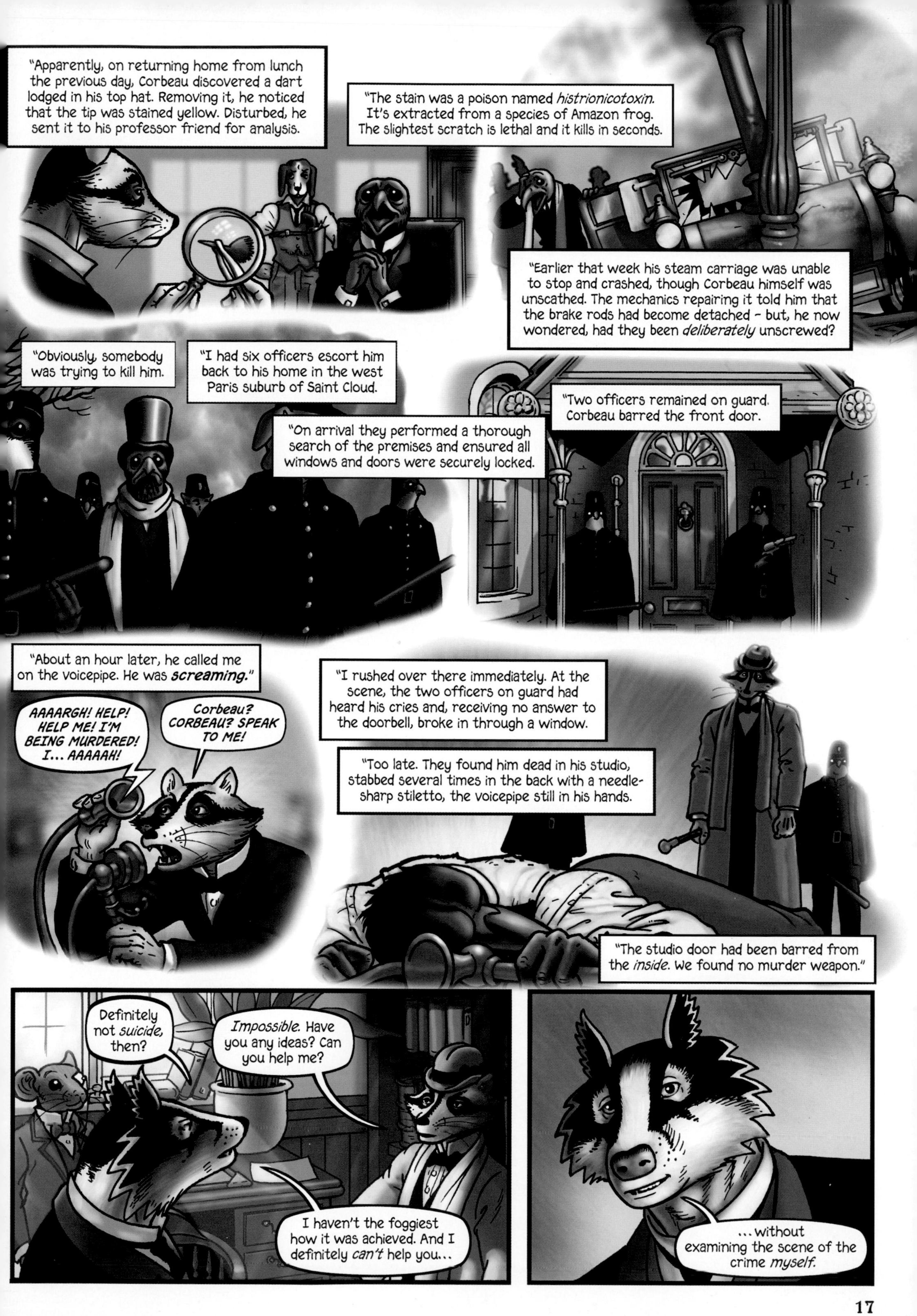
"Apparently, on returning home from lunch the previous day, Corbeau discovered a dart lodged in his top hat. Removing it, he noticed that the tip was stained yellow. Disturbed, he sent it to his professor friend for analysis.
"The stain was a poison named *histrionicotoxin*. It's extracted from a species of Amazon frog. The slightest scratch is lethal and it kills in seconds.
"Earlier that week his steam carriage was unable to stop and crashed, though Corbeau himself was unscathed. The mechanics repairing it told him that the brake rods had become detached – but, he now wondered, had they been *deliberately* unscrewed?
"Obviously, somebody was trying to kill him.
"I had six officers escort him back to his home in the west Paris suburb of Saint Cloud.
"On arrival they performed a thorough search of the premises and ensured all windows and doors were securely locked.
"Two officers remained on guard. Corbeau barred the front door.
"About an hour later, he called me on the voicepipe. He was ***screaming.***"
AAAARGH! HELP! HELP ME! I'M BEING MURDERED! I... AAAAAH!
Corbeau? CORBEAU? SPEAK TO ME!
"I rushed over there immediately. At the scene, the two officers on guard had heard his cries and, receiving no answer to the doorbell, broke in through a window.
"Too late. They found him dead in his studio, stabbed several times in the back with a needle-sharp stiletto, the voicepipe still in his hands.
"The studio door had been barred from the *inside*. We found no murder weapon."
Definitely not *suicide*, then?
Impossible. Have you any ideas? Can you help me?
I haven't the foggiest how it was achieved. And I definitely *can't* help you...
...without examining the scene of the crime *myself*.

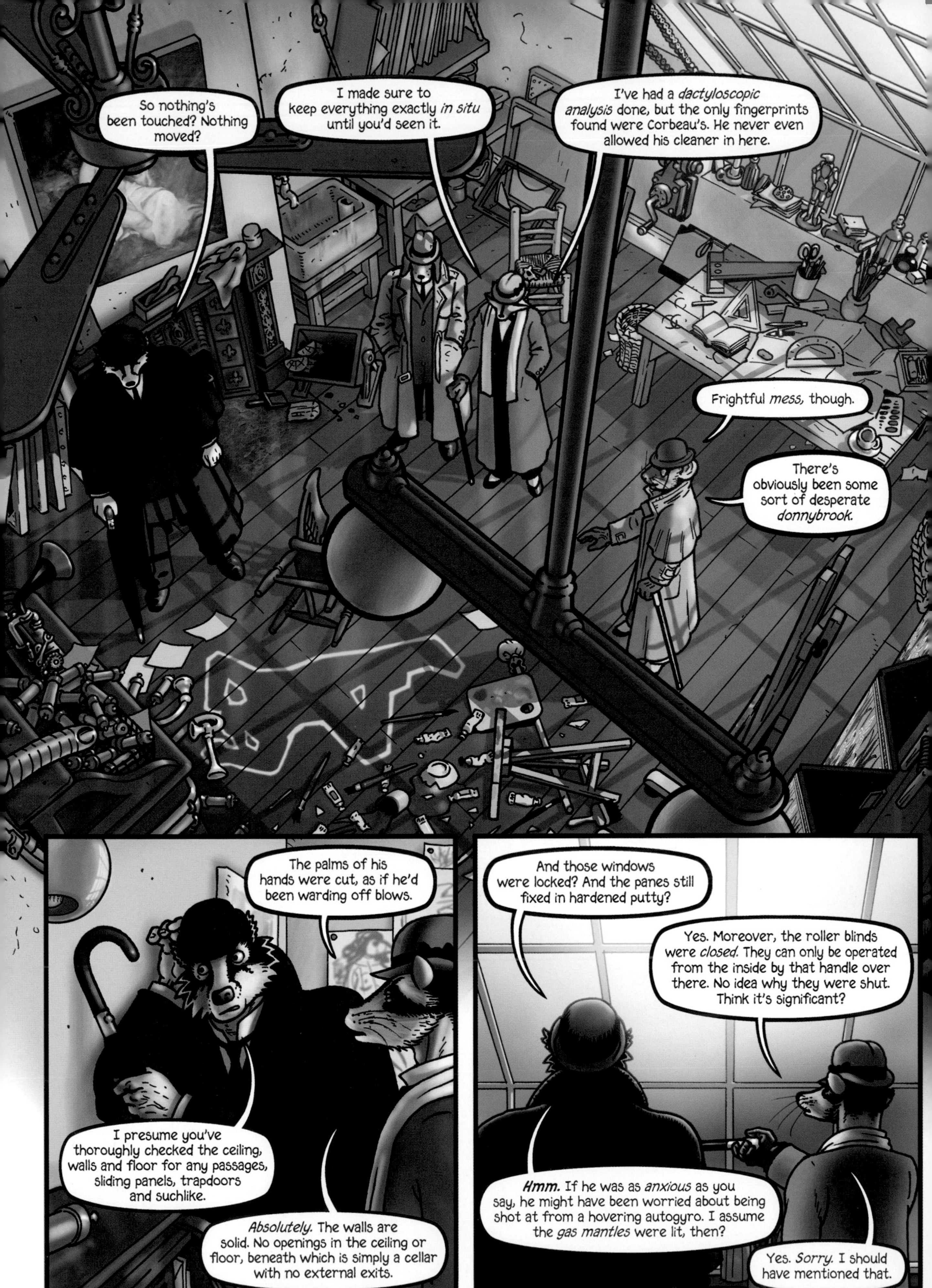

So nothing's been touched? Nothing moved?
I made sure to keep everything exactly *in situ* until you'd seen it.
I've had a *dactyloscopic analysis* done, but the only fingerprints found were Corbeau's. He never even allowed his cleaner in here.
Frightful *mess,* though.
There's obviously been some sort of desperate *donnybrook.*
The palms of his hands were cut, as if he'd been warding off blows.
I presume you've thoroughly checked the ceiling, walls and floor for any passages, sliding panels, trapdoors and suchlike.
Absolutely. The walls are solid. No openings in the ceiling or floor, beneath which is simply a cellar with no external exits.
And those windows were locked? And the panes still fixed in hardened putty?
Yes. Moreover, the roller blinds were *closed.* They can only be operated from the inside by that handle over there. No idea why they were shut. Think it's significant?
Hmm. If he was as *anxious* as you say, he might have been worried about being shot at from a hovering autogyro. I assume the *gas mantles* were lit, then?
Yes. *Sorry.* I should have mentioned that.

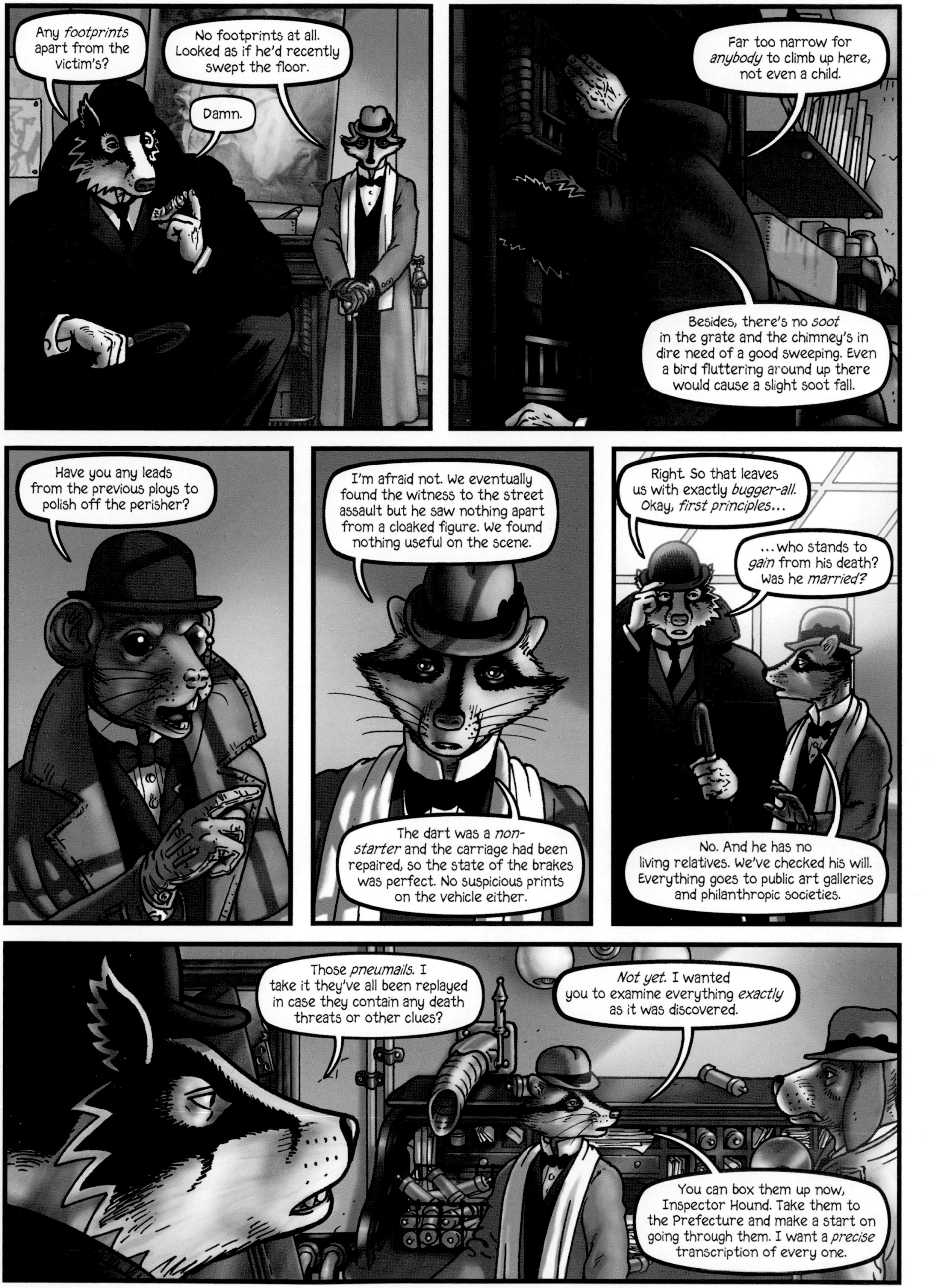

Any *footprints* apart from the victim's?
No footprints at all. Looked as if he'd recently swept the floor.
Damn.
Far too narrow for *anybody* to climb up here, not even a child.
Besides, there's no *soot* in the grate and the chimney's in dire need of a good sweeping. Even a bird fluttering around up there would cause a slight soot fall.
Have you any leads from the previous ploys to polish off the perisher?
I'm afraid not. We eventually found the witness to the street assault but he saw nothing apart from a cloaked figure. We found nothing useful on the scene.
The dart was a *non-starter* and the carriage had been repaired, so the state of the brakes was perfect. No suspicious prints on the vehicle either.
Right. So that leaves us with exactly *bugger-all*. Okay, *first principles*...
...who stands to *gain* from his death? Was he *married?*
No. And he has no living relatives. We've checked his will. Everything goes to public art galleries and philanthropic societies.
Those *pneumails*. I take it they've all been replayed in case they contain any death threats or other clues?
Not yet. I wanted you to examine everything *exactly* as it was discovered.
You can box them up now, Inspector Hound. Take them to the Prefecture and make a start on going through them. I want a *precise* transcription of every one.

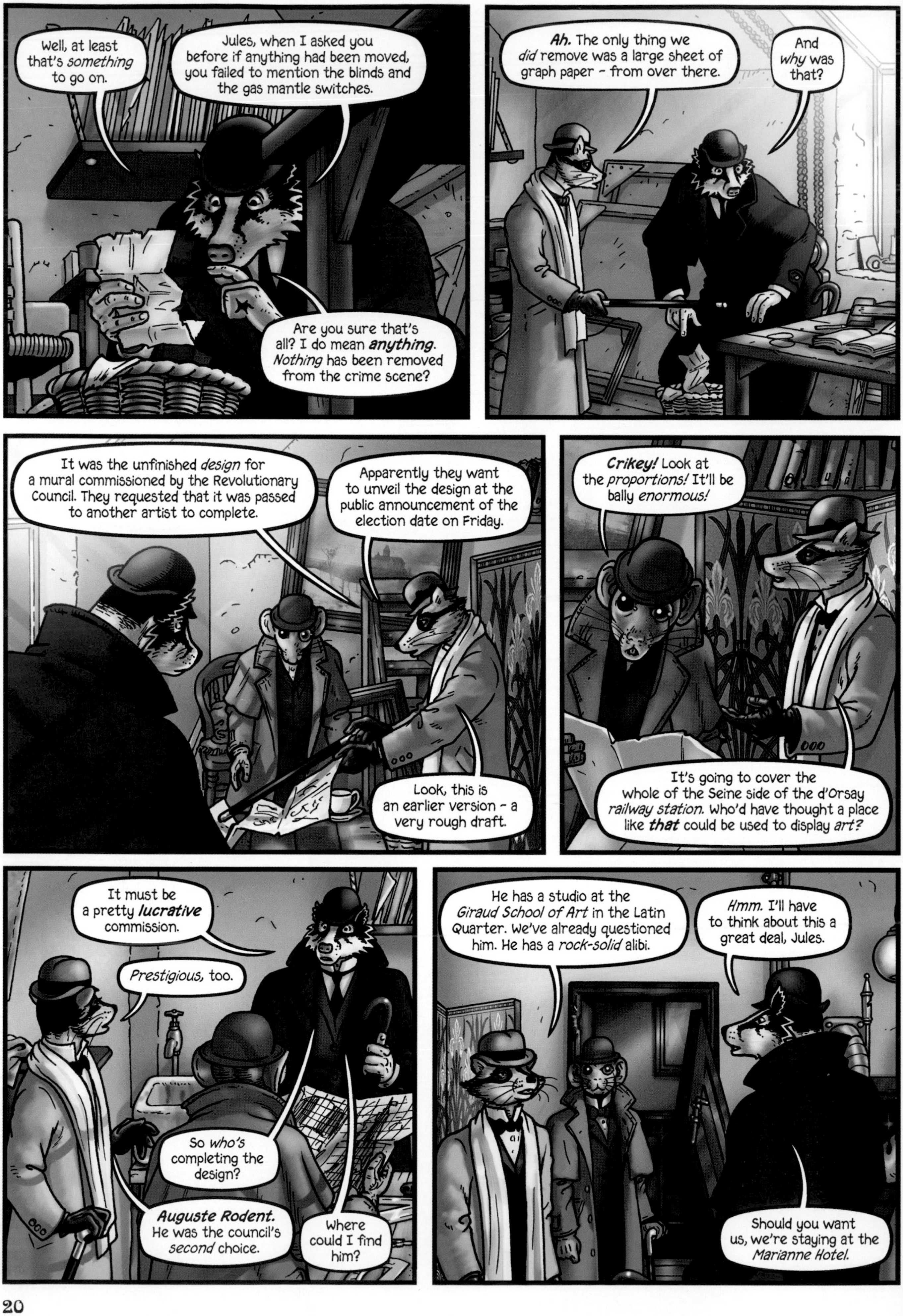

Well, at least that's *something* to go on.
Jules, when I asked you before if anything had been moved, you failed to mention the blinds and the gas mantle switches.
Are you sure that's all? I do mean ***anything***. *Nothing* has been removed from the crime scene?
Ah. The only thing we *did* remove was a large sheet of graph paper - from over there.
And *why* was that?
It was the unfinished *design* for a mural commissioned by the Revolutionary Council. They requested that it was passed to another artist to complete.
Apparently they want to unveil the design at the public announcement of the election date on Friday.
Look, this is an earlier version - a very rough draft.
Crikey! Look at the *proportions!* It'll be bally *enormous!*
It's going to cover the whole of the Seine side of the d'Orsay *railway station.* Who'd have thought a place like ***that*** could be used to display *art?*
It must be a pretty ***lucrative*** commission.
Prestigious, too.
So *who's* completing the design?
Auguste Rodent. He was the council's *second* choice.
Where could I find him?
He has a studio at the *Giraud School of Art* in the Latin Quarter. We've already questioned him. He has a *rock-solid* alibi.
Hmm. I'll have to think about this a great deal, Jules.
Should you want us, we're staying at the *Marianne Hotel.*

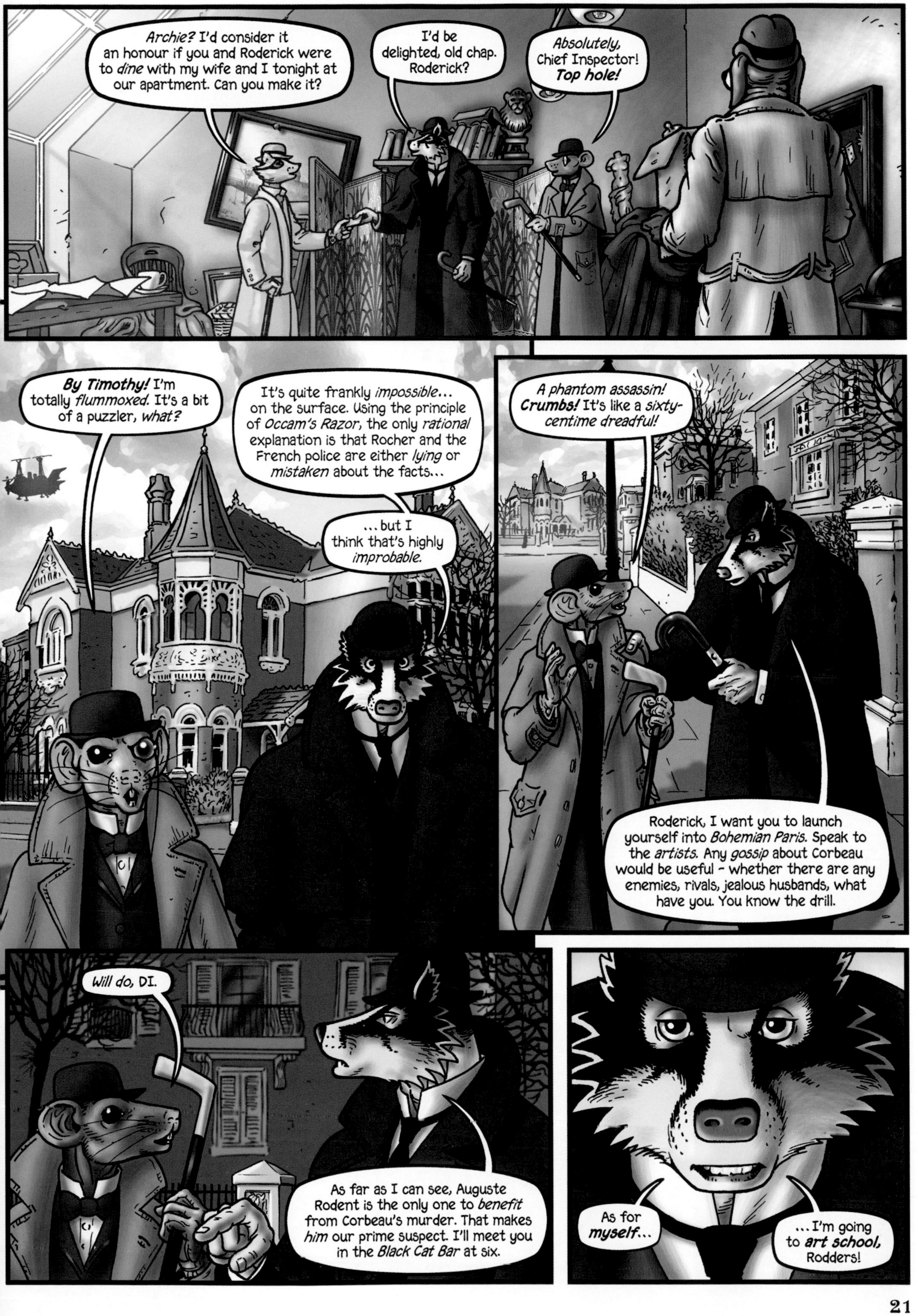
Archie? I'd consider it an honour if you and Roderick were to dine with my wife and I tonight at our apartment. Can you make it?
I'd be delighted, old chap. Roderick?
Absolutely, Chief Inspector! Top hole!
By Timothy! I'm totally flummoxed. It's a bit of a puzzler, what?
It's quite frankly impossible... on the surface. Using the principle of Occam's Razor, the only rational explanation is that Rocher and the French police are either lying or mistaken about the facts...
...but I think that's highly improbable.
A phantom assassin! Crumbs! It's like a sixty-centime dreadful!
Roderick, I want you to launch yourself into Bohemian Paris. Speak to the artists. Any gossip about Corbeau would be useful - whether there are any enemies, rivals, jealous husbands, what have you. You know the drill.
Will do, DI.
As far as I can see, Auguste Rodent is the only one to benefit from Corbeau's murder. That makes him our prime suspect. I'll meet you in the Black Cat Bar at six.
As for myself...
...I'm going to art school, Rodders!

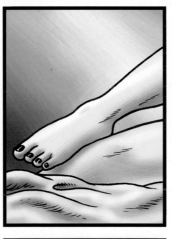

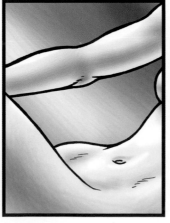

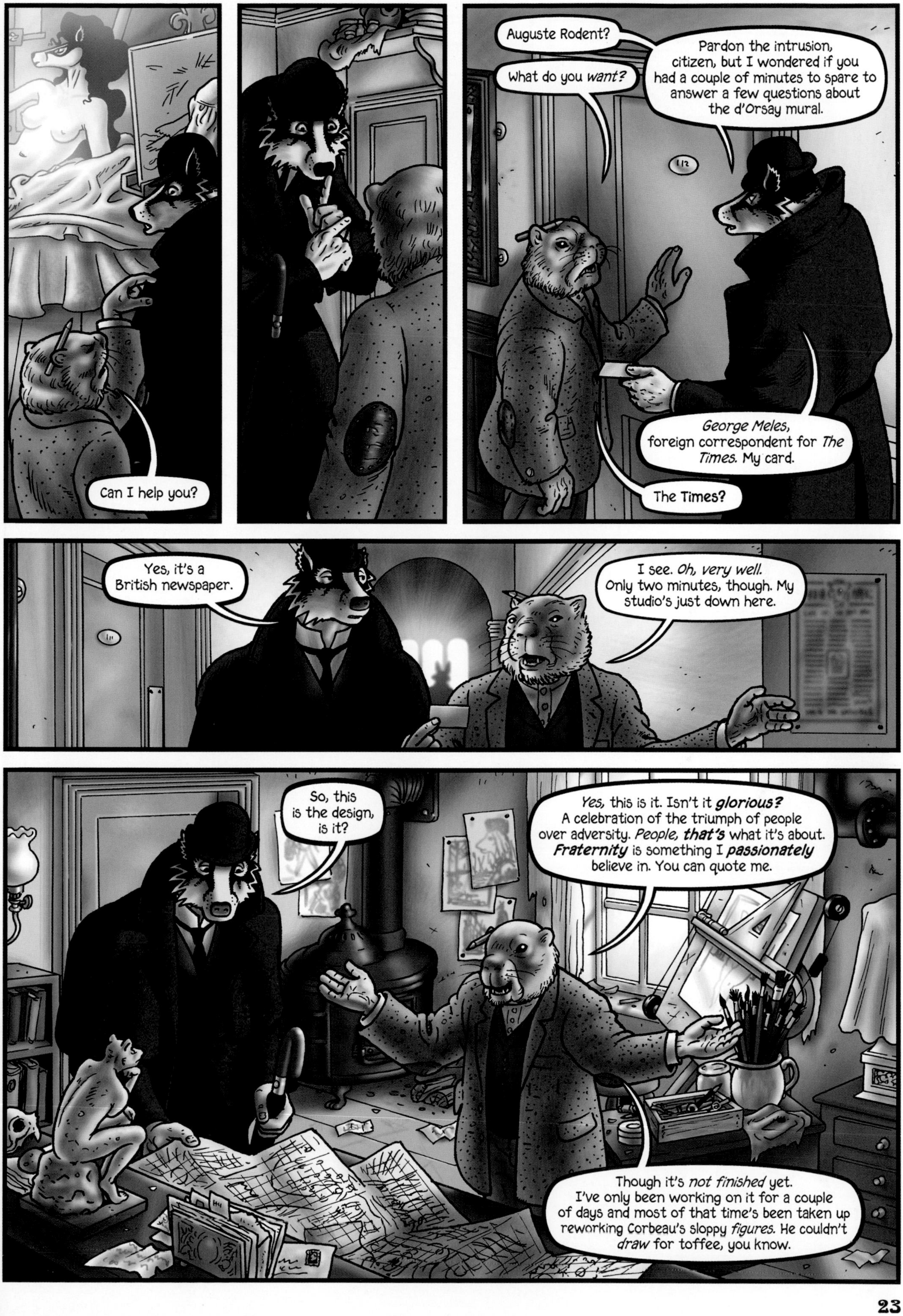
Can I help you?
Auguste Rodent?
What do you *want?*
Pardon the intrusion, citizen, but I wondered if you had a couple of minutes to spare to answer a few questions about the d'Orsay mural.
George Meles, foreign correspondent for *The Times.* My card.
The Times?
Yes, it's a British newspaper.
I see. *Oh, very well.* Only two minutes, though. My studio's just down here.
So, this is the design, is it?
Yes, this is it. Isn't it ***glorious?*** A celebration of the triumph of people over adversity. *People,* ***that's*** what it's about. ***Fraternity*** is something I ***passionately*** believe in. You can quote me.
Though it's *not finished* yet. I've only been working on it for a couple of days and most of that time's been taken up reworking Corbeau's sloppy *figures.* He couldn't *draw* for toffee, you know.

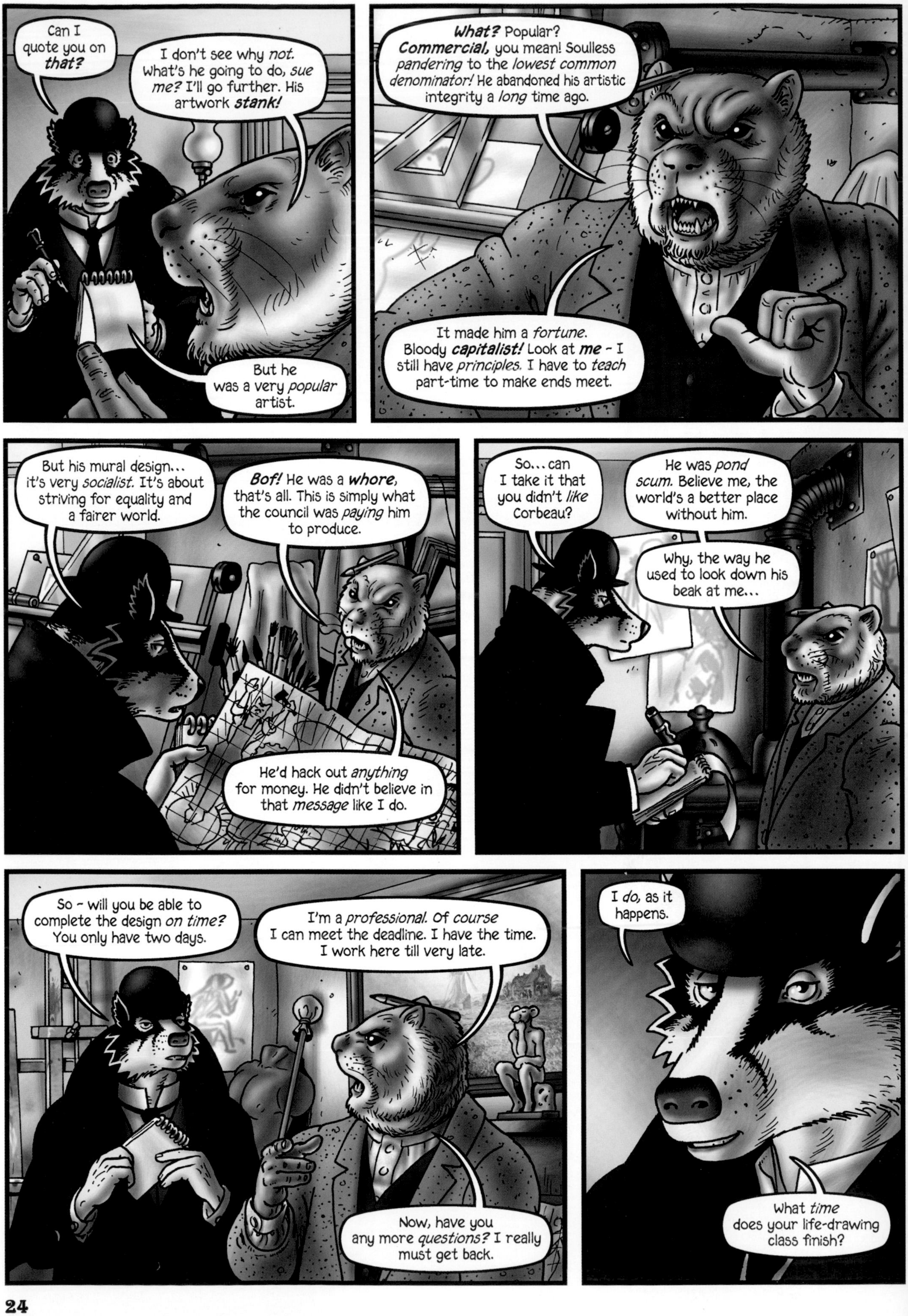
Can I quote you on *that?*
I don't see why *not.* What's he going to do, *sue me?* I'll go further. His artwork **stank!**
But he was a very *popular* artist.
What? Popular? ***Commercial,*** you mean! Soulless *pandering* to the *lowest common denominator!* He abandoned his artistic integrity a *long* time ago.
It made him a *fortune.* Bloody ***capitalist!*** Look at ***me*** – I still have *principles.* I have to *teach* part-time to make ends meet.
But his mural design... it's very *socialist.* It's about striving for equality and a fairer world.
Bof! He was a ***whore,*** that's all. This is simply what the council was *paying* him to produce.
He'd hack out *anything* for money. He didn't believe in that *message* like I do.
So... can I take it that you didn't *like* Corbeau?
He was *pond scum.* Believe me, the world's a better place without him.
Why, the way he used to look down his beak at me...
So – will you be able to complete the design *on time?* You only have two days.
I'm a *professional.* Of *course* I can meet the deadline. I have the time. I work here till very late.
Now, have you any more *questions?* I really must get back.
I *do,* as it happens.
What *time* does your life-drawing class finish?

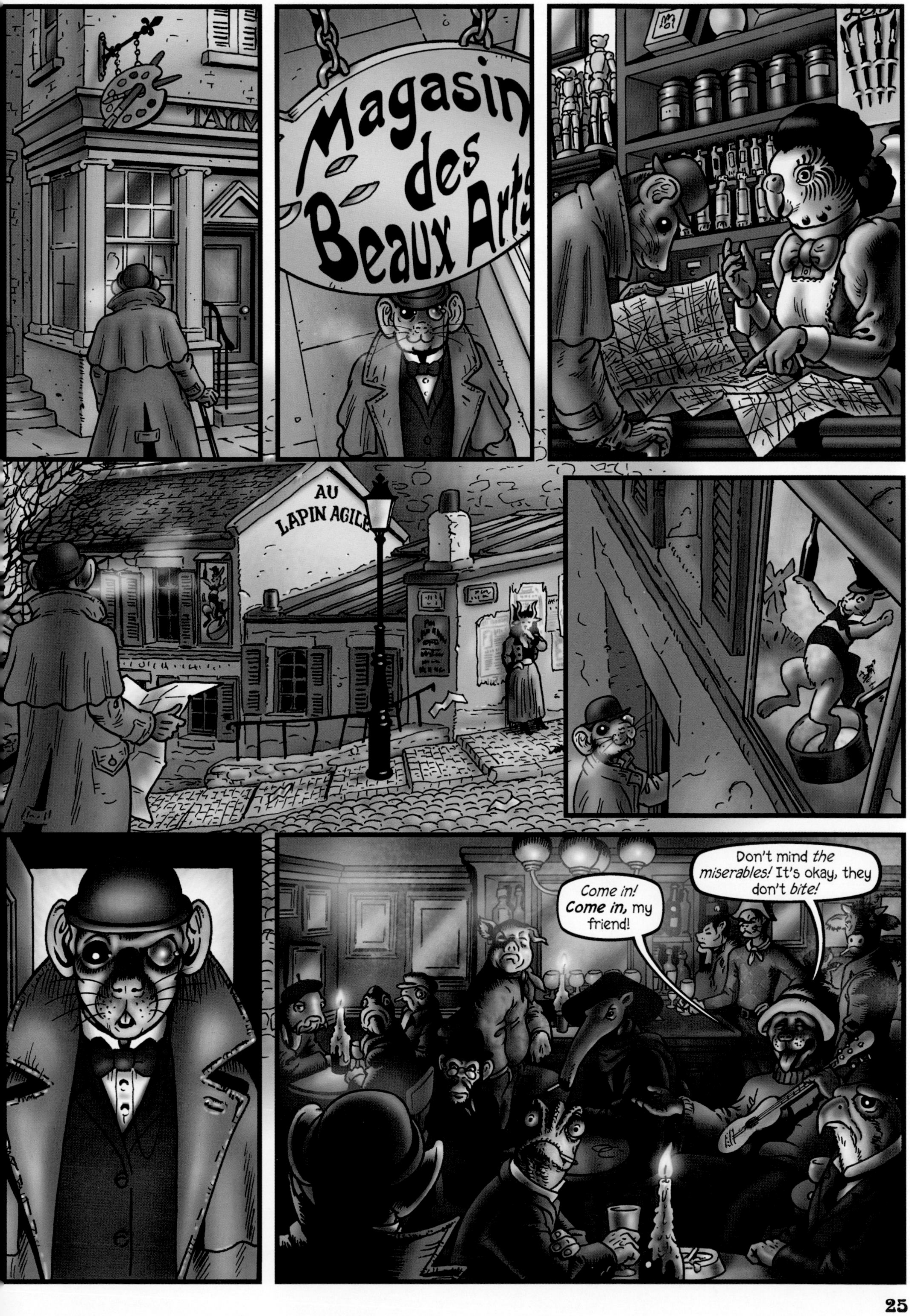
Magasin des Beaux Arts
AU LAPIN AGILE
Come in! **Come in,** my friend!
Don't mind *the miserables!* It's okay, they don't *bite!*

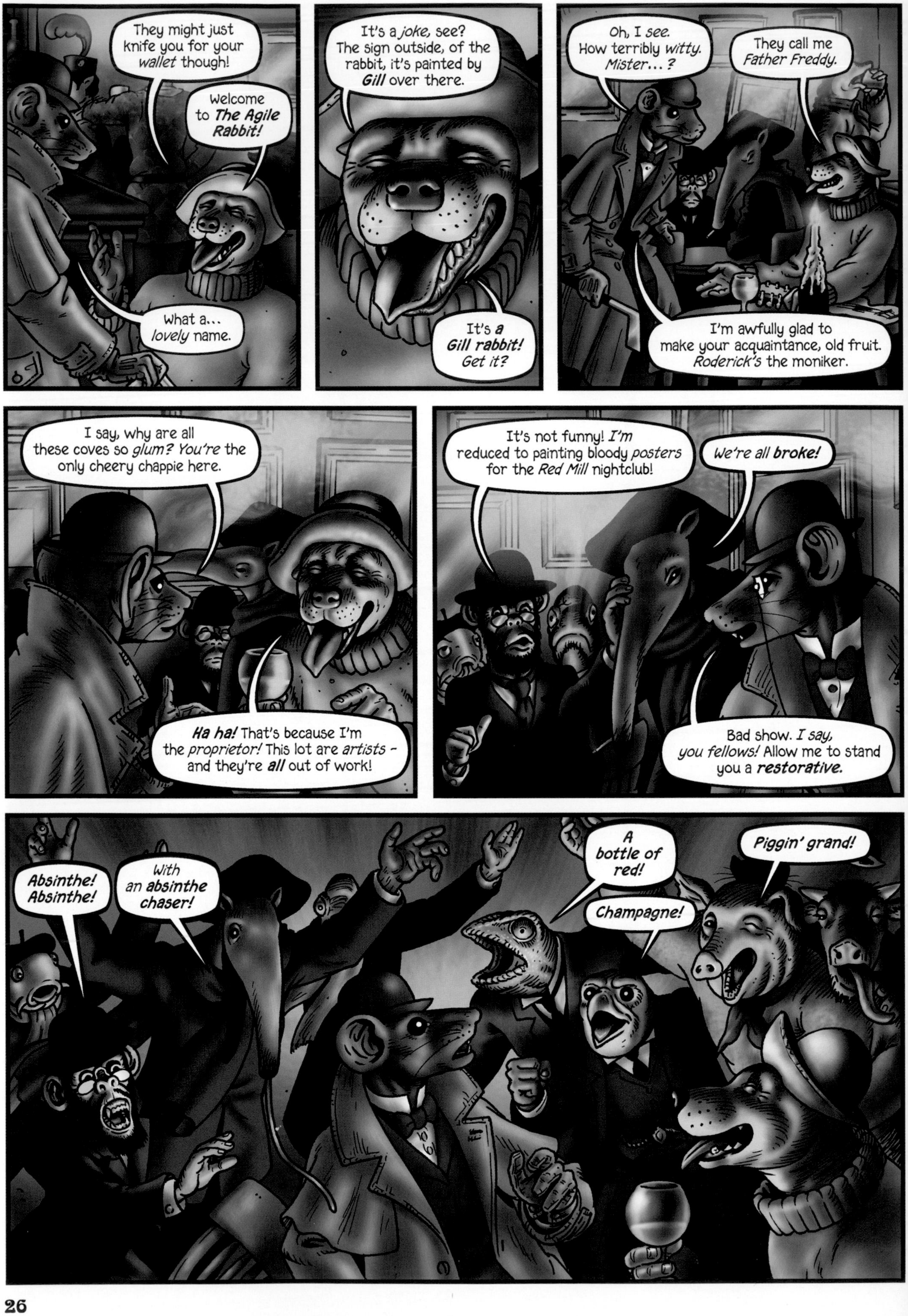

They might just knife you for your *wallet* though!
Welcome to ***The Agile Rabbit!***
What a... *lovely* name.
It's a *joke,* see? The sign outside, of the rabbit, it's painted by ***Gill*** over there.
It's ***a Gill rabbit!*** *Get it?*
Oh, I *see.* How terribly *witty.* *Mister...?*
They call me *Father Freddy.*
I'm awfully glad to make your acquaintance, old fruit. *Roderick's* the moniker.
I say, why are all these coves so *glum? You're* the only cheery chappie here.
Ha ha! That's because I'm the *proprietor!* This lot are *artists* - and they're ***all*** out of work!
It's not funny! *I'm* reduced to painting bloody *posters* for the *Red Mill* nightclub!
We're all ***broke!***
Bad show. *I say, you fellows!* Allow me to stand you a ***restorative.***
Absinthe! Absinthe!
With an ***absinthe chaser!***
A bottle of red!
Champagne!
Piggin' grand!

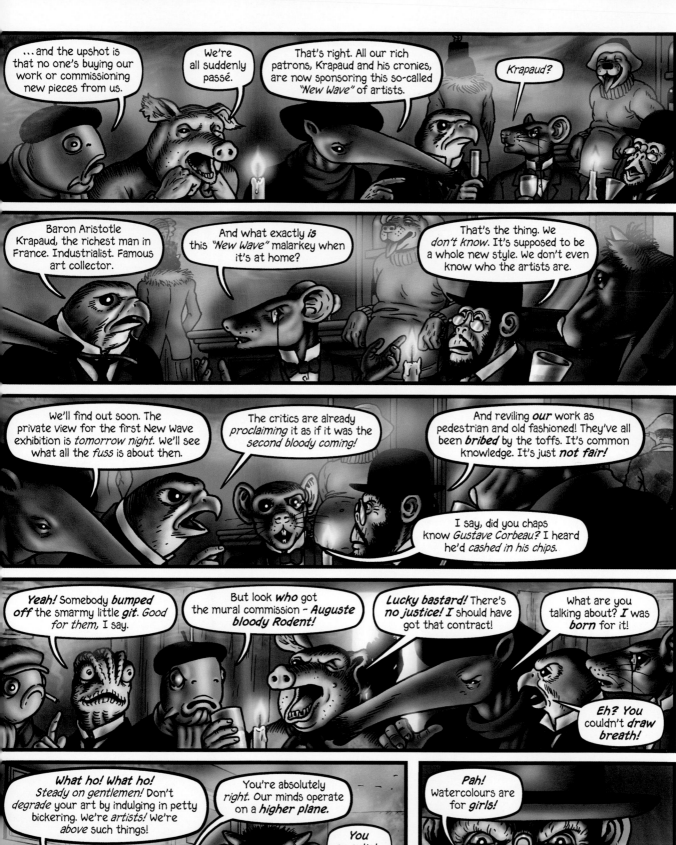

...and the upshot is that no one's buying our work or commissioning new pieces from us.

We're all suddenly passé.

That's right. All our rich patrons, Krapaud and his cronies, are now sponsoring this so-called *"New Wave"* of artists.

Krapaud?

Baron Aristotle Krapaud, the richest man in France. Industrialist. Famous art collector.

And what exactly *is* this *"New Wave"* malarkey when it's at home?

That's the thing. We *don't know*. It's supposed to be a whole new style. We don't even know who the artists are.

We'll find out soon. The private view for the first New Wave exhibition is *tomorrow night*. We'll see what all the *fuss* is about then.

The critics are already *proclaiming* it as if it was the *second bloody coming!*

And reviling *our* work as pedestrian and old fashioned! They've all been *bribed* by the toffs. It's common knowledge. It's just *not fair!*

I say, did you chaps know *Gustave Corbeau*? I heard he'd *cashed in his chips.*

Yeah! Somebody *bumped off* the smarmy little *git. Good for them*, I say.

But look *who* got the mural commission – *Auguste bloody Rodent!*

Lucky bastard! There's *no justice! I* should have got that contract!

What are you talking about? *I* was *born* for it!

Eh? You couldn't *draw breath!*

What ho! What ho! Steady on gentlemen! Don't *degrade* your art by indulging in petty bickering. We're *artists!* We're *above* such things!

You're absolutely *right.* Our minds operate on a *higher plane.*

You an artist, then?

Yes, well, *er*, strictly on an *amateur level*, don't you know. I dabble in *watercolours* for a lark.

Pah! Watercolours are for *girls!*

Real men use *oils!*

27

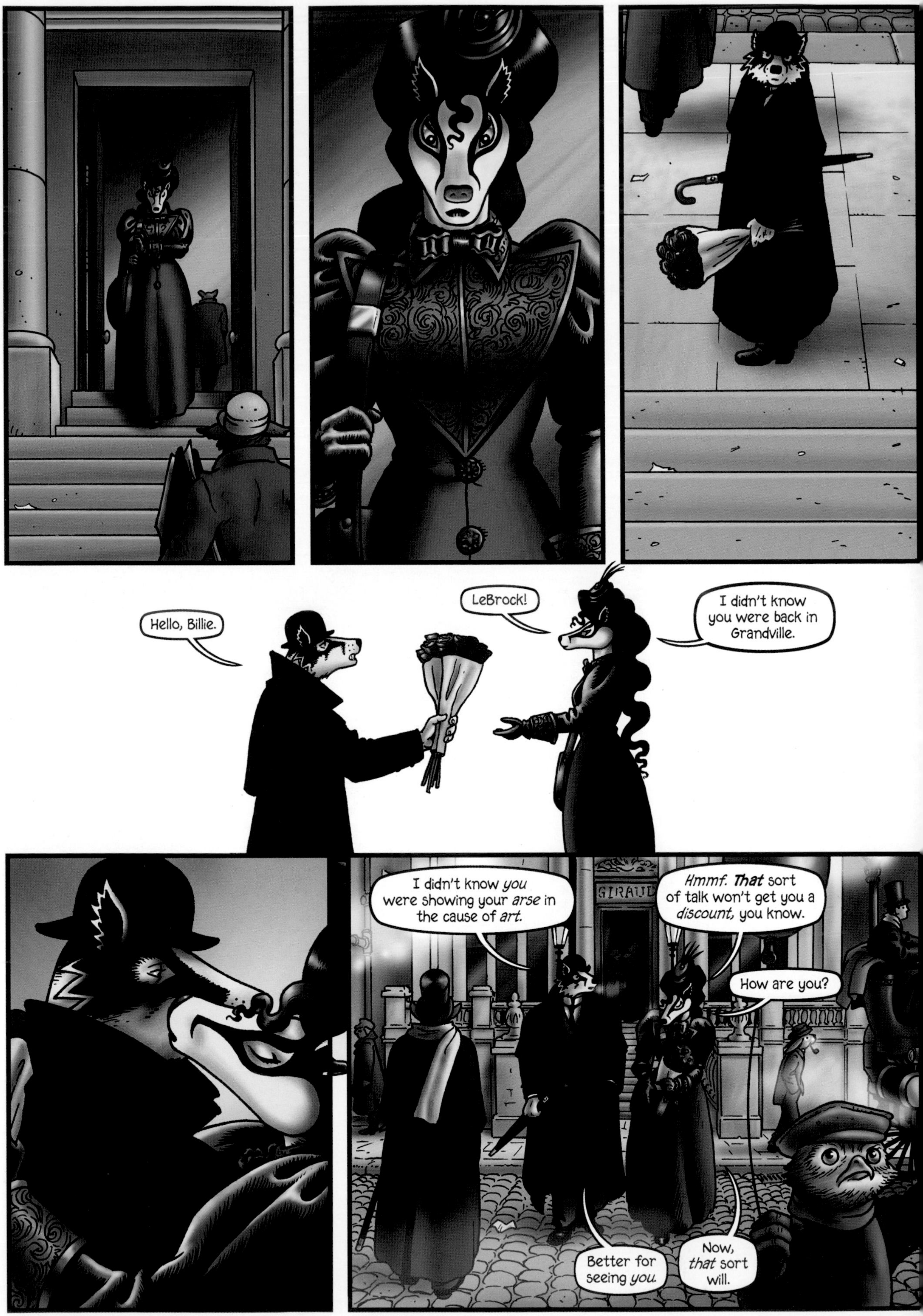
Hello, Billie.
LeBrock!
I didn't know you were back in Grandville.
I didn't know *you* were showing your *arse* in the cause of *art*.
Hmmf. ***That*** sort of talk won't get you a *discount,* you know.
How are you?
Better for seeing *you.*
Now, *that* sort will.

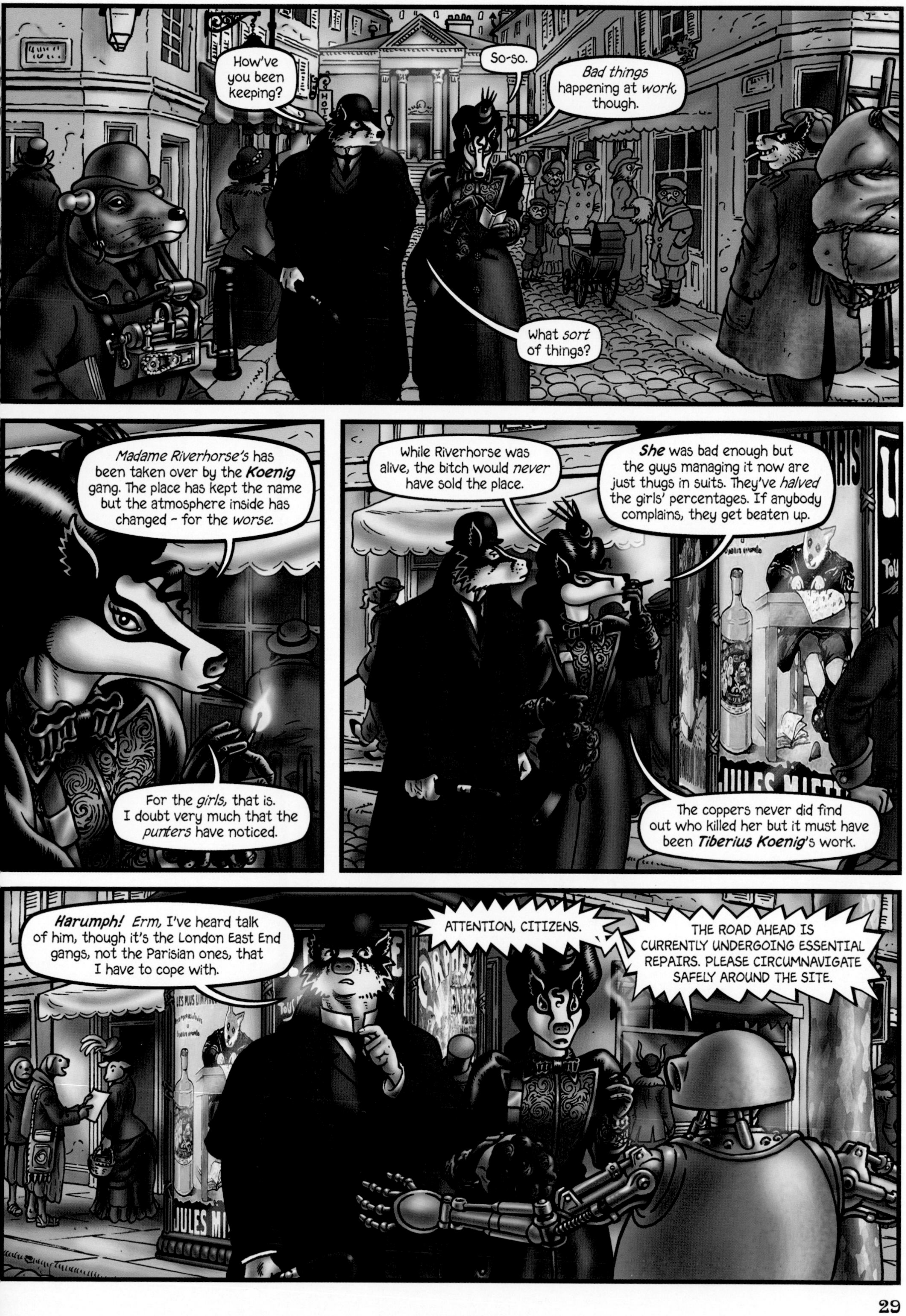
How've you been keeping?
So-so.
Bad things happening at *work*, though.
What *sort* of things?
Madame Riverhorse's has been taken over by the ***Koenig*** gang. The place has kept the name but the atmosphere inside has changed – for the *worse*.
For the *girls*, that is. I doubt very much that the *punters* have noticed.
While Riverhorse was alive, the bitch would *never* have sold the place.
She was bad enough but the guys managing it now are just thugs in suits. They've *halved* the girls' percentages. If anybody complains, they get beaten up.
The coppers never did find out who killed her but it must have been ***Tiberius Koenig***'s work.
Harumph! *Erm*, I've heard talk of him, though it's the London East End gangs, not the Parisian ones, that I have to cope with.
ATTENTION, CITIZENS.
THE ROAD AHEAD IS CURRENTLY UNDERGOING ESSENTIAL REPAIRS. PLEASE CIRCUMNAVIGATE SAFELY AROUND THE SITE.

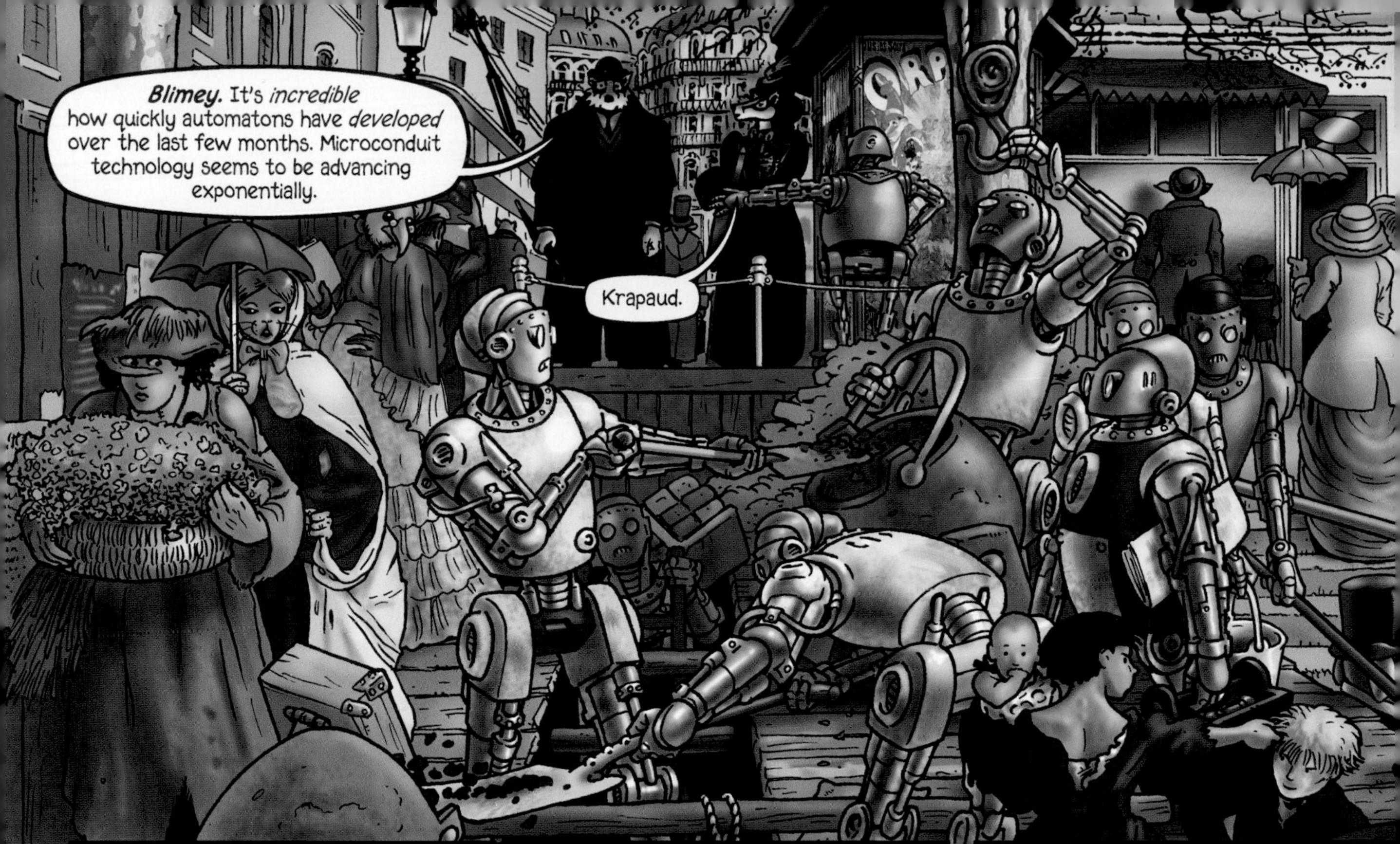
Blimey. It's incredible how quickly automatons have developed over the last few months. Microconduit technology seems to be advancing exponentially.
Krapaud.

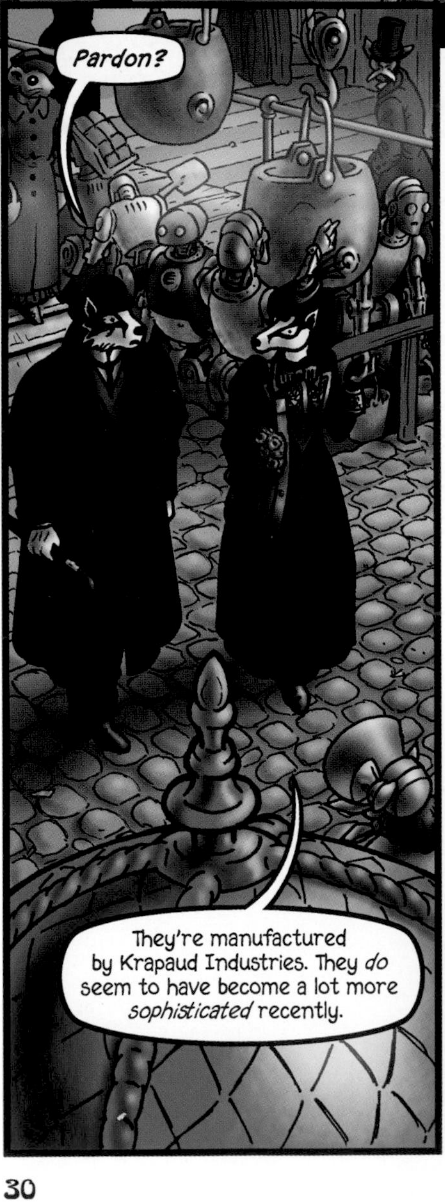
Pardon?
They're manufactured by Krapaud Industries. They do seem to have become a lot more sophisticated recently.

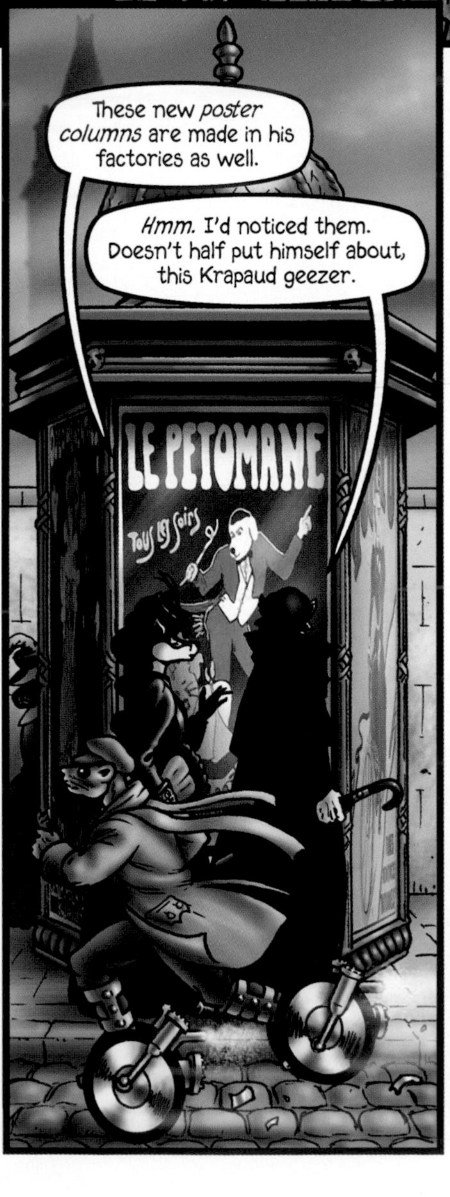
These new poster columns are made in his factories as well.
Hmm. I'd noticed them. Doesn't half put himself about, this Krapaud geezer.
LE PETOMANE
Tous les soirs

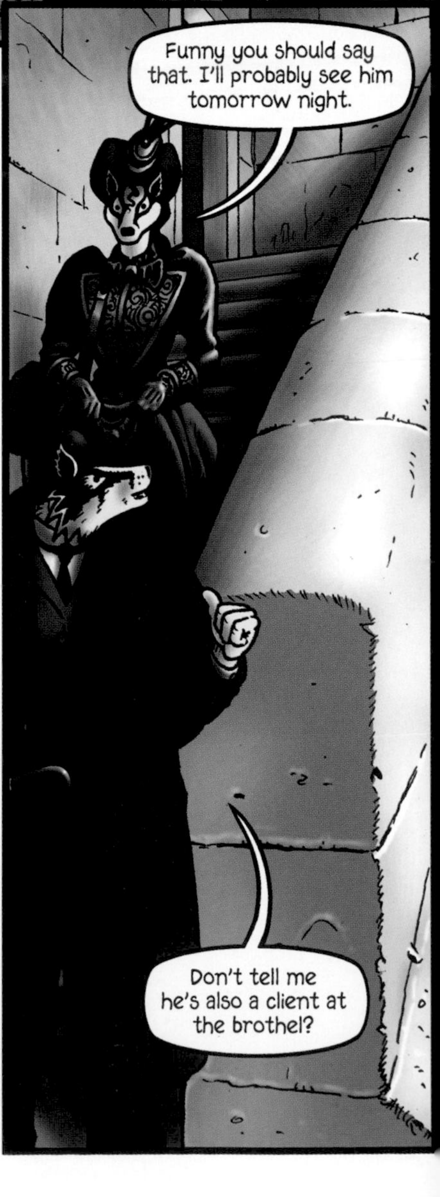
Funny you should say that. I'll probably see him tomorrow night.
Don't tell me he's also a client at the brothel?

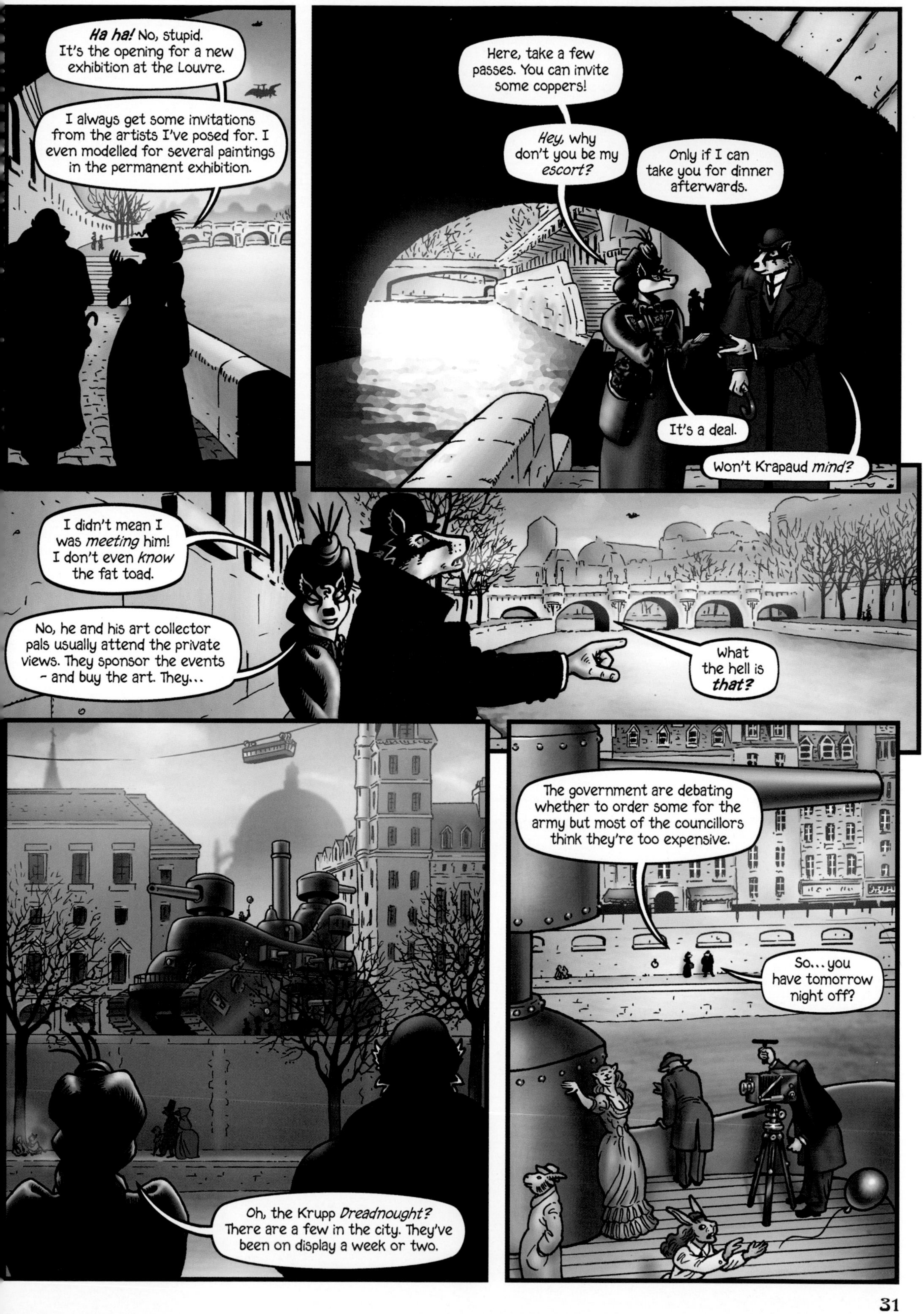

Ha ha! No, stupid. It's the opening for a new exhibition at the Louvre.
I always get some invitations from the artists I've posed for. I even modelled for several paintings in the permanent exhibition.
Here, take a few passes. You can invite some coppers!
Hey, why don't you be my *escort?*
Only if I can take you for dinner afterwards.
It's a deal.
Won't Krapaud *mind?*
I didn't mean I was *meeting* him! I don't even *know* the fat toad.
No, he and his art collector pals usually attend the private views. They sponsor the events - and buy the art. They...
What the hell is *that?*
Oh, the Krupp *Dreadnought?* There are a few in the city. They've been on display a week or two.
The government are debating whether to order some for the army but most of the councillors think they're too expensive.
So... you have tomorrow night off?

I'm on the day shift for a while.

If you're accompanying me at the Louvre tomorrow night, I'm not having you *showing me up*. You will dress *properly*, won't you?

What do you mean?

You'll be wearing *full evening dress,* not that old suit?

It's the *only* one I've got!

I've even had the *bullet holes* repaired!

Well, you better get another one if you want to escort *me.*

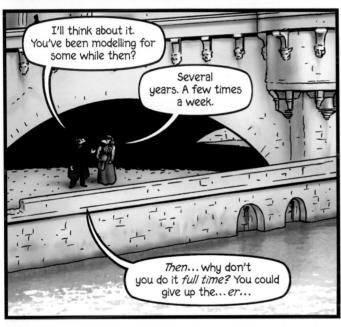

I'll think about it. You've been modelling for some while then?

Several years. A few times a week.

Then... why don't you do it *full time?* You could give up the...*er...*

Whoring? Modelling pays a *pittance.* I couldn't *live* off it.

Anyway, what's it to *you?*

You... you know, Billie...you're a beautiful, intelligent woman. You...you should get *married...* settle down.

What the *hell* are you *talking* about? You know what I *am!* What *respectable man* would marry a woman like *me?*

Well? Did you *hear* what I said? *LeBrock!*

Yes.

I heard you.

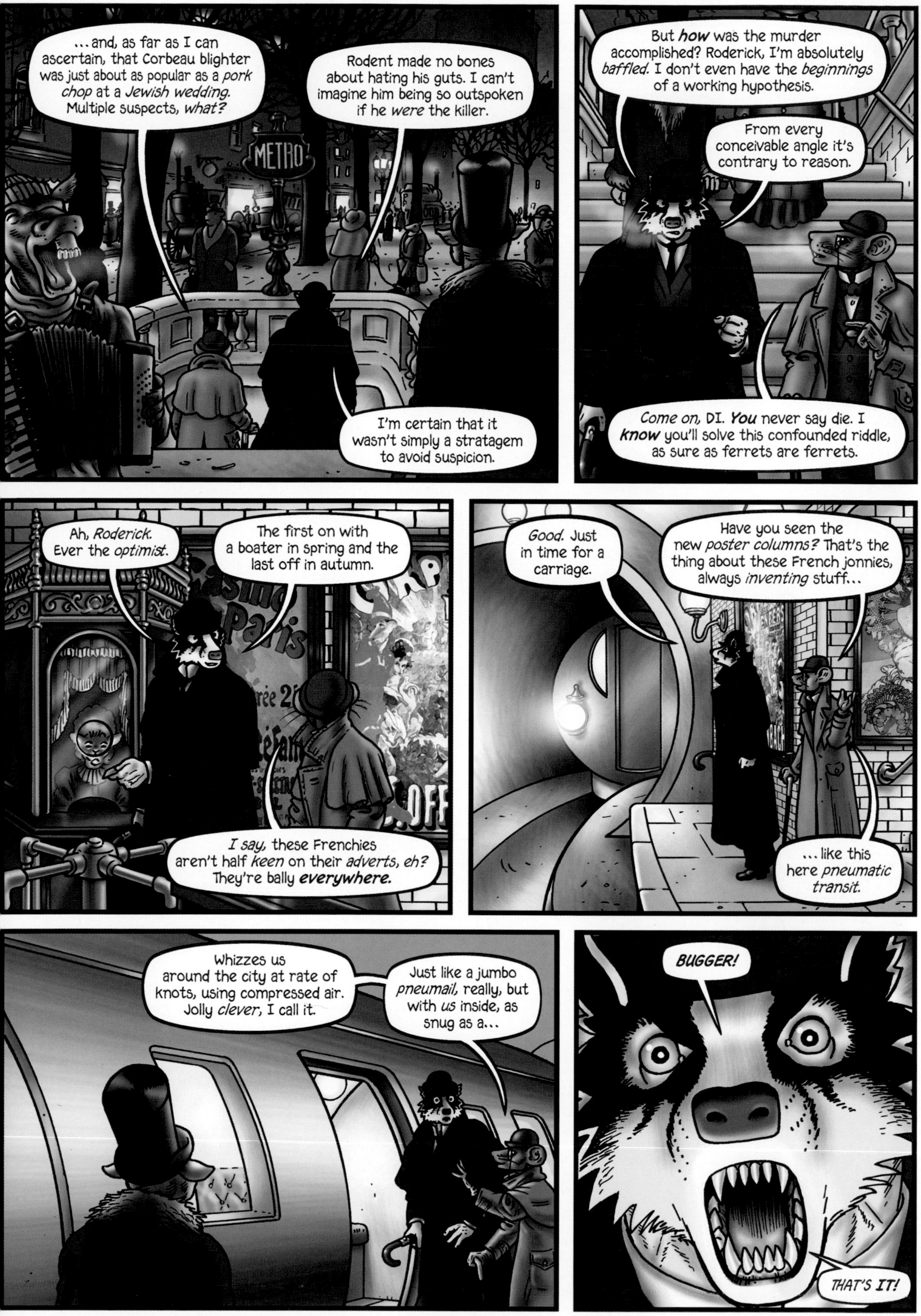

...and, as far as I can ascertain, that Corbeau blighter was just about as popular as a *pork chop* at a *Jewish wedding.* Multiple suspects, *what?*
Rodent made no bones about hating his guts. I can't imagine him being so outspoken if he *were* the killer.
METRO
I'm certain that it wasn't simply a stratagem to avoid suspicion.
But ***how*** was the murder accomplished? Roderick, I'm absolutely *baffled.* I don't even have the *beginnings* of a working hypothesis.
From every conceivable angle it's contrary to reason.
Come on, DI. ***You*** never say die. I ***know*** you'll solve this confounded riddle, as sure as ferrets are ferrets.
Ah, *Roderick.* Ever the *optimist.*
The first on with a boater in spring and the last off in autumn.
I say, these Frenchies aren't half *keen* on their *adverts, eh?* They're bally ***everywhere.***
Good. Just in time for a carriage.
Have you seen the new *poster columns?* That's the thing about these French jonnies, always *inventing* stuff...
...like this here *pneumatic transit.*
Whizzes us around the city at rate of knots, using compressed air. Jolly *clever,* I call it.
Just like a jumbo *pneumail,* really, but with *us* inside, as snug as a...
BUGGER!
THAT'S ***IT!***

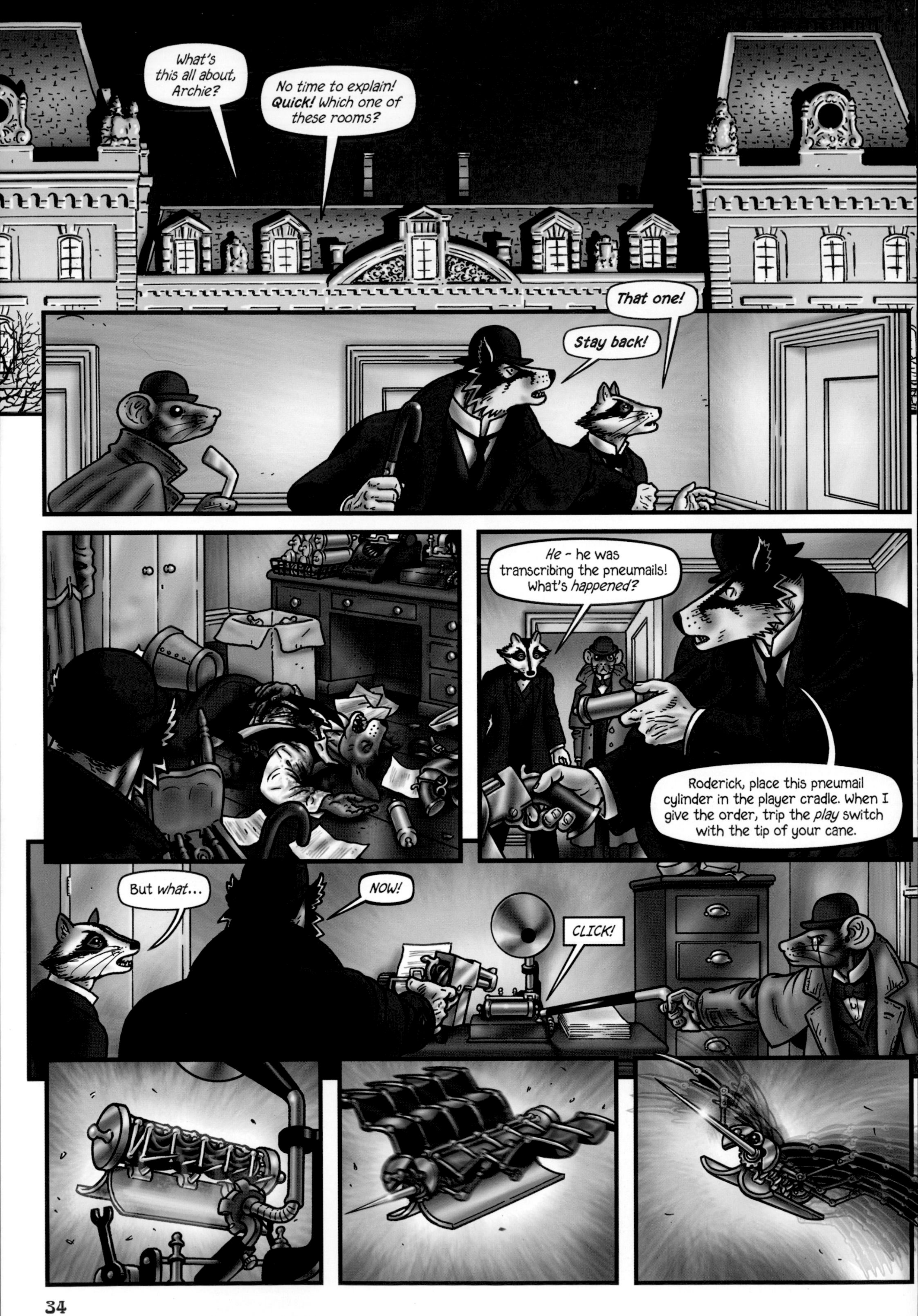

What's this all about, Archie?
No time to explain! **Quick!** Which one of these rooms?
That one!
Stay back!
He - he was transcribing the pneumails! What's *happened?*
Roderick, place this pneumail cylinder in the player cradle. When I give the order, trip the *play* switch with the tip of your cane.
But *what*...
NOW!
CLICK!

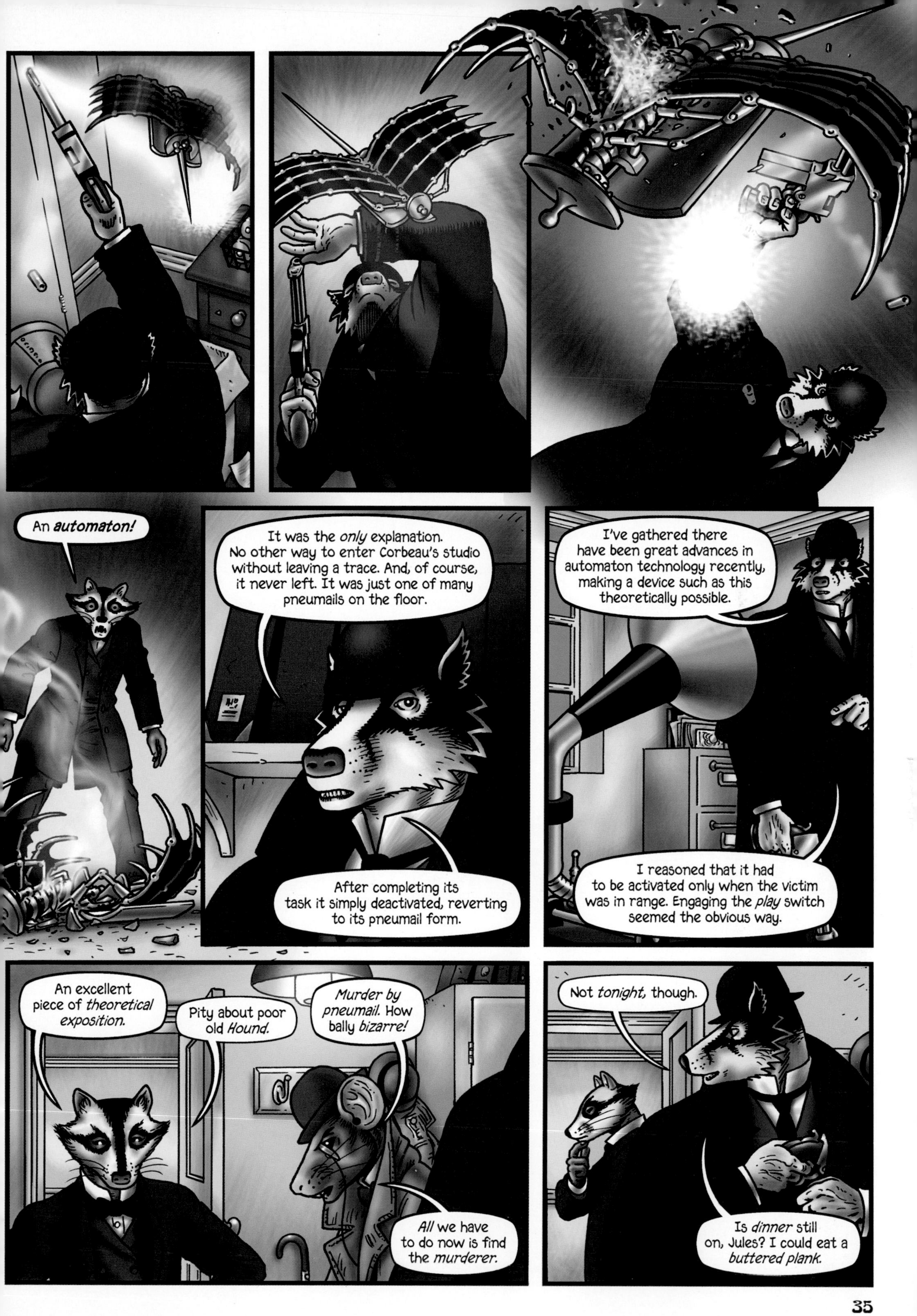
An *automaton!*
It was the *only* explanation. No other way to enter Corbeau's studio without leaving a trace. And, of course, it never left. It was just one of many pneumails on the floor.
After completing its task it simply deactivated, reverting to its pneumail form.
I've gathered there have been great advances in automaton technology recently, making a device such as this theoretically possible.
I reasoned that it had to be activated only when the victim was in range. Engaging the *play* switch seemed the obvious way.
An excellent piece of *theoretical exposition.*
Pity about poor old *Hound.*
Murder by pneumail. How bally *bizarre!*
All we have to do now is find the *murderer.*
Not *tonight,* though.
Is *dinner* still on, Jules? I could eat a *buttered plank.*

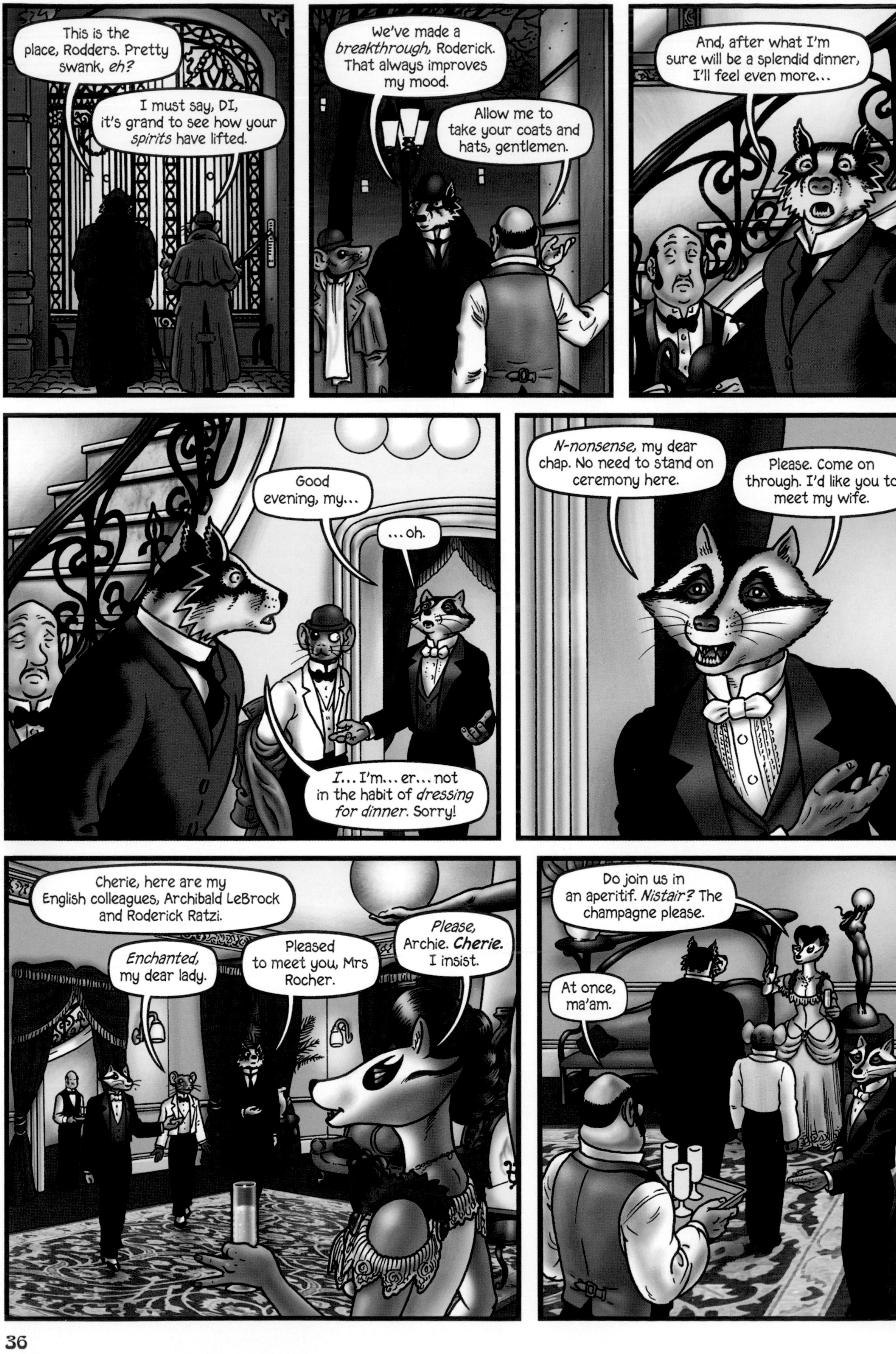
This is the place, Rodders. Pretty swank, *eh?*
I must say, DI, it's grand to see how your *spirits* have lifted.
We've made a *breakthrough*, Roderick. That always improves my mood.
Allow me to take your coats and hats, gentlemen.
And, after what I'm sure will be a splendid dinner, I'll feel even more...
Good evening, my...
...oh.
I... I'm... er... not in the habit of *dressing for dinner*. Sorry!
N-nonsense, my dear chap. No need to stand on ceremony here.
Please. Come on through. I'd like you to meet my wife.
Cherie, here are my English colleagues, Archibald LeBrock and Roderick Ratzi.
Enchanted, my dear lady.
Pleased to meet you, Mrs Rocher.
Please, Archie. ***Cherie***. I insist.
Do join us in an aperitif. *Nistair?* The champagne please.
At once, ma'am.

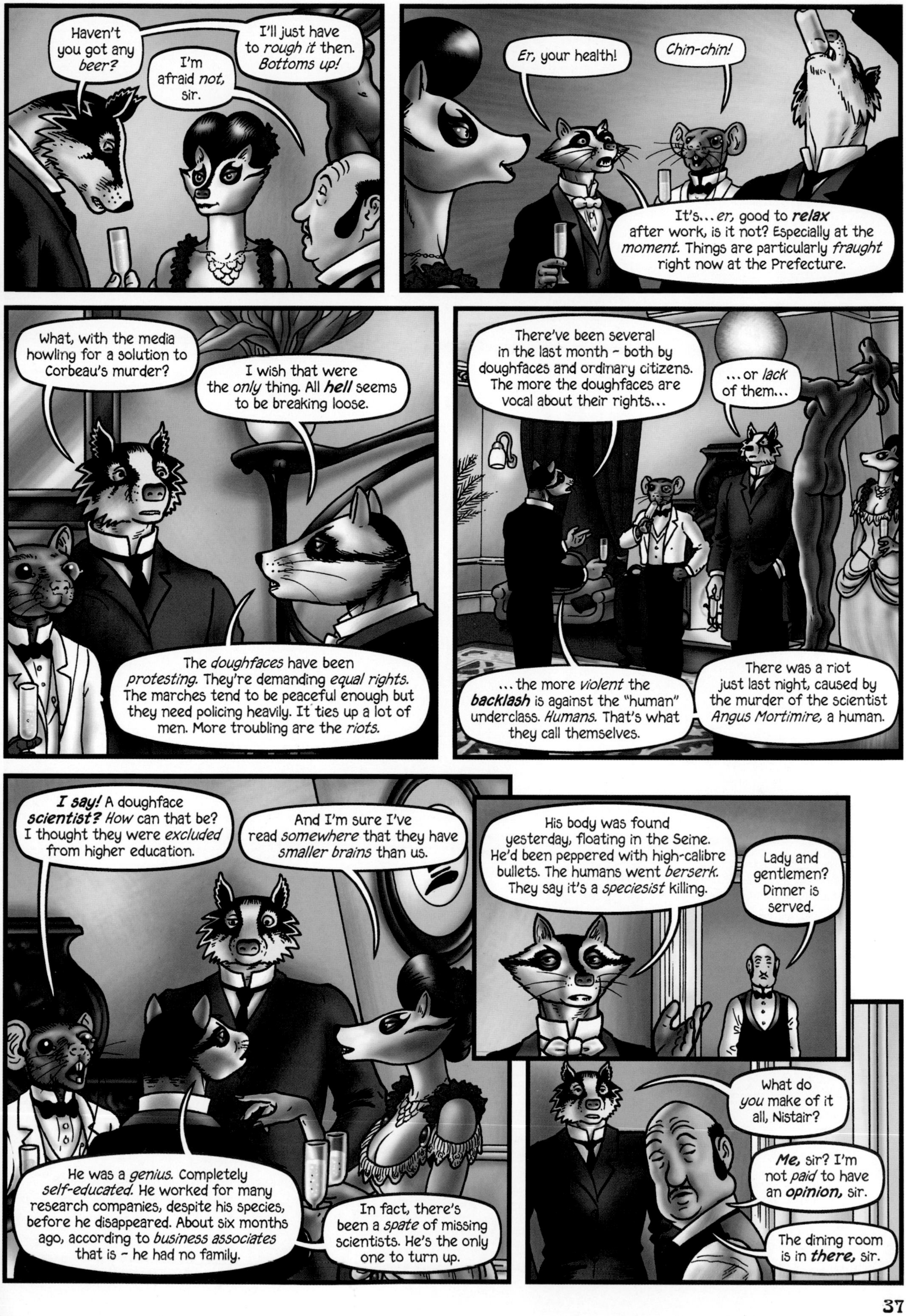
Haven't you got any *beer?*
I'm afraid *not,* sir.
I'll just have to *rough it* then. *Bottoms up!*
Er, your health!
Chin-chin!
It's... *er,* good to ***relax*** after work, is it not? Especially at the *moment.* Things are particularly *fraught* right now at the Prefecture.
What, with the media howling for a solution to Corbeau's murder?
I wish that were the *only* thing. All ***hell*** seems to be breaking loose.
The *doughfaces* have been *protesting.* They're demanding *equal rights.* The marches tend to be peaceful enough but they need policing heavily. It ties up a lot of men. More troubling are the *riots.*
There've been several in the last month – both by doughfaces and ordinary citizens. The more the doughfaces are vocal about their rights...
...or *lack* of them...
...the more *violent* the ***backlash*** is against the "human" underclass. *Humans.* That's what they call themselves.
There was a riot just last night, caused by the murder of the scientist *Angus Mortimire,* a human.
I say! A doughface ***scientist?*** *How* can that be? I thought they were *excluded* from higher education.
And I'm sure I've read *somewhere* that they have *smaller brains* than us.
He was a *genius.* Completely *self-educated.* He worked for many research companies, despite his species, before he disappeared. About six months ago, according to *business associates* that is – he had no family.
In fact, there's been a *spate* of missing scientists. He's the only one to turn up.
His body was found yesterday, floating in the Seine. He'd been peppered with high-calibre bullets. The humans went *berserk.* They say it's a *speciesist* killing.
Lady and gentlemen? Dinner is served.
What do *you* make of it all, Nistair?
Me, sir? I'm not *paid* to have an ***opinion,*** sir.
The dining room is in ***there,*** sir.

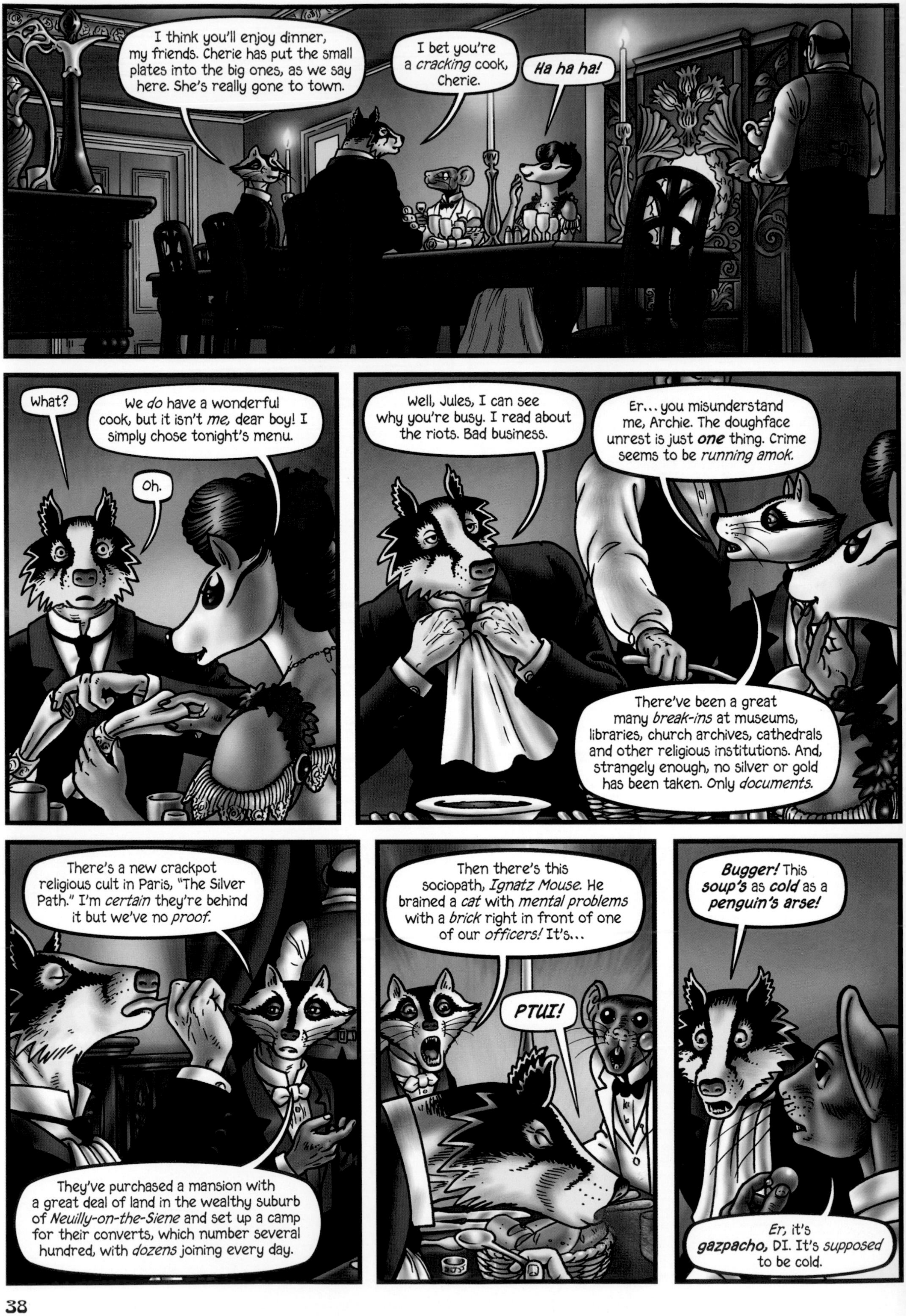

I think you'll enjoy dinner, my friends. Cherie has put the small plates into the big ones, as we say here. She's really gone to town.
I bet you're a *cracking* cook, Cherie.
Ha ha ha!
What?
We *do* have a wonderful cook, but it isn't *me,* dear boy! I simply chose tonight's menu.
Oh.
Well, Jules, I can see why you're busy. I read about the riots. Bad business.
Er... you misunderstand me, Archie. The doughface unrest is just ***one*** thing. Crime seems to be *running amok.*
There've been a great many *break-ins* at museums, libraries, church archives, cathedrals and other religious institutions. And, strangely enough, no silver or gold has been taken. Only *documents.*
There's a new crackpot religious cult in Paris, "The Silver Path." I'm *certain* they're behind it but we've no *proof.*
They've purchased a mansion with a great deal of land in the wealthy suburb of *Neuilly-on-the-Siene* and set up a camp for their converts, which number several hundred, with *dozens* joining every day.
Then there's this sociopath, *Ignatz Mouse.* He brained a *cat* with *mental problems* with a *brick* right in front of one of our *officers!* It's...
PTUI!
Bugger! This ***soup's*** as ***cold*** as a ***penguin's arse!***
Er, it's ***gazpacho,*** DI. It's *supposed* to be cold.

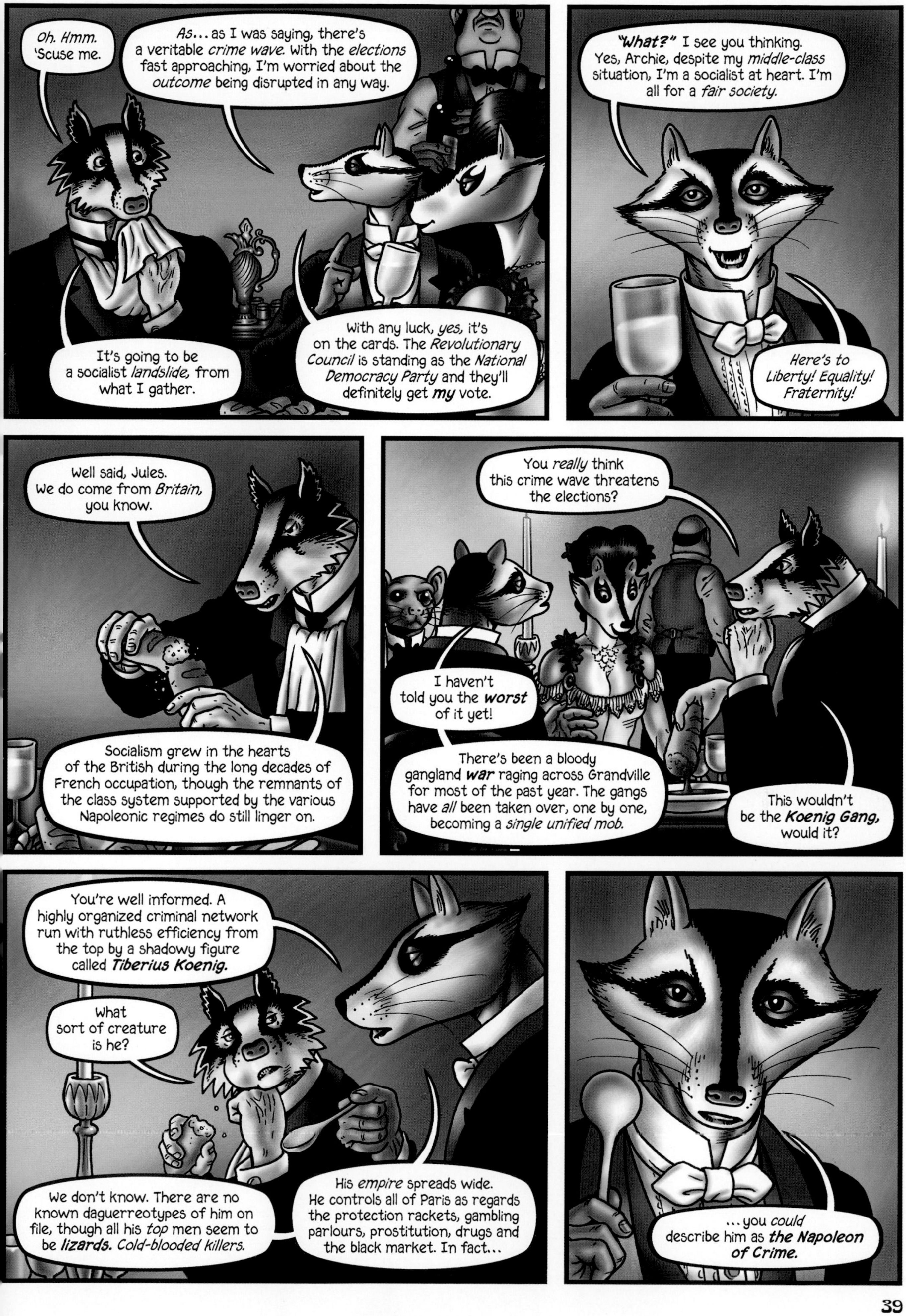

Oh. Hmm. 'Scuse me.
As... as I was saying, there's a veritable crime wave. With the elections fast approaching, I'm worried about the outcome being disrupted in any way.
It's going to be a socialist landslide, from what I gather.
With any luck, yes, it's on the cards. The Revolutionary Council is standing as the National Democracy Party and they'll definitely get my vote.
"What?" I see you thinking. Yes, Archie, despite my middle-class situation, I'm a socialist at heart. I'm all for a fair society.
Here's to Liberty! Equality! Fraternity!
Well said, Jules. We do come from Britain, you know.
Socialism grew in the hearts of the British during the long decades of French occupation, though the remnants of the class system supported by the various Napoleonic regimes do still linger on.
You really think this crime wave threatens the elections?
I haven't told you the worst of it yet!
There's been a bloody gangland war raging across Grandville for most of the past year. The gangs have all been taken over, one by one, becoming a single unified mob.
This wouldn't be the Koenig Gang, would it?
You're well informed. A highly organized criminal network run with ruthless efficiency from the top by a shadowy figure called Tiberius Koenig.
What sort of creature is he?
We don't know. There are no known daguerreotypes of him on file, though all his top men seem to be lizards. Cold-blooded killers.
His empire spreads wide. He controls all of Paris as regards the protection rackets, gambling parlours, prostitution, drugs and the black market. In fact...
...you could describe him as the Napoleon of Crime.

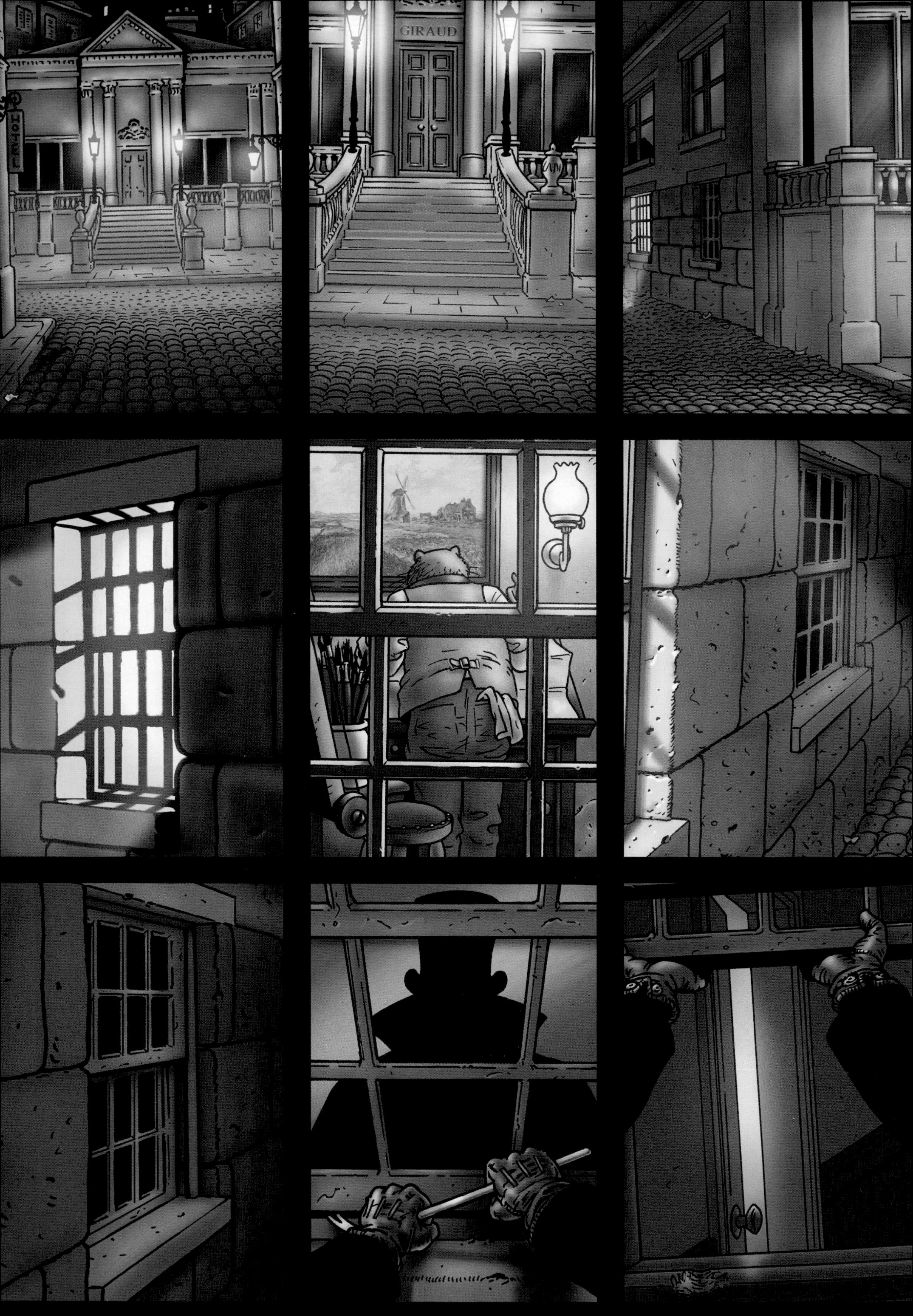
HOTEL
GIRAUD

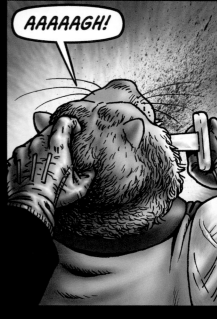

AAAAAGH!

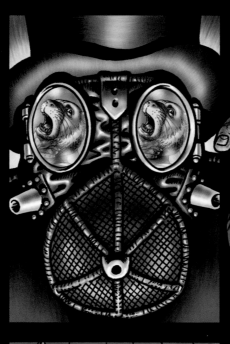

41

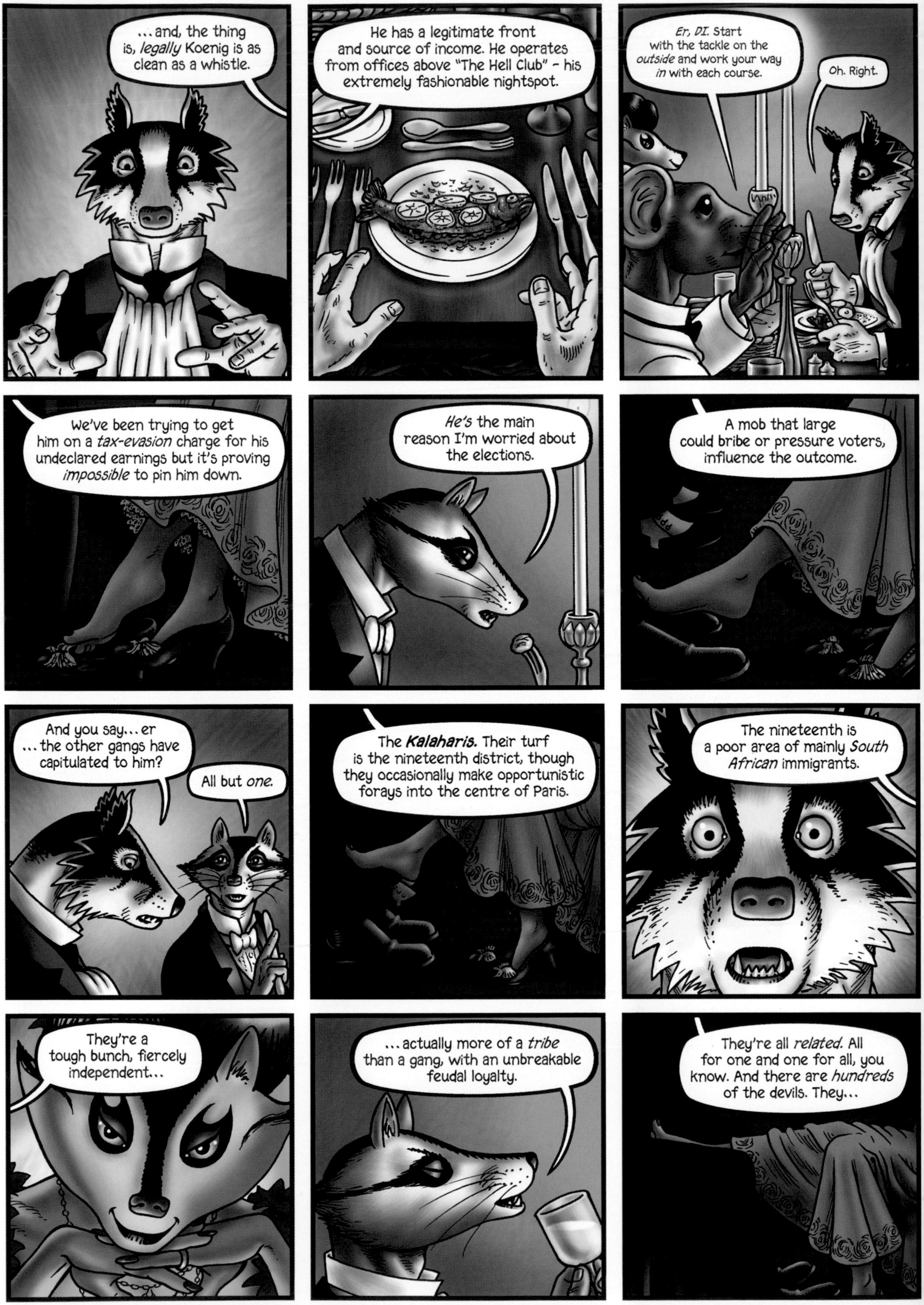
...and, the thing is, *legally* Koenig is as clean as a whistle.
He has a legitimate front and source of income. He operates from offices above "The Hell Club" – his extremely fashionable nightspot.
Er, DI. Start with the tackle on the *outside* and work your way *in* with each course.
Oh. Right.
We've been trying to get him on a *tax-evasion* charge for his undeclared earnings but it's proving *impossible* to pin him down.
He's the main reason I'm worried about the elections.
A mob that large could bribe or pressure voters, influence the outcome.
And you say... er ... the other gangs have capitulated to him?
All but *one.*
The ***Kalaharis.*** Their turf is the nineteenth district, though they occasionally make opportunistic forays into the centre of Paris.
The nineteenth is a poor area of mainly *South African* immigrants.
They're a tough bunch, fiercely independent...
...actually more of a *tribe* than a gang, with an unbreakable feudal loyalty.
They're all *related.* All for one and one for all, you know. And there are *hundreds* of the devils. They...

STOP! Er... f-for a moment - and let Roderick tell you what he *discovered* at *The Agile Rabbit!*

Do they, by God?

Does this make him a possible suspect, *Archibald?*

E-enough to necessitate questioning him. It's a definite *connection.*

Eh? *Oh,* yes. All those bohemian johnnies seem to think that this billionaire bounder *Krapaud* and his filthy rich amigos are out to get them.

I'm afraid he's a famously hard man to get to see. And we don't have any legal way to *force* him to be interviewed if we've no evidence of any link.

How would you like to attend a private view at the *Louvre* tomorrow night? Krapaud will most likely be there. It'll be an opportunity to question the bugger.

I have some invitations right here.

Ha ha! My friend, you *really* are a *magician!* **How** on earth...

Pardon me, sir. You're wanted *urgently* on the voicepipe. It's the *Prefecture.*

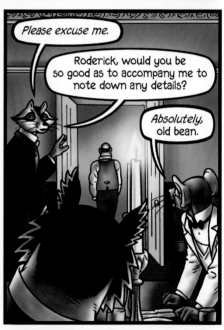

Please excuse me.

Roderick, would you be so good as to accompany me to note down any details?

Absolutely, old bean.

Would you like to know something, my *dear* Archie?

I can't *bear* the thought of you *languishing* all *alone* in your hotel room. You know, if you're *ever* at a bit of a...*loose end...*

...*do* let me know. I could go for a big strapping badger like...

Rodent's been *murdered!* I must leave *immediately!*

No! I mean - *wait* for me!

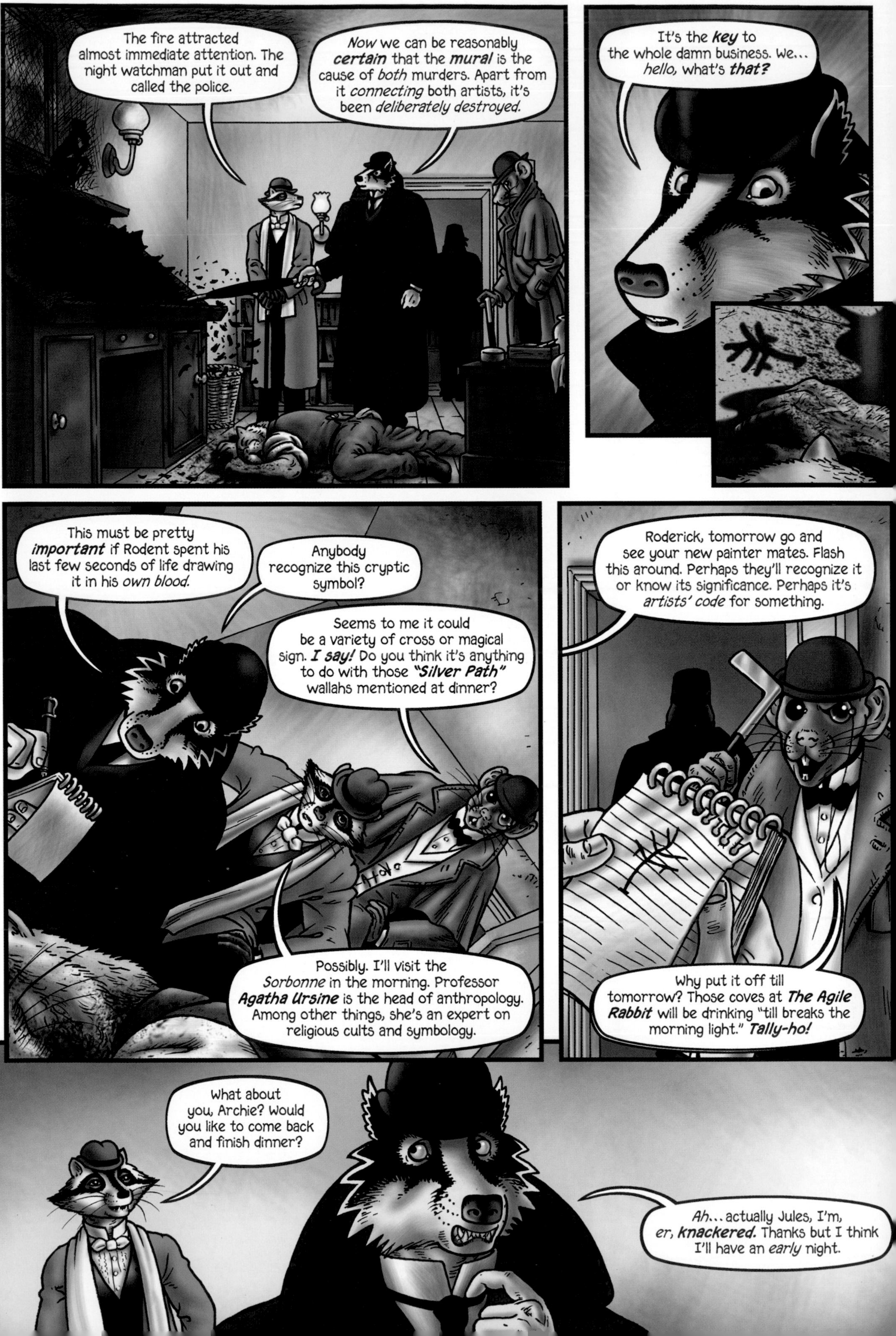

The fire attracted almost immediate attention. The night watchman put it out and called the police.
Now we can be reasonably ***certain*** that the ***mural*** is the cause of *both* murders. Apart from it *connecting* both artists, it's been *deliberately destroyed.*
It's the ***key*** to the whole damn business. We... *hello,* what's ***that?***
This must be pretty ***important*** if Rodent spent his last few seconds of life drawing it in his *own blood.*
Anybody recognize this cryptic symbol?
Seems to me it could be a variety of cross or magical sign. ***I say!*** Do you think it's anything to do with those ***"Silver Path"*** wallahs mentioned at dinner?
Possibly. I'll visit the *Sorbonne* in the morning. Professor ***Agatha Ursine*** is the head of anthropology. Among other things, she's an expert on religious cults and symbology.
Roderick, tomorrow go and see your new painter mates. Flash this around. Perhaps they'll recognize it or know its significance. Perhaps it's *artists' code* for something.
Why put it off till tomorrow? Those coves at ***The Agile Rabbit*** will be drinking "till breaks the morning light." ***Tally-ho!***
What about you, Archie? Would you like to come back and finish dinner?
Ah... actually Jules, I'm, *er,* ***knackered.*** Thanks but I think I'll have an *early* night.

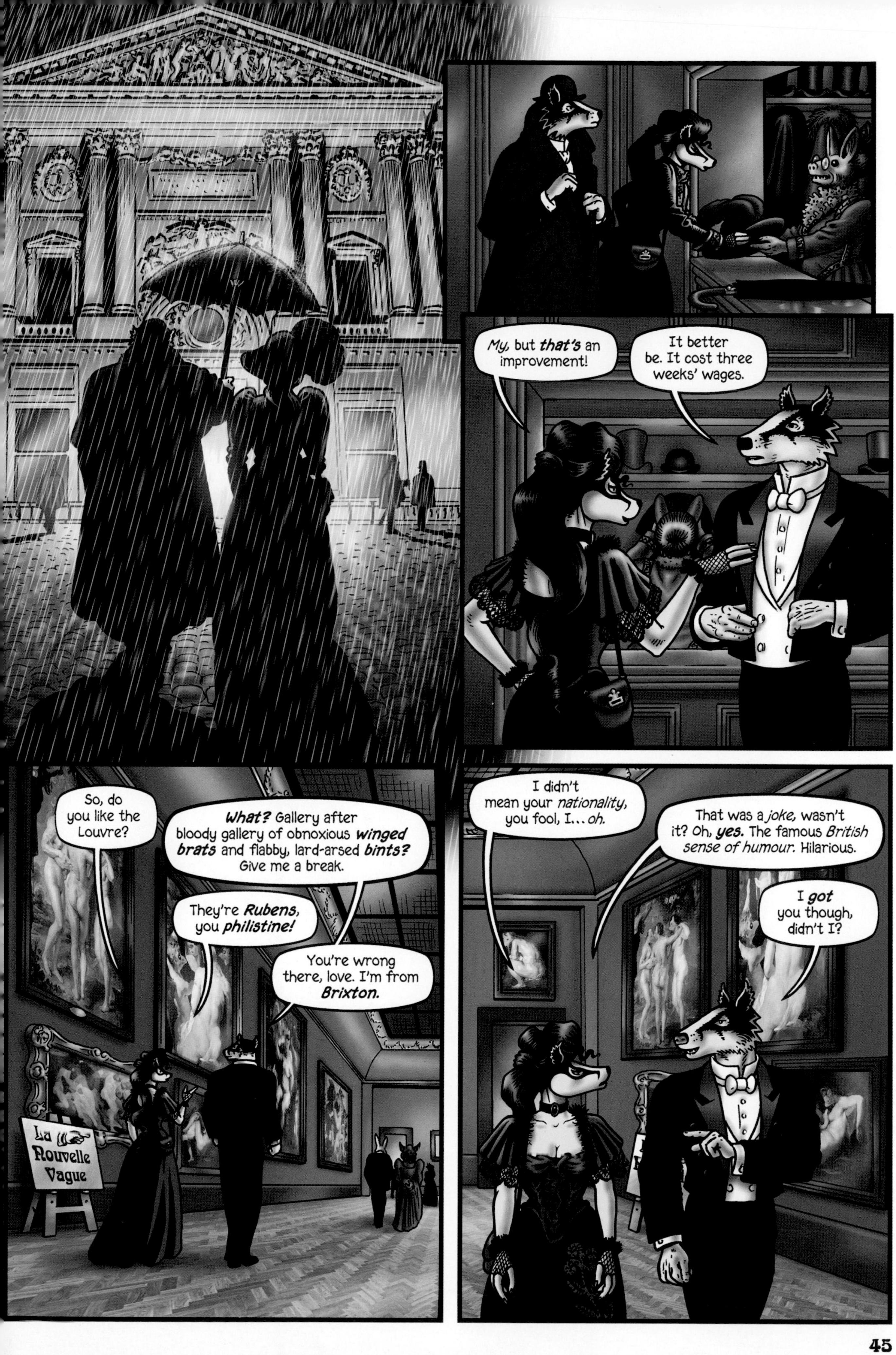
My, but that's an improvement!
It better be. It cost three weeks' wages.
So, do you like the Louvre?
What? Gallery after bloody gallery of obnoxious winged brats and flabby, lard-arsed bints? Give me a break.
They're Rubens, you philistine!
You're wrong there, love. I'm from Brixton.
La Nouvelle Vague
I didn't mean your nationality, you fool, I... oh.
That was a joke, wasn't it? Oh, yes. The famous British sense of humour. Hilarious.
I got you though, didn't I?

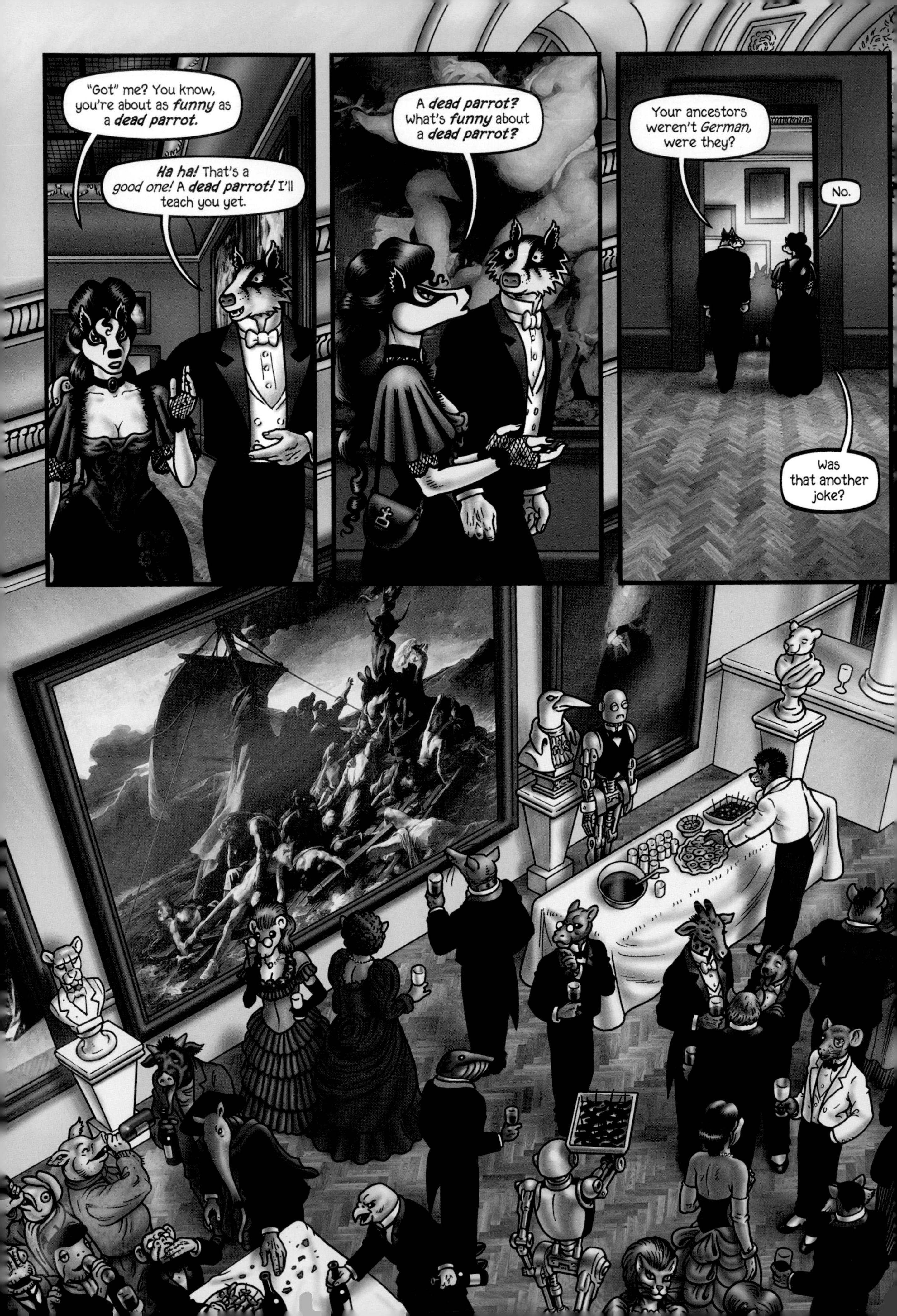
"Got" me? You know, you're about as *funny* as a *dead parrot.*
Ha ha! That's a *good one!* A ***dead parrot!*** I'll teach you yet.
A ***dead parrot?*** What's ***funny*** about a ***dead parrot?***
Your ancestors weren't *German,* were they?
No.
Was that another joke?

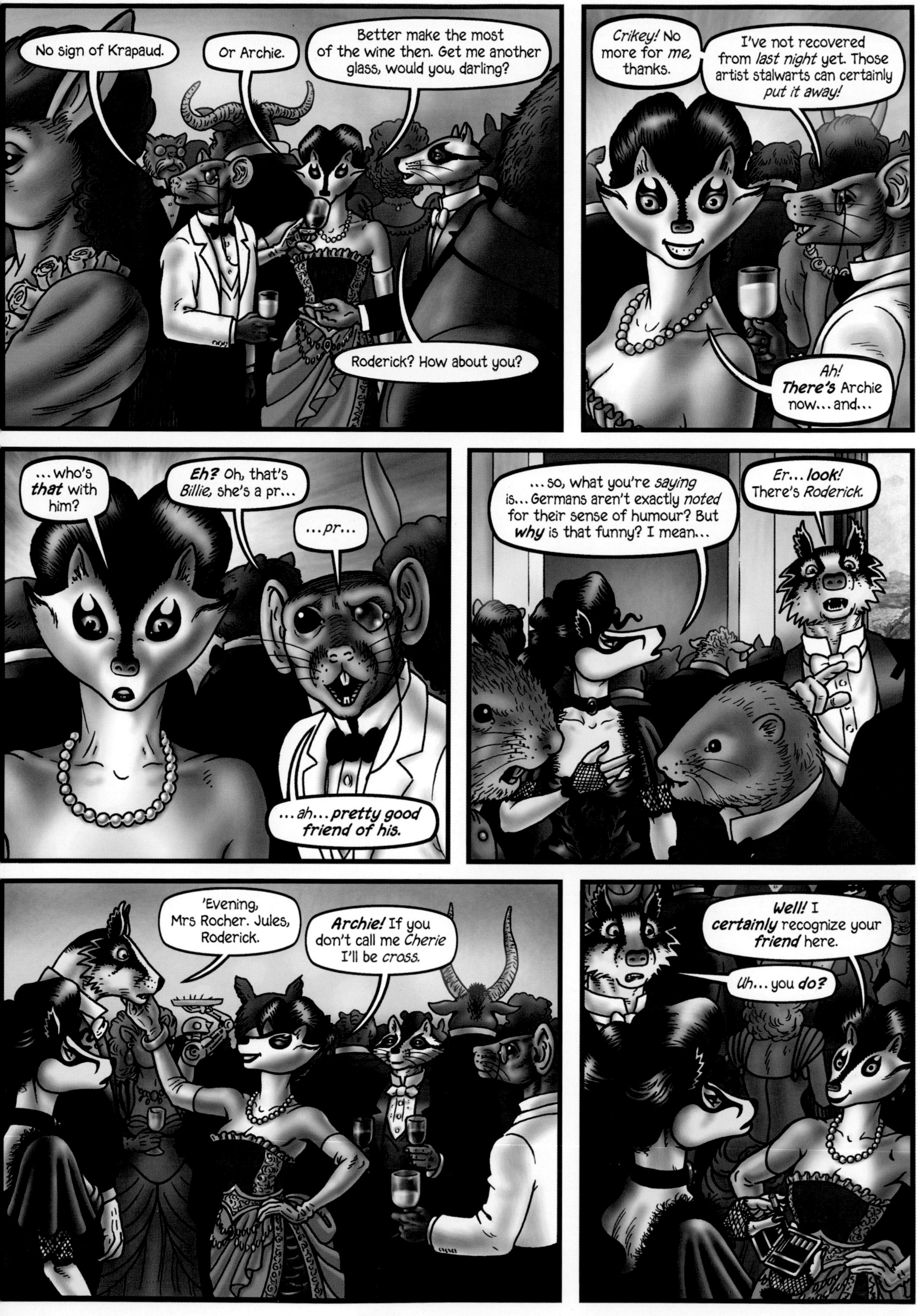
No sign of Krapaud.
Or Archie.
Better make the most of the wine then. Get me another glass, would you, darling?
Roderick? How about you?
Crikey! No more for *me*, thanks.
I've not recovered from *last night* yet. Those artist stalwarts can certainly *put it away!*
*Ah! **There's** Archie now... and...*
...who's ***that*** with him?
Eh? Oh, that's *Billie*, she's a pr...
...pr...
*...ah... **pretty good friend of his.***
...so, what you're *saying* is... Germans aren't exactly *noted* for their sense of humour? But ***why*** is that funny? I mean...
*Er... **look!*** There's *Roderick.*
'Evening, Mrs Rocher. Jules, Roderick.
Archie! If you don't call me *Cherie* I'll be *cross.*
Well! I ***certainly*** recognize your ***friend*** here.
Uh... you ***do?***

Doesn't *everybody* here? No need to imagine what *you* look like naked, darling!

I'm not ashamed of my body.

Neither am I, dear, but I'm not so **common** as to **flaunt** it in the face of every Tom, Dick and...

Harumph! Er, *Jules*, any luck with your professor?

Not really. You know, it all depends upon how *accurate* Rodent's drawing was. *Bleeding to death* tends to impede one's abilities.

Given that he was most likely in shock and shaking uncontrollably, Agatha suggests that he could have been attempting to draw any one of *these*.

For example, "H" in the *Theban* alphabet, apparently used in *witchcraft*, and the *Viking rune* for the letter "Z".

It's similar to the alchemical symbol for *"cinere clavelati"*, whatever *that* means, and the classic *Slavonic cross*. It's comparable to the *"suastika"* too.

The **what?**

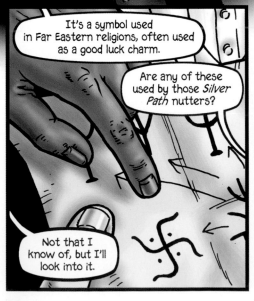

It's a symbol used in Far Eastern religions, often used as a good luck charm.

Are any of these used by those *Silver Path* nutters?

Not that I know of, but I'll look into it.

How about you, Rodders? Any of your artist chums recognize it?

Not a one, DI. Vincent over there suggested it could be a badly drawn *Christmas tree*.

Though he **was** fairly *blotto* at the time.

Great. Where's *Krapaud?*

48

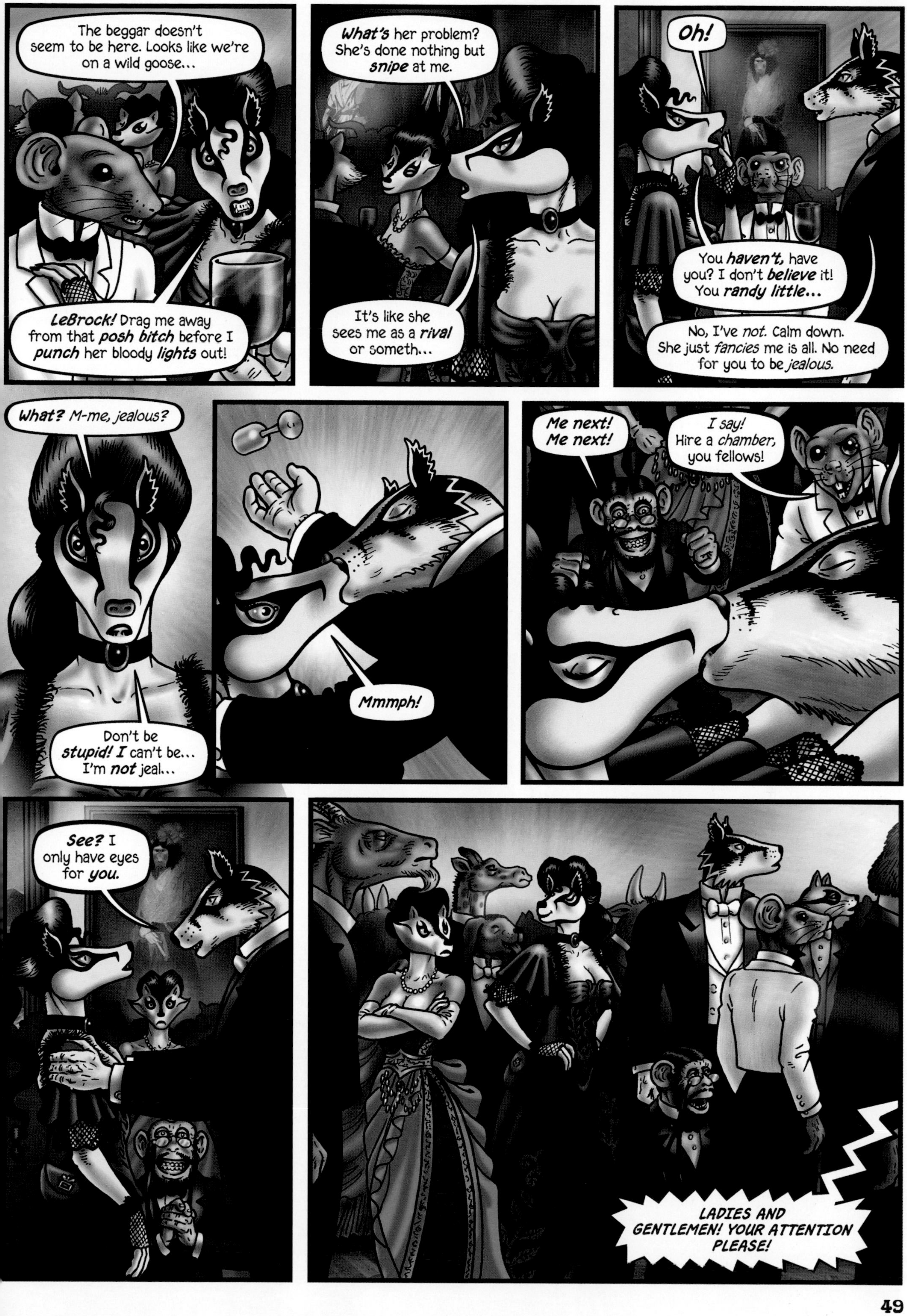

The beggar doesn't seem to be here. Looks like we're on a wild goose...
LeBrock! Drag me away from that posh bitch before I punch her bloody lights out!
What's her problem? She's done nothing but snipe at me.
It's like she sees me as a rival or someth...
Oh!
You haven't, have you? I don't believe it! You randy little...
No, I've not. Calm down. She just fancies me is all. No need for you to be jealous.
What? M-me, jealous?
Don't be stupid! I can't be... I'm not jeal...
Mmmph!
Me next! Me next!
I say! Hire a chamber, you fellows!
See? I only have eyes for you.
LADIES AND GENTLEMEN! YOUR ATTENTION PLEASE!

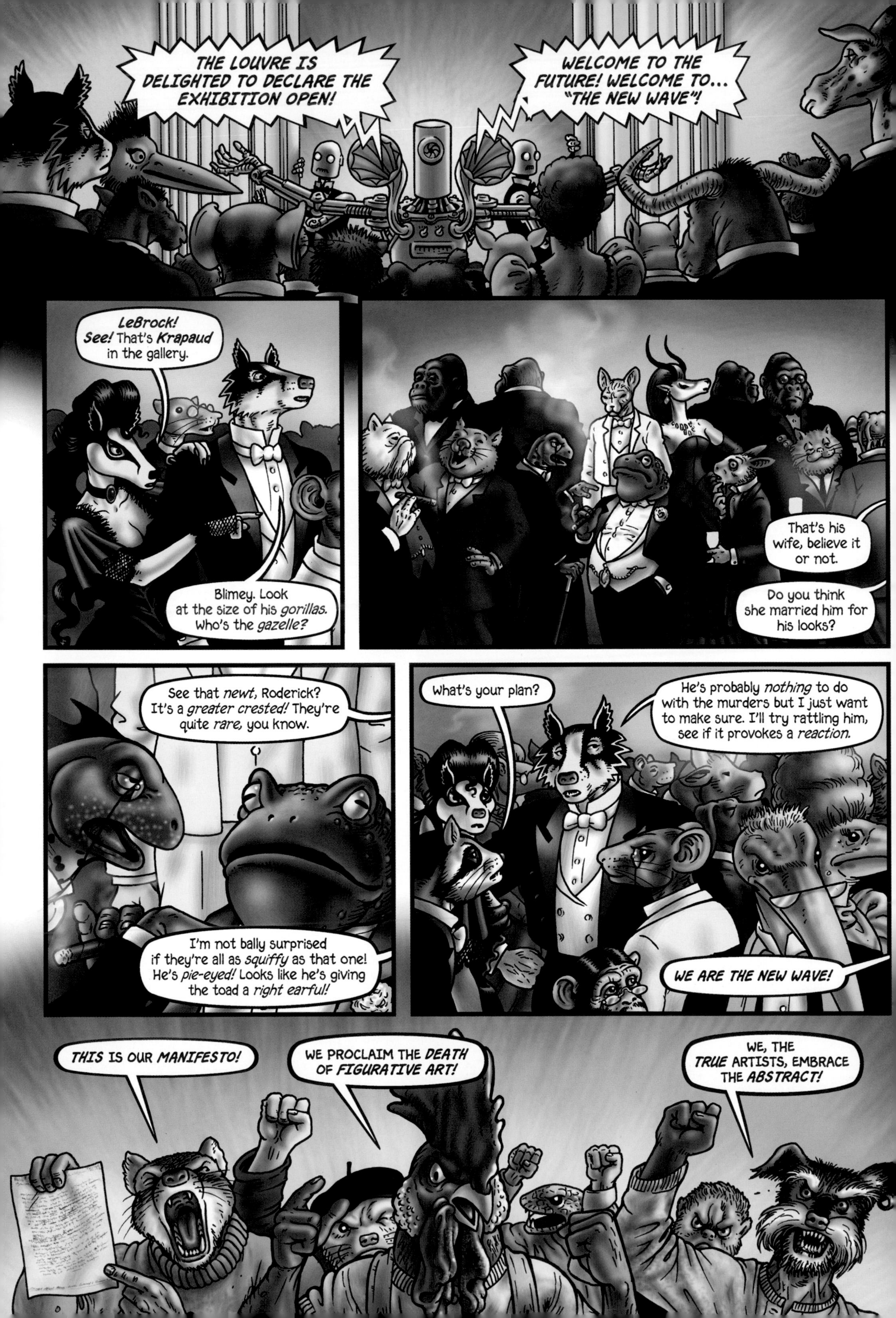
THE LOUVRE IS DELIGHTED TO DECLARE THE EXHIBITION OPEN!
WELCOME TO THE FUTURE! WELCOME TO... "THE NEW WAVE"!
LeBrock! See! That's Krapaud in the gallery.
Blimey. Look at the size of his gorillas. Who's the gazelle?
That's his wife, believe it or not.
Do you think she married him for his looks?
See that newt, Roderick? It's a greater crested! They're quite rare, you know.
I'm not bally surprised if they're all as squiffy as that one! He's pie-eyed! Looks like he's giving the toad a right earful!
What's your plan?
He's probably nothing to do with the murders but I just want to make sure. I'll try rattling him, see if it provokes a reaction.
WE ARE THE NEW WAVE!
THIS IS OUR MANIFESTO!
WE PROCLAIM THE DEATH OF FIGURATIVE ART!
WE, THE TRUE ARTISTS, EMBRACE THE ABSTRACT!

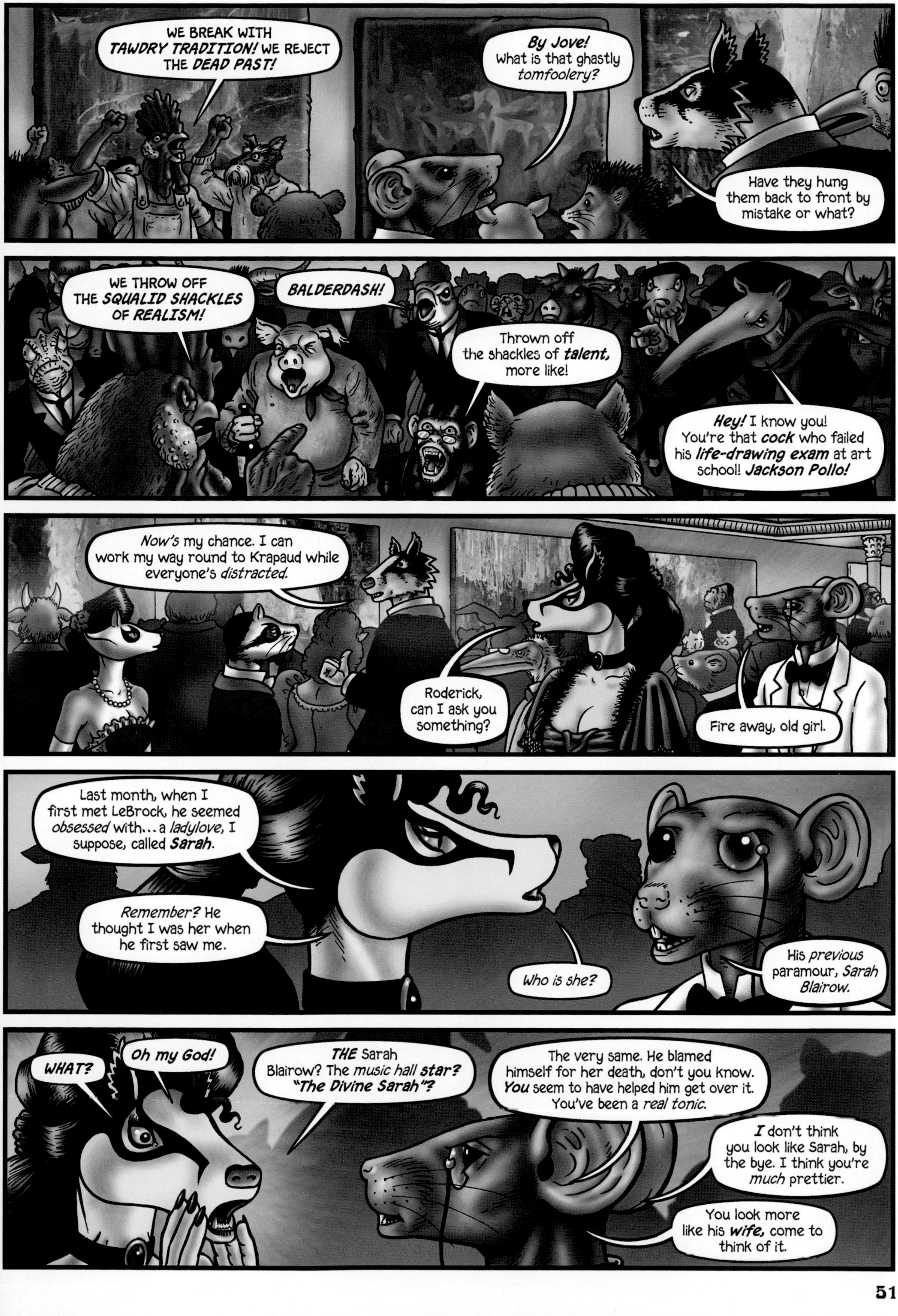
WE BREAK WITH *TAWDRY TRADITION!* WE REJECT THE *DEAD PAST!*
By Jove! What is that ghastly *tomfoolery?*
Have they hung them back to front by mistake or what?
WE THROW OFF THE *SQUALID SHACKLES* OF *REALISM!*
BALDERDASH!
Thrown off the shackles of ***talent,*** more like!
Hey! I know you! You're that ***cock*** who failed his ***life-drawing exam*** at art school! ***Jackson Pollo!***
Now's my chance. I can work my way round to Krapaud while everyone's *distracted.*
Roderick, can I ask you something?
Fire away, old girl.
Last month, when I first met LeBrock, he seemed *obsessed* with... a *ladylove,* I suppose, called ***Sarah.***
Remember? He thought I was her when he first saw me.
Who is she?
His *previous* paramour, *Sarah Blairow.*
WHAT?
Oh my God!
THE Sarah Blairow? The *music hall* ***star? "The Divine Sarah"?***
The very same. He blamed himself for her death, don't you know. ***You*** seem to have helped him get over it. You've been a *real tonic.*
I don't think you look like Sarah, by the bye. I think you're *much* prettier.
You look more like his ***wife,*** come to think of it.

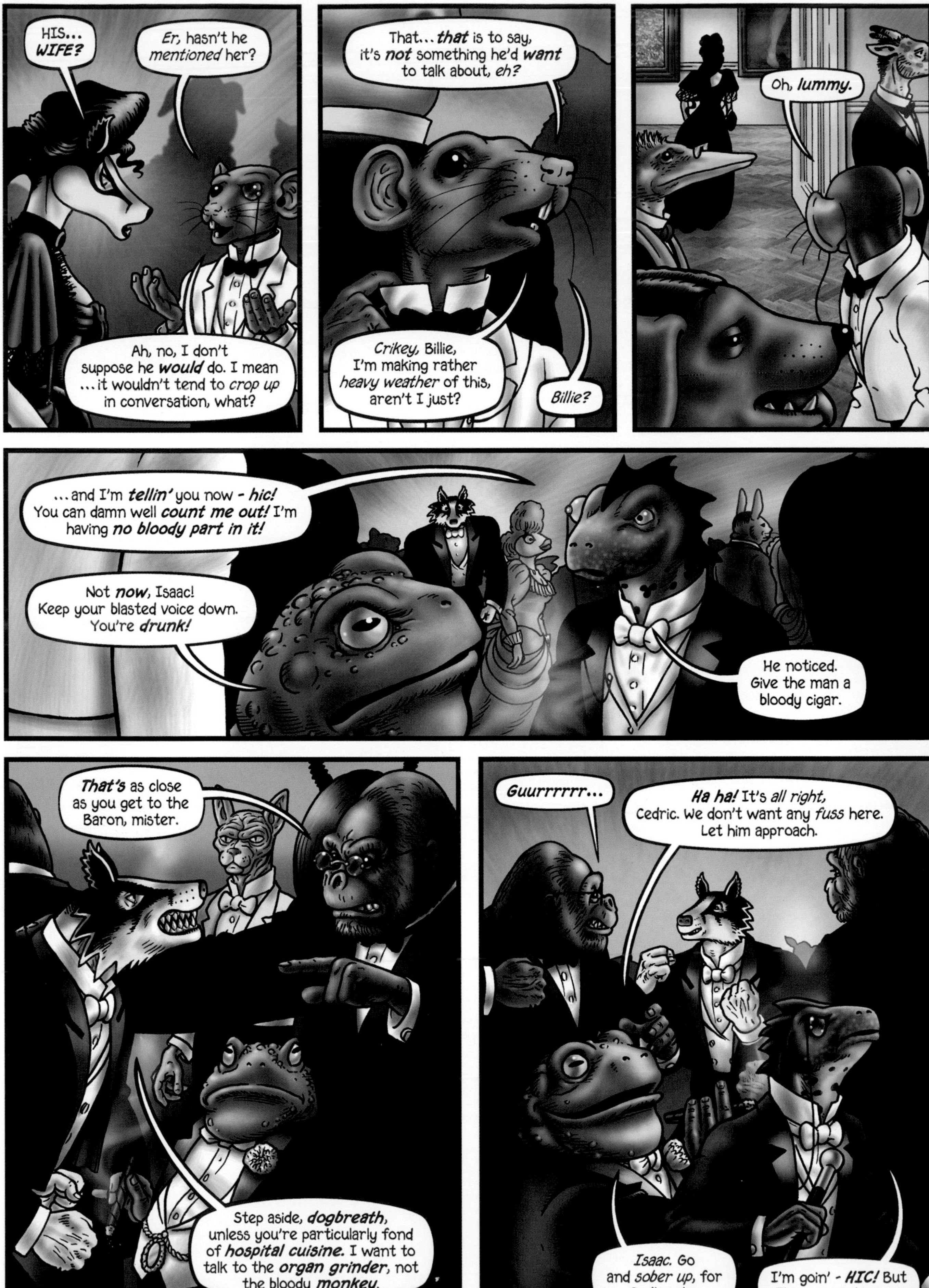
HIS... WIFE?
Er, hasn't he mentioned her?
Ah, no, I don't suppose he would do. I mean ...it wouldn't tend to crop up in conversation, what?
That... that is to say, it's not something he'd want to talk about, eh?
Crikey, Billie, I'm making rather heavy weather of this, aren't I just?
Billie?
Oh, lummy.
...and I'm tellin' you now - hic! You can damn well count me out! I'm having no bloody part in it!
Not now, Isaac! Keep your blasted voice down. You're drunk!
He noticed. Give the man a bloody cigar.
That's as close as you get to the Baron, mister.
Step aside, dogbreath, unless you're particularly fond of hospital cuisine. I want to talk to the organ grinder, not the bloody monkey.
Guurrrrrr...
Ha ha! It's all right, Cedric. We don't want any fuss here. Let him approach.
Isaac. Go and sober up, for God's sake.
I'm goin' - HIC! But I'm warnin' you...

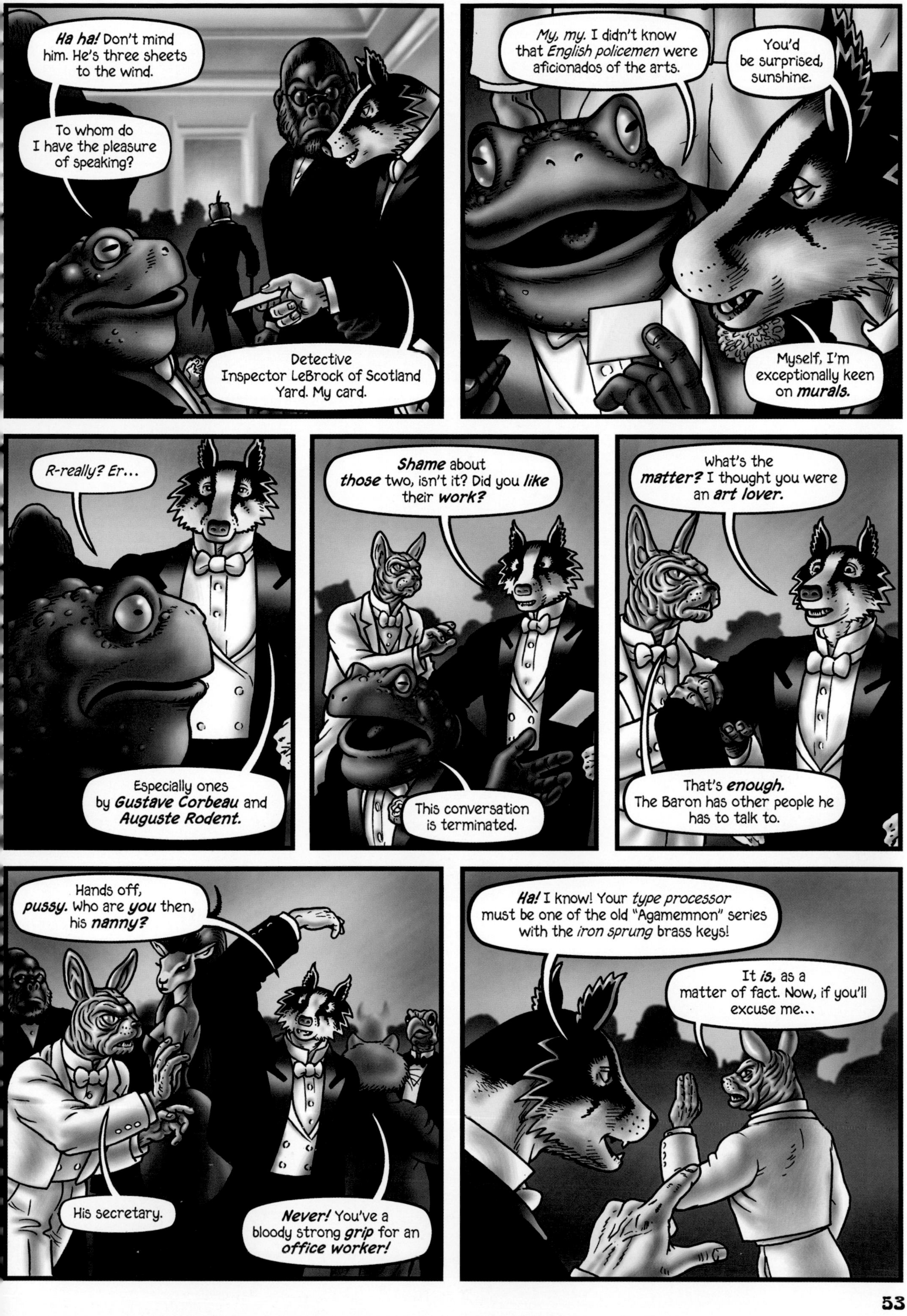

Ha ha! Don't mind him. He's three sheets to the wind.
To whom do I have the pleasure of speaking?
Detective Inspector LeBrock of Scotland Yard. My card.
My, my. I didn't know that *English policemen* were aficionados of the arts.
You'd be surprised, sunshine.
Myself, I'm exceptionally keen on ***murals.***
R-really? Er...
Especially ones by ***Gustave Corbeau*** and ***Auguste Rodent.***
Shame about ***those*** two, isn't it? Did you ***like*** their ***work?***
This conversation is terminated.
What's the ***matter?*** I thought you were an ***art lover.***
That's ***enough.*** The Baron has other people he has to talk to.
Hands off, ***pussy.*** Who are ***you*** then, his ***nanny?***
His secretary.
Never! You've a bloody strong ***grip*** for an ***office worker!***
Ha! I know! Your *type processor* must be one of the old "Agamemnon" series with the *iron sprung* brass keys!
It ***is,*** as a matter of fact. Now, if you'll excuse me...

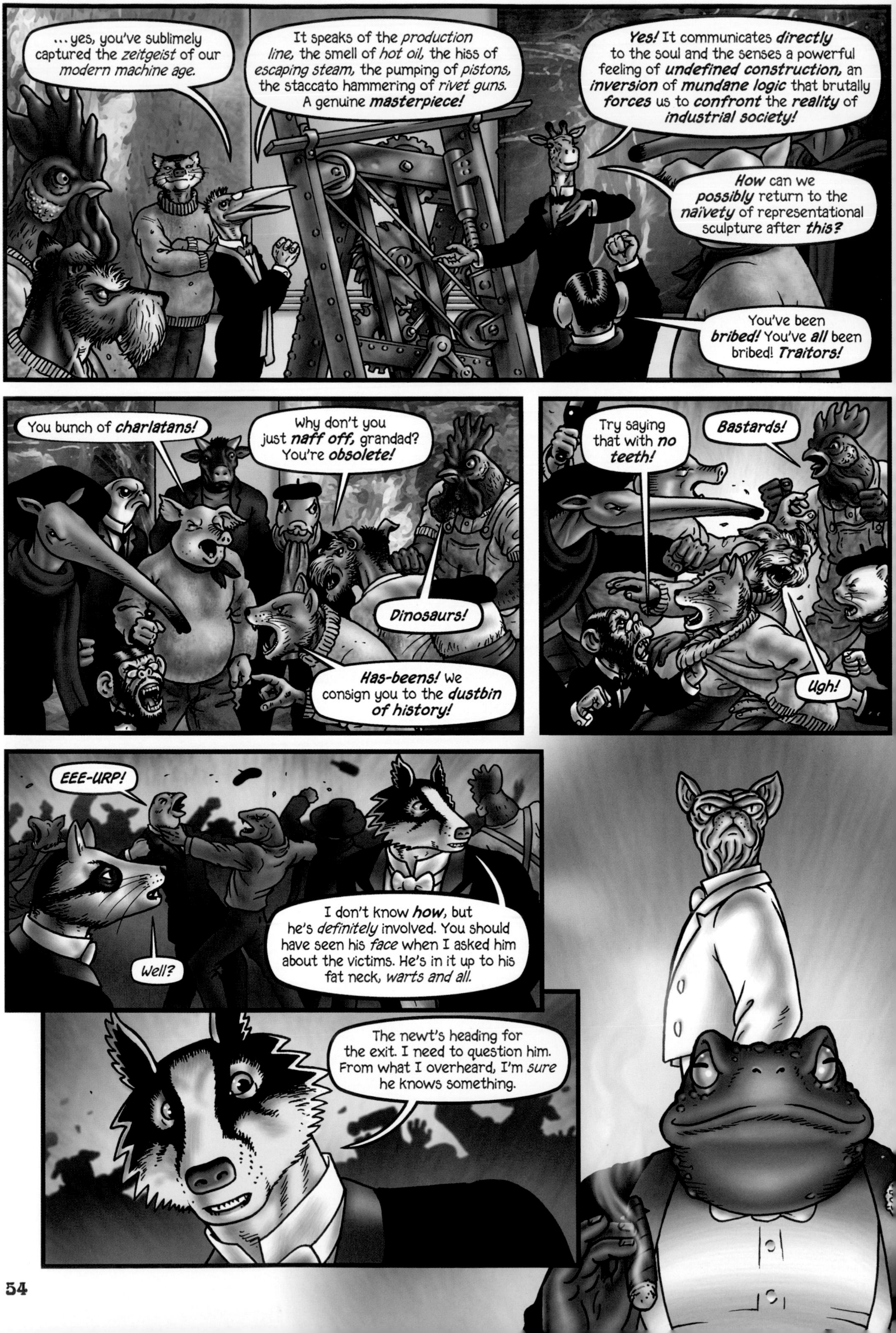

...yes, you've sublimely captured the *zeitgeist* of our *modern machine age.*
It speaks of the *production line,* the smell of *hot oil,* the hiss of *escaping steam,* the pumping of *pistons,* the staccato hammering of *rivet guns.* A genuine ***masterpiece!***
Yes! It communicates ***directly*** to the soul and the senses a powerful feeling of ***undefined construction,*** an ***inversion*** of ***mundane logic*** that brutally ***forces*** us to ***confront*** the ***reality*** of ***industrial society!***
How can we ***possibly*** return to the ***naïvety*** of representational sculpture after ***this?***
You've been ***bribed!*** You've ***all*** been bribed! ***Traitors!***
You bunch of ***charlatans!***
Why don't you just ***naff off,*** grandad? You're ***obsolete!***
Dinosaurs!
Has-beens! We consign you to the ***dustbin of history!***
Try saying that with ***no teeth!***
Bastards!
Ugh!
EEE-URP!
I don't know ***how,*** but he's *definitely* involved. You should have seen his *face* when I asked him about the victims. He's in it up to his fat neck, *warts and all.*
Well?
The newt's heading for the exit. I need to question him. From what I overheard, I'm *sure* he knows something.

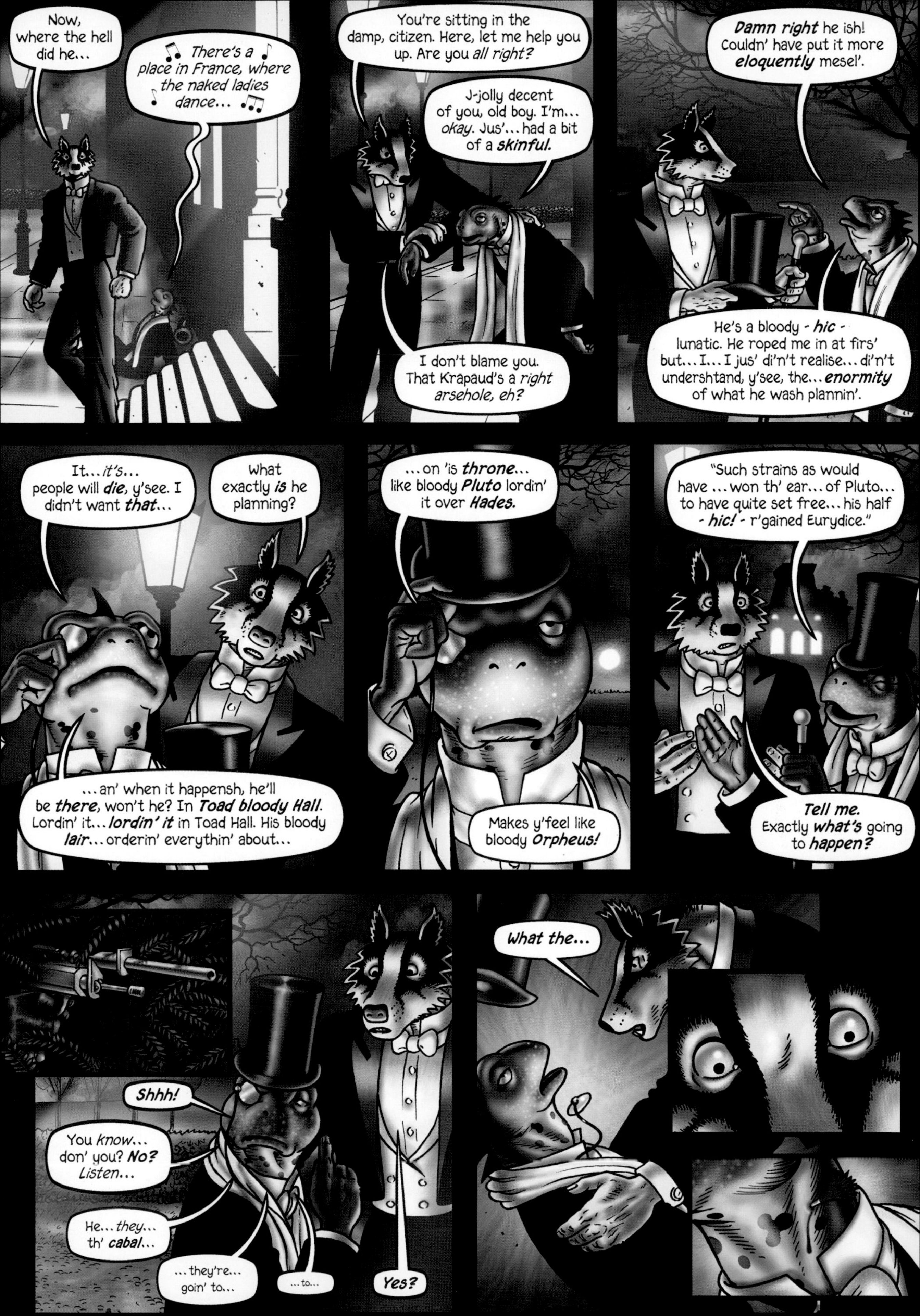
Now, where the hell did he...
There's a place in France, where the naked ladies dance...
You're sitting in the damp, citizen. Here, let me help you up. Are you *all right?*
J-jolly decent of you, old boy. I'm... *okay*. Jus'... had a bit of a **skinful.**
I don't blame you. That Krapaud's a *right arsehole, eh?*
Damn right he ish! Couldn' have put it more **eloquently** mesel'.
He's a bloody - **hic** - lunatic. He roped me in at firs' but... I... I jus' di'n't realise... di'n't undershtand, y'see, the... **enormity** of what he wash plannin'.
It... *it's*... people will **die**, y'see. I didn't want **that**...
What exactly **is** he planning?
...an' when it happensh, he'll be **there**, won't he? In **Toad bloody Hall**. Lordin' it... **lordin' it** in Toad Hall. His bloody **lair**... orderin' everythin' about...
...on 'is **throne**... like bloody **Pluto** lordin' it over **Hades.**
Makes y'feel like bloody **Orpheus!**
"Such strains as would have ... won th' ear... of Pluto... to have quite set free... his half - **hic!** - r'gained Eurydice."
Tell me. Exactly **what's** going to **happen?**
Shhh!
You *know*... don' you? **No?** *Listen*...
He... *they*... th' **cabal**...
... they're... goin' to...
...to...
Yes?
What the...

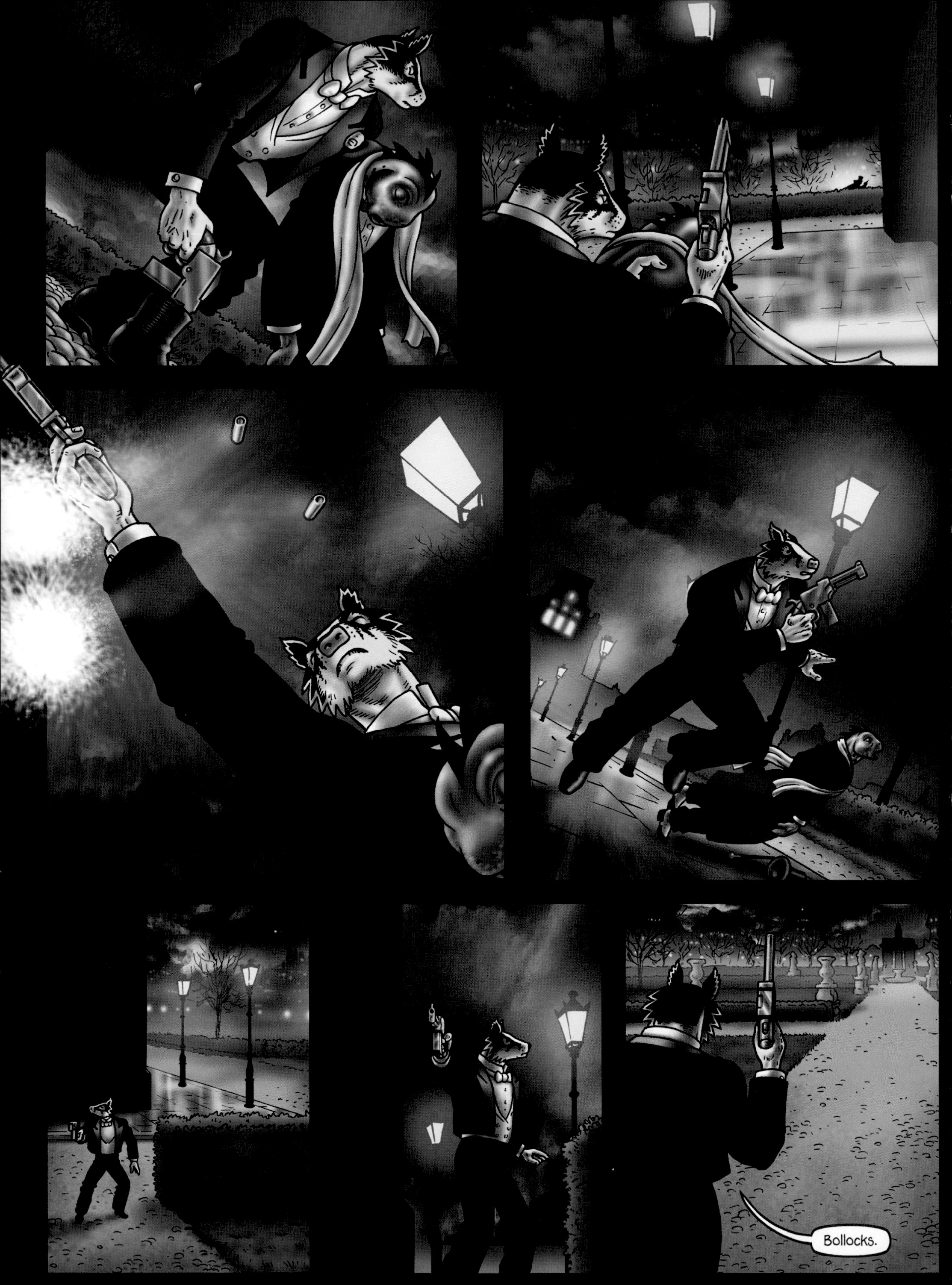
Bollocks.

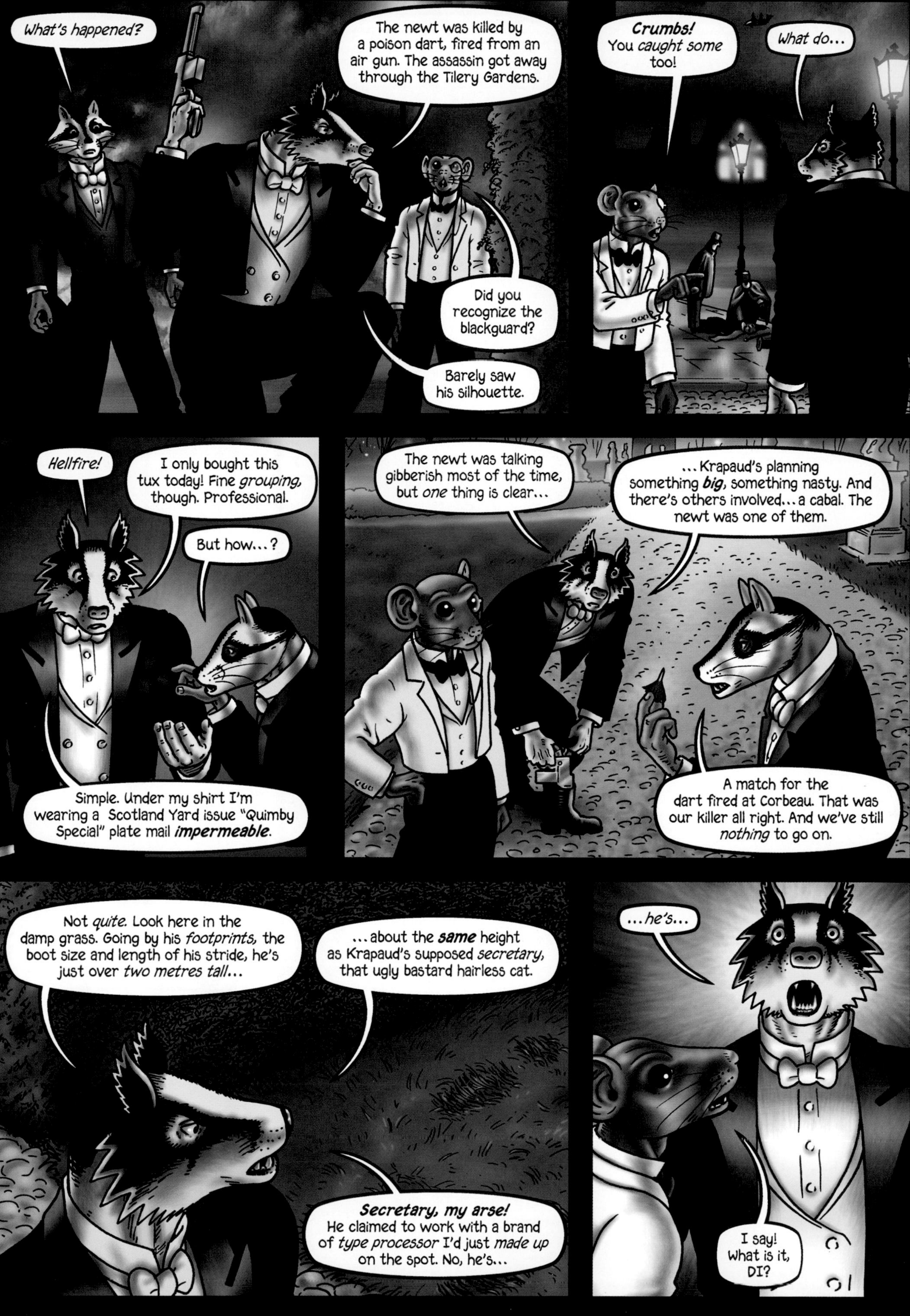

What's happened?
The newt was killed by a poison dart, fired from an air gun. The assassin got away through the Tilery Gardens.
Did you recognize the blackguard?
Barely saw his silhouette.
Crumbs! You *caught some* too!
What do...
Hellfire!
I only bought this tux today! Fine *grouping*, though. Professional.
But how...?
Simple. Under my shirt I'm wearing a Scotland Yard issue "Quimby Special" plate mail ***impermeable***.
The newt was talking gibberish most of the time, but *one* thing is clear...
...Krapaud's planning something ***big***, something nasty. And there's others involved...a cabal. The newt was one of them.
A match for the dart fired at Corbeau. That was our killer all right. And we've still *nothing* to go on.
Not *quite*. Look here in the damp grass. Going by his *footprints*, the boot size and length of his stride, he's just over *two metres tall*...
...about the ***same*** height as Krapaud's supposed *secretary*, that ugly bastard hairless cat.
Secretary, my arse! He claimed to work with a brand of *type processor* I'd just *made up* on the spot. No, he's...
...he's...
I say! What is it, DI?

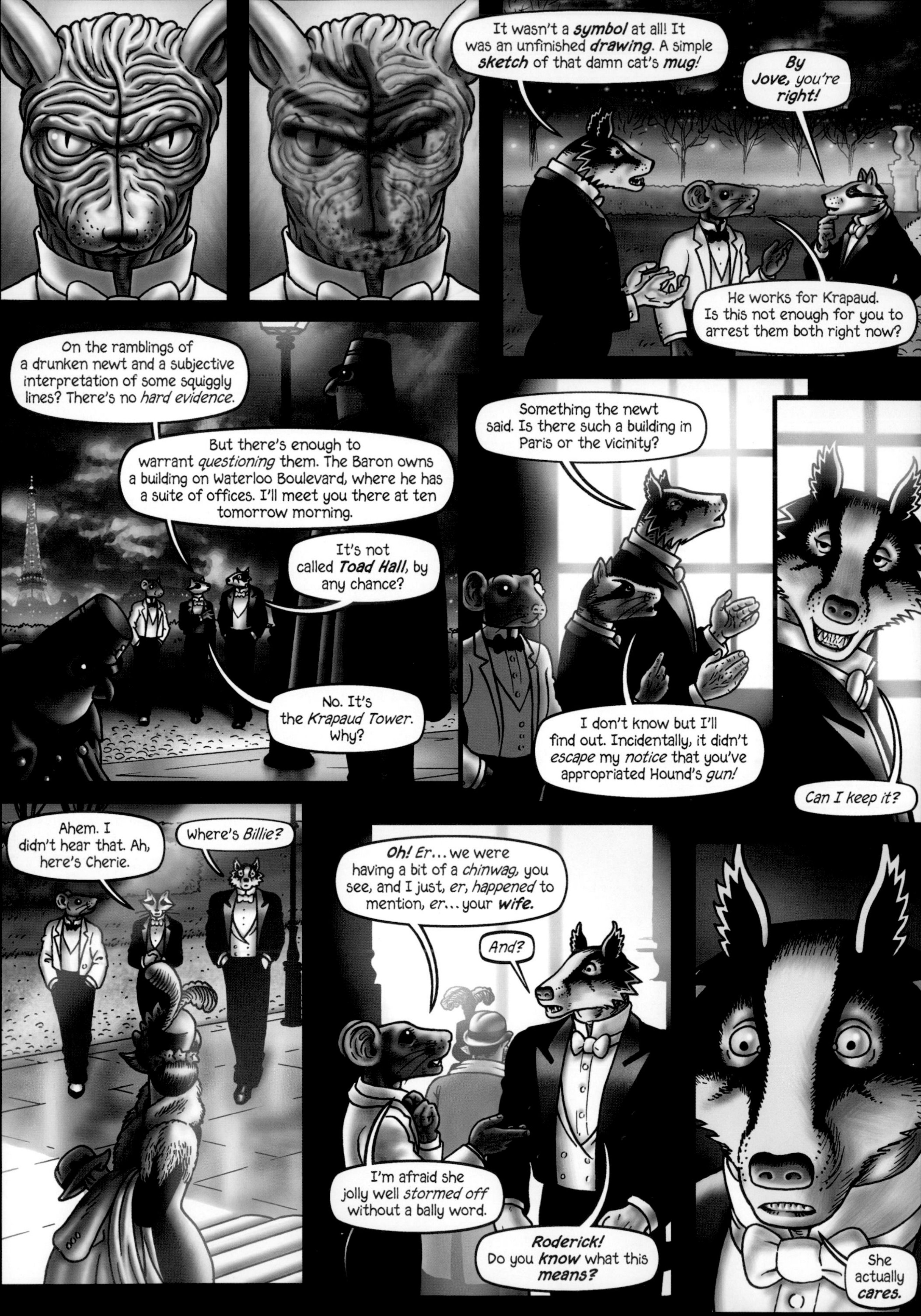

It wasn't a symbol at all! It was an unfinished drawing. A simple sketch of that damn cat's mug!
By Jove, you're right!
He works for Krapaud. Is this not enough for you to arrest them both right now?
On the ramblings of a drunken newt and a subjective interpretation of some squiggly lines? There's no hard evidence.
But there's enough to warrant questioning them. The Baron owns a building on Waterloo Boulevard, where he has a suite of offices. I'll meet you there at ten tomorrow morning.
It's not called Toad Hall, by any chance?
No. It's the Krapaud Tower. Why?
Something the newt said. Is there such a building in Paris or the vicinity?
I don't know but I'll find out. Incidentally, it didn't escape my notice that you've appropriated Hound's gun!
Can I keep it?
Ahem. I didn't hear that. Ah, here's Cherie.
Where's Billie?
Oh! Er... we were having a bit of a chinwag, you see, and I just, er, happened to mention, er... your wife.
And?
I'm afraid she jolly well stormed off without a bally word.
Roderick! Do you know what this means?
She actually cares.

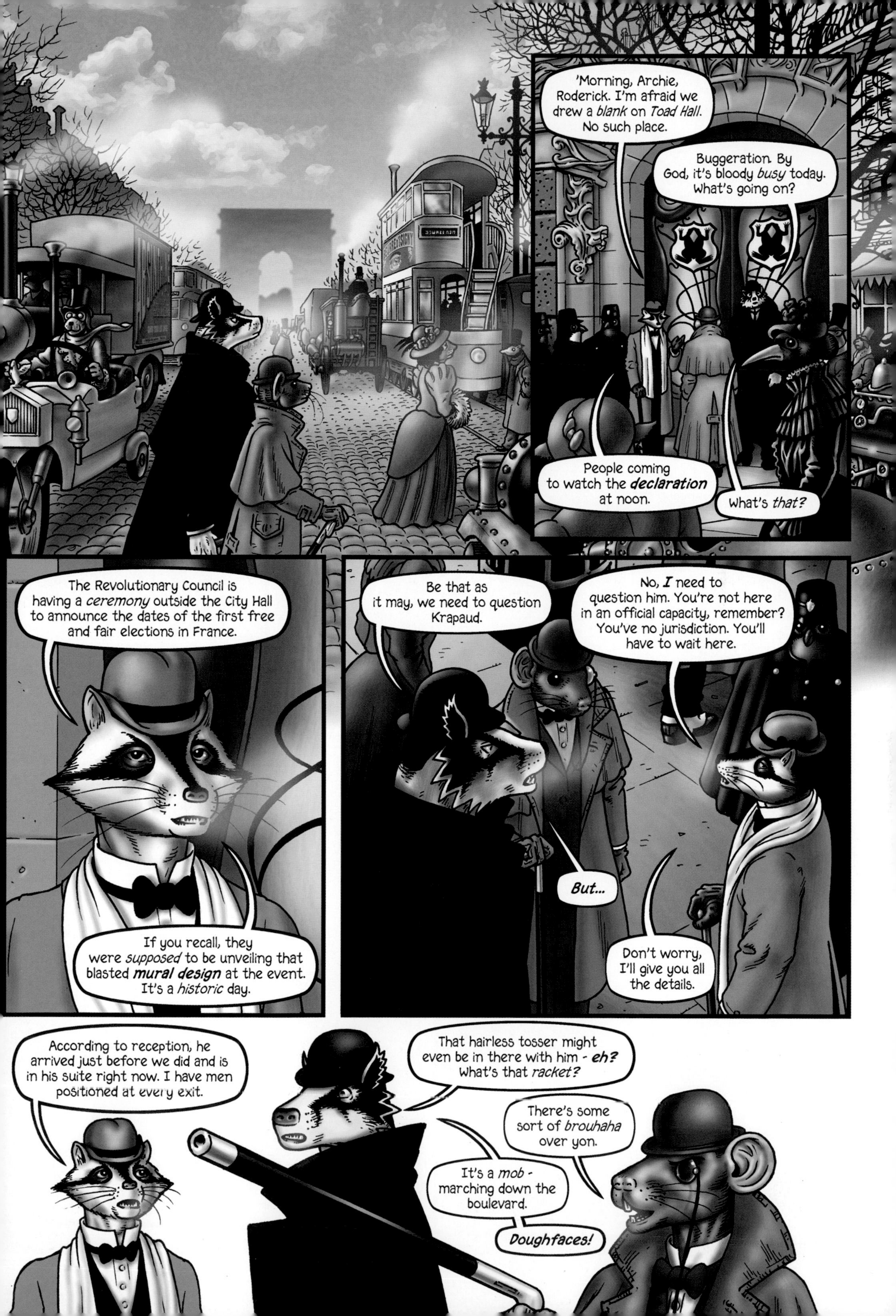
'Morning, Archie, Roderick. I'm afraid we drew a *blank* on *Toad Hall*. No such place.
Buggeration. By God, it's bloody *busy* today. What's going on?
People coming to watch the ***declaration*** at noon.
What's *that?*
The Revolutionary Council is having a *ceremony* outside the City Hall to announce the dates of the first free and fair elections in France.
If you recall, they were *supposed* to be unveiling that blasted ***mural design*** at the event. It's a *historic* day.
Be that as it may, we need to question Krapaud.
No, ***I*** need to question him. You're not here in an official capacity, remember? You've no jurisdiction. You'll have to wait here.
But...
Don't worry, I'll give you all the details.
According to reception, he arrived just before we did and is in his suite right now. I have men positioned at every exit.
That hairless tosser might even be in there with him - ***eh?*** What's that *racket?*
There's some sort of *brouhaha* over yon.
It's a *mob* - marching down the boulevard.
Doughfaces!

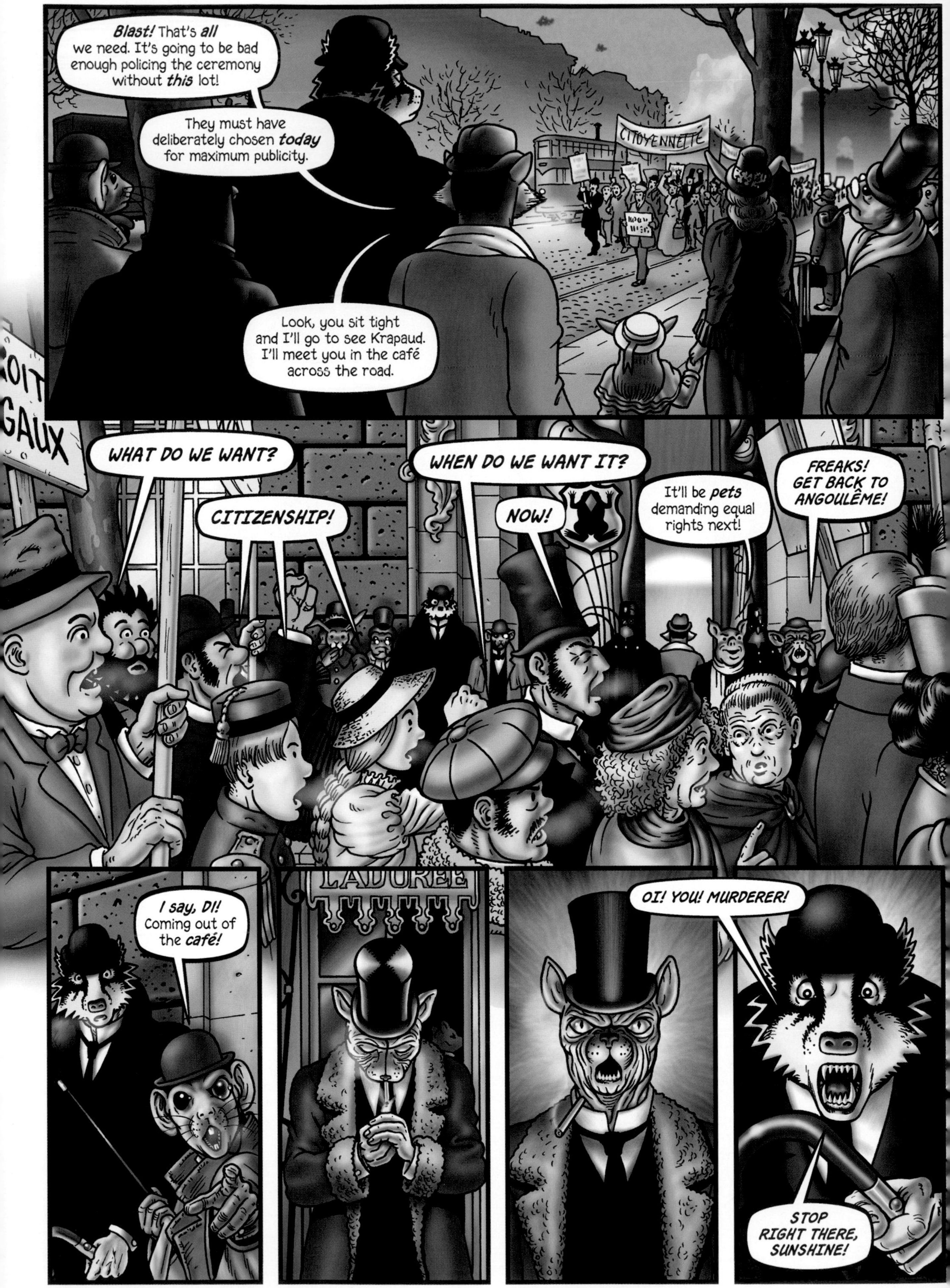
Blast! That's *all* we need. It's going to be bad enough policing the ceremony without *this* lot!
They must have deliberately chosen *today* for maximum publicity.
CITOYENNETÉ
Look, you sit tight and I'll go to see Krapaud. I'll meet you in the café across the road.
WHAT DO WE WANT?
CITIZENSHIP!
WHEN DO WE WANT IT?
NOW!
It'll be *pets* demanding equal rights next!
FREAKS! GET BACK TO ANGOULÊME!
I say, DI! Coming out of the *café!*
LADUREE
OI! YOU! MURDERER!
STOP RIGHT THERE, SUNSHINE!

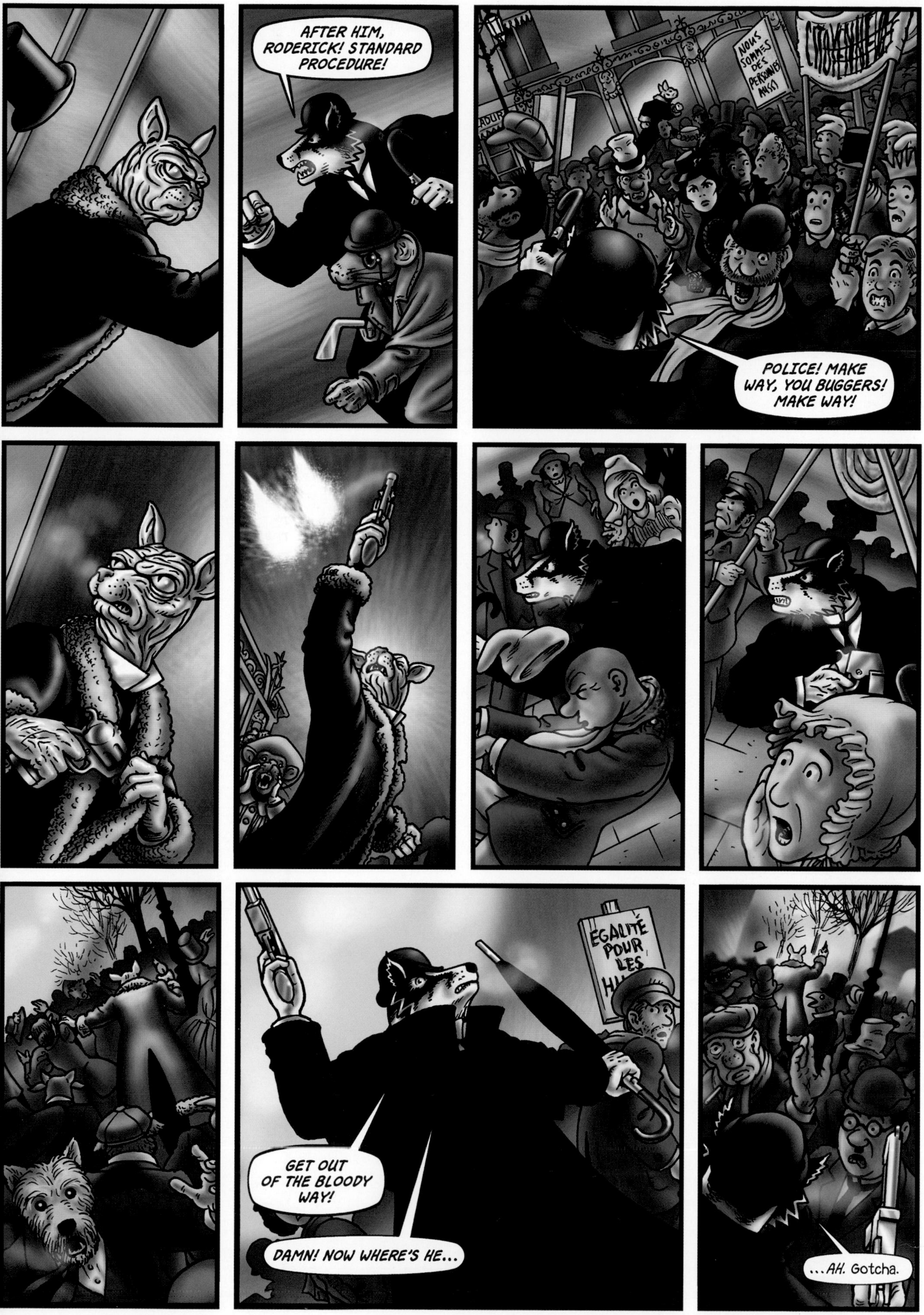
AFTER HIM, RODERICK! STANDARD PROCEDURE!
NOUS SOMMES DES
POLICE! MAKE WAY, YOU BUGGERS! MAKE WAY!
EGALITÉ POUR LES
GET OUT OF THE BLOODY WAY!
DAMN! NOW WHERE'S HE...
...AH. Gotcha.

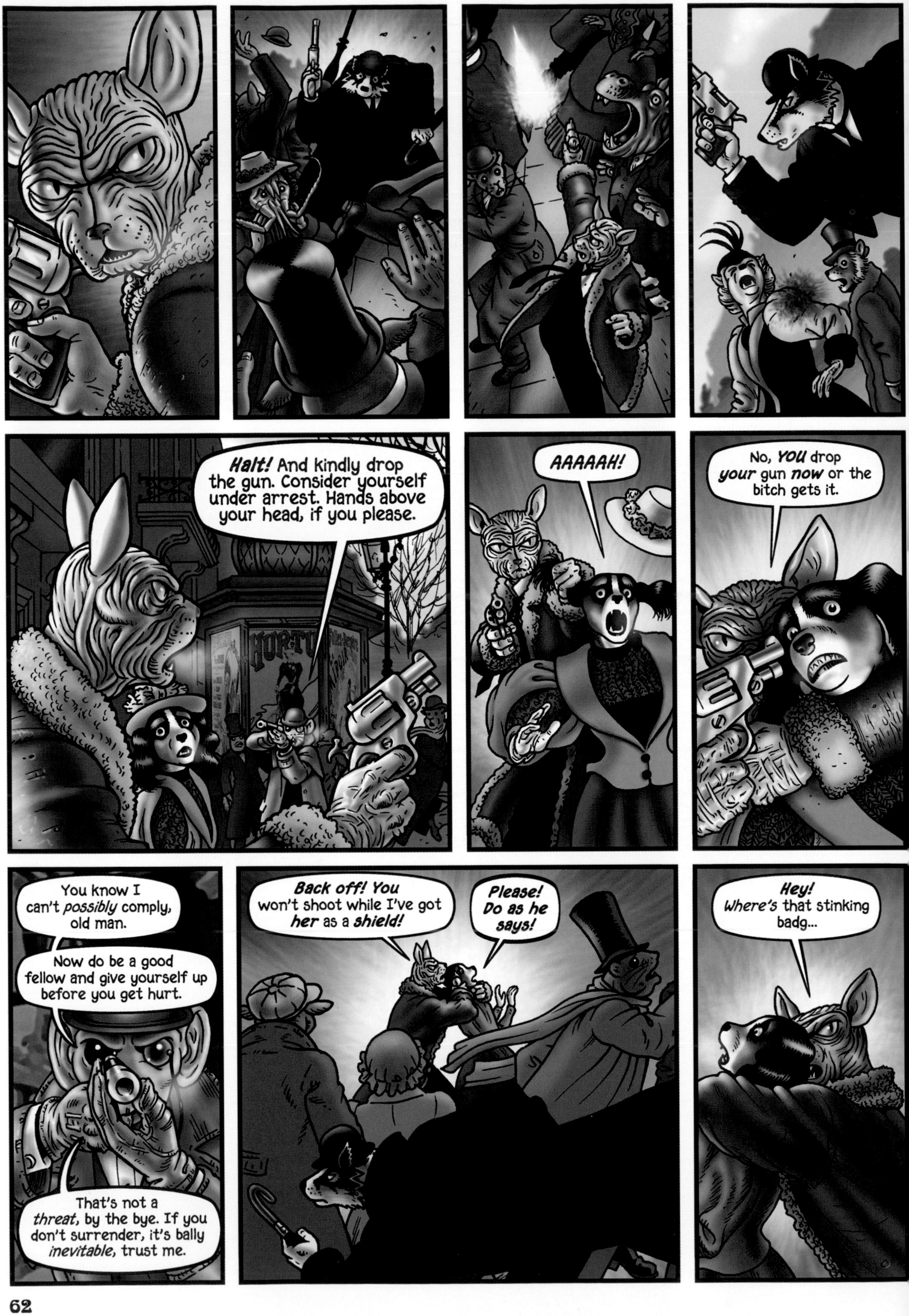
Halt! And kindly drop the gun. Consider yourself under arrest. Hands above your head, if you please.
AAAAAH!
No, YOU drop your gun now or the bitch gets it.
You know I can't possibly comply, old man.
Now do be a good fellow and give yourself up before you get hurt.
That's not a threat, by the bye. If you don't surrender, it's bally inevitable, trust me.
Back off! You won't shoot while I've got her as a shield!
Please! Do as he says!
Hey! Where's that stinking badg...

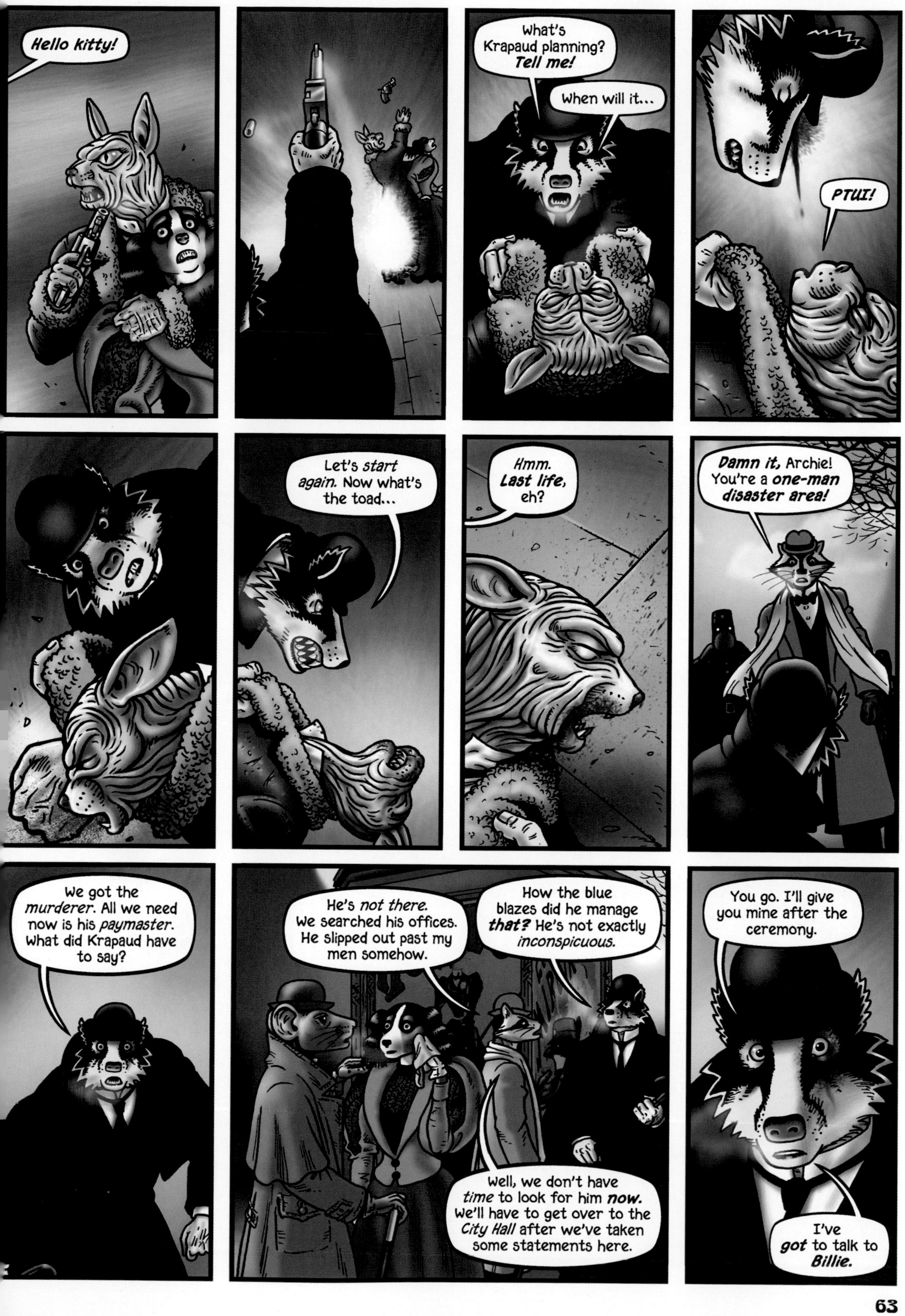

Hello kitty!
What's Krapaud planning? Tell me!
When will it...
PTUI!
Let's start again. Now what's the toad...
Hmm. Last life, eh?
Damn it, Archie! You're a one-man disaster area!
We got the murderer. All we need now is his paymaster. What did Krapaud have to say?
He's not there. We searched his offices. He slipped out past my men somehow.
How the blue blazes did he manage that? He's not exactly inconspicuous.
Well, we don't have time to look for him now. We'll have to get over to the City Hall after we've taken some statements here.
You go. I'll give you mine after the ceremony.
I've got to talk to Billie.

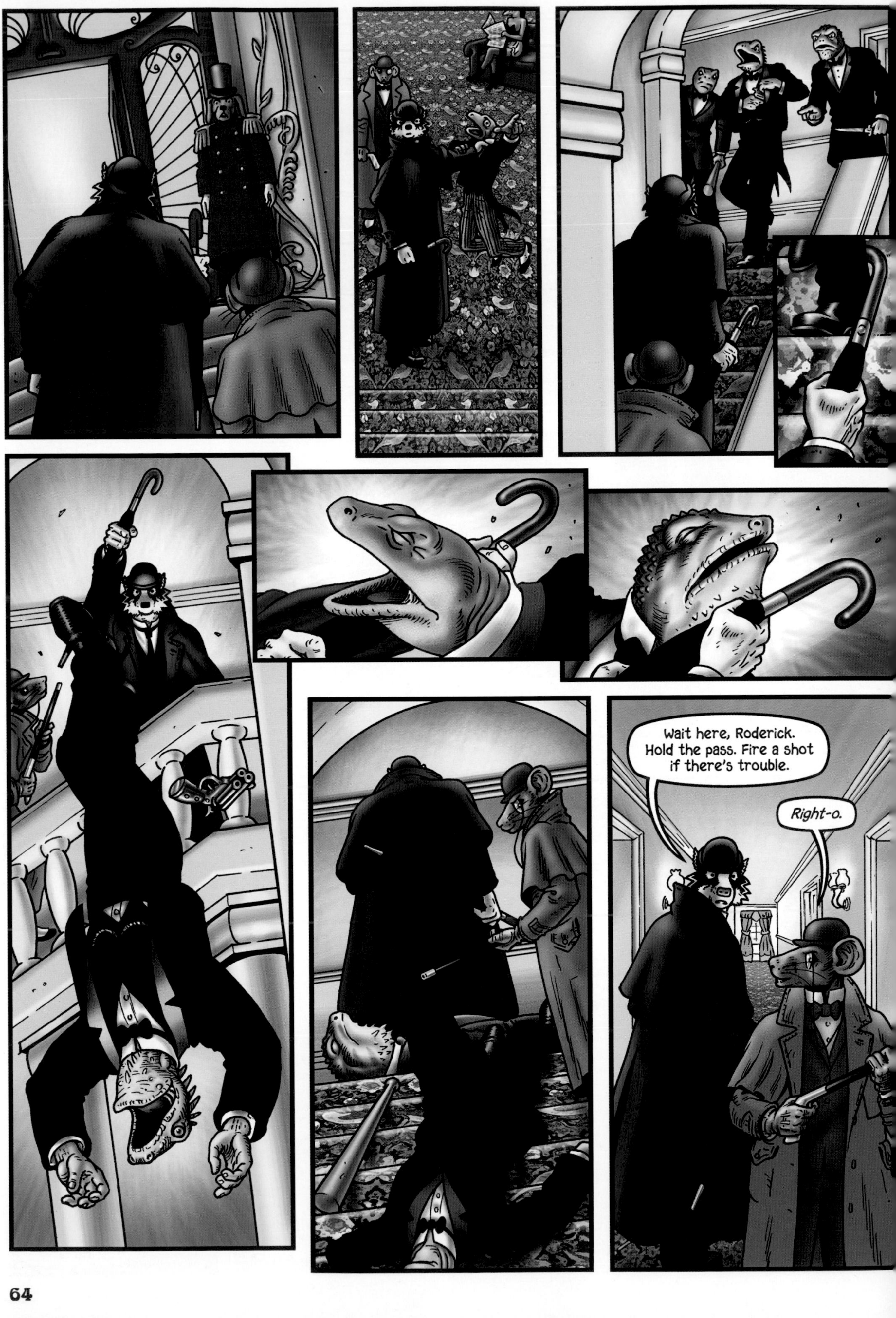
Wait here, Roderick. Hold the pass. Fire a shot if there's trouble.
Right-o.

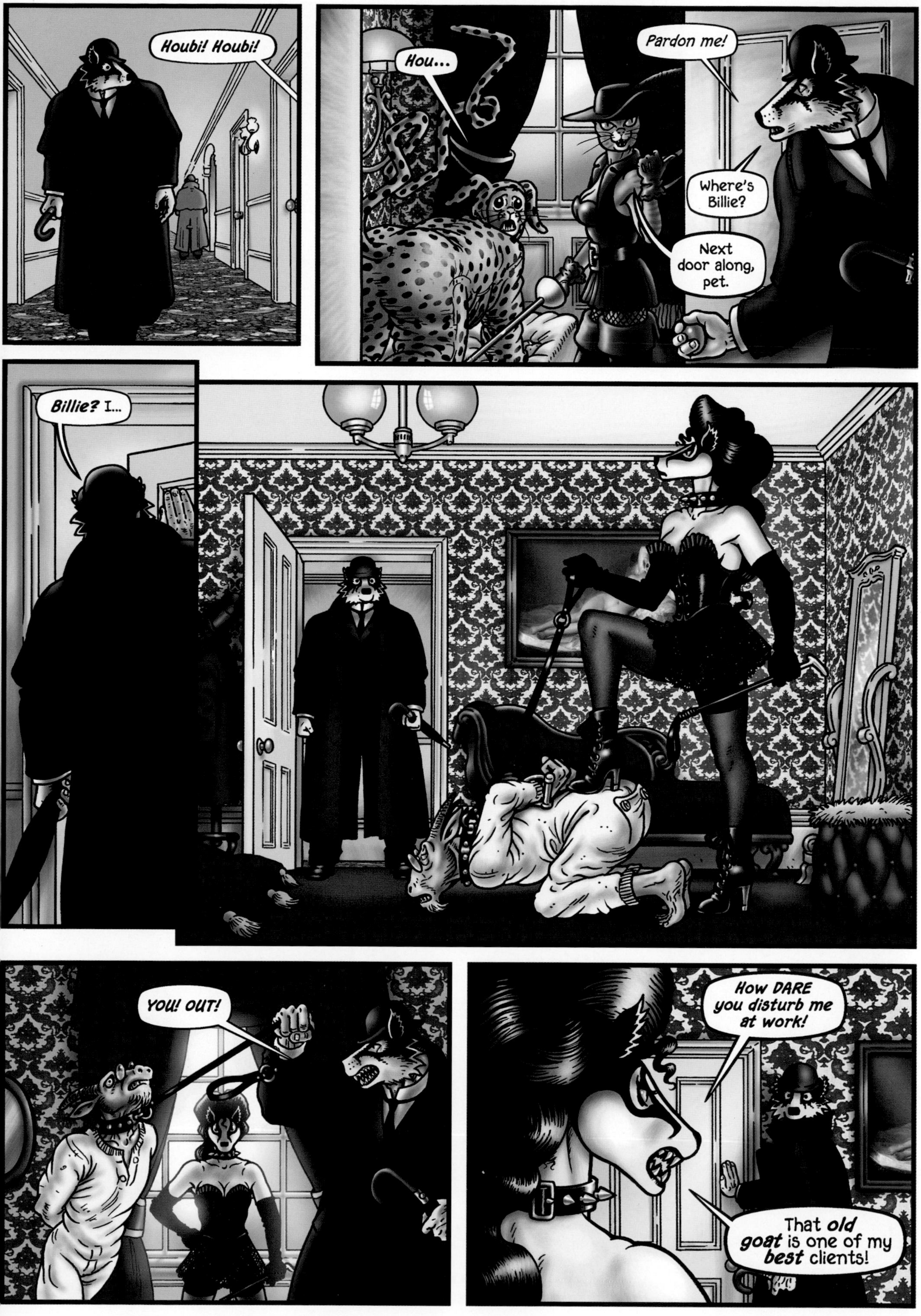
Houbi! Houbi!
Hou...
Pardon me!
Where's Billie?
Next door along, pet.
Billie? I...
YOU! OUT!
How DARE you disturb me at work!
That old goat is one of my best clients!

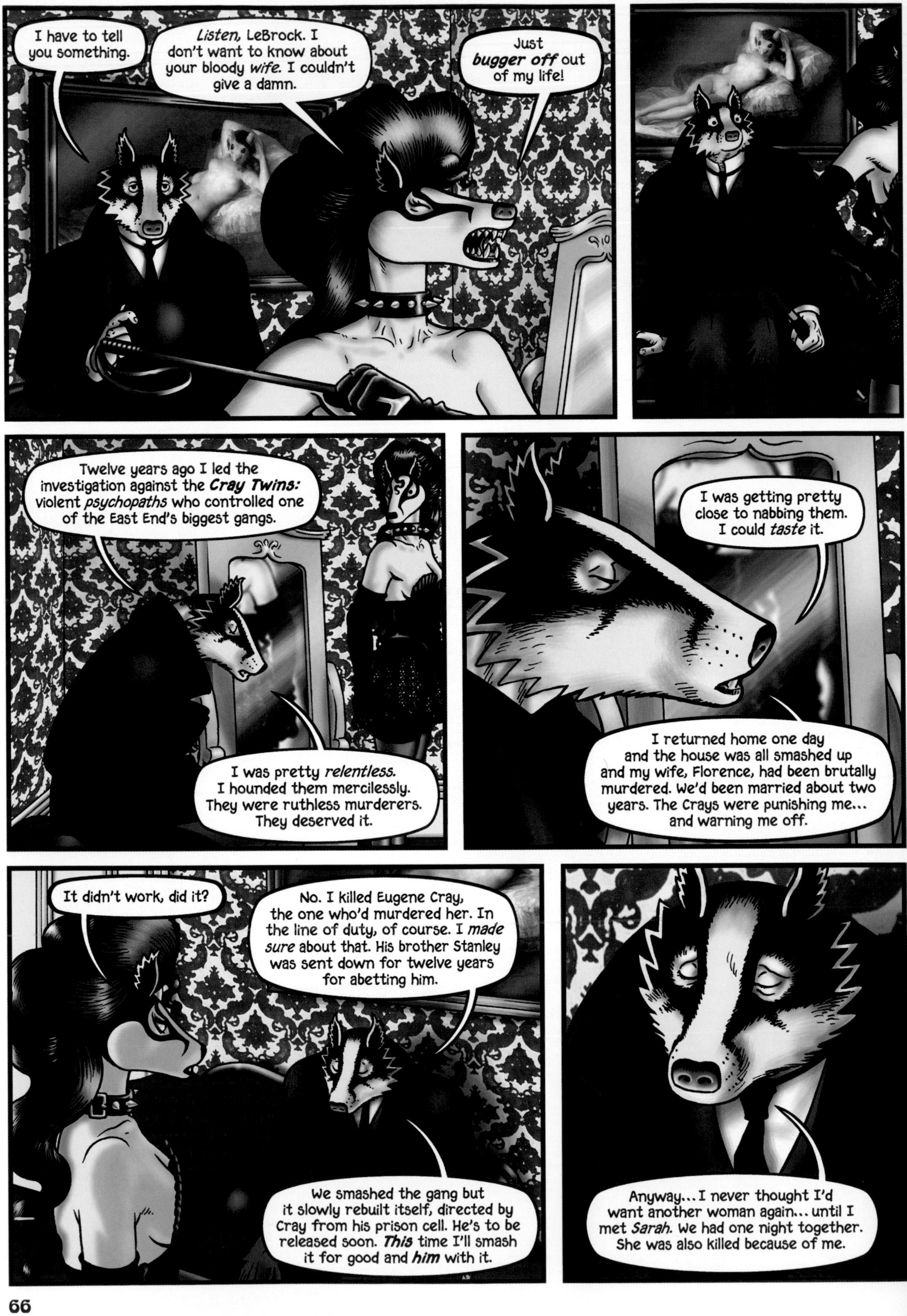
I have to tell you something.
Listen, LeBrock. I don't want to know about your bloody *wife*. I couldn't give a damn.
Just **bugger off** out of my life!
Twelve years ago I led the investigation against the ***Cray Twins:*** violent *psychopaths* who controlled one of the East End's biggest gangs.
I was pretty *relentless.* I hounded them mercilessly. They were ruthless murderers. They deserved it.
I was getting pretty close to nabbing them. I could *taste* it.
I returned home one day and the house was all smashed up and my wife, Florence, had been brutally murdered. We'd been married about two years. The Crays were punishing me... and warning me off.
It didn't work, did it?
No. I killed Eugene Cray, the one who'd murdered her. In the line of duty, of course. I *made sure* about that. His brother Stanley was sent down for twelve years for abetting him.
We smashed the gang but it slowly rebuilt itself, directed by Cray from his prison cell. He's to be released soon. ***This*** time I'll smash it for good and ***him*** with it.
Anyway... I never thought I'd want another woman again... until I met *Sarah.* We had one night together. She was also killed because of me.

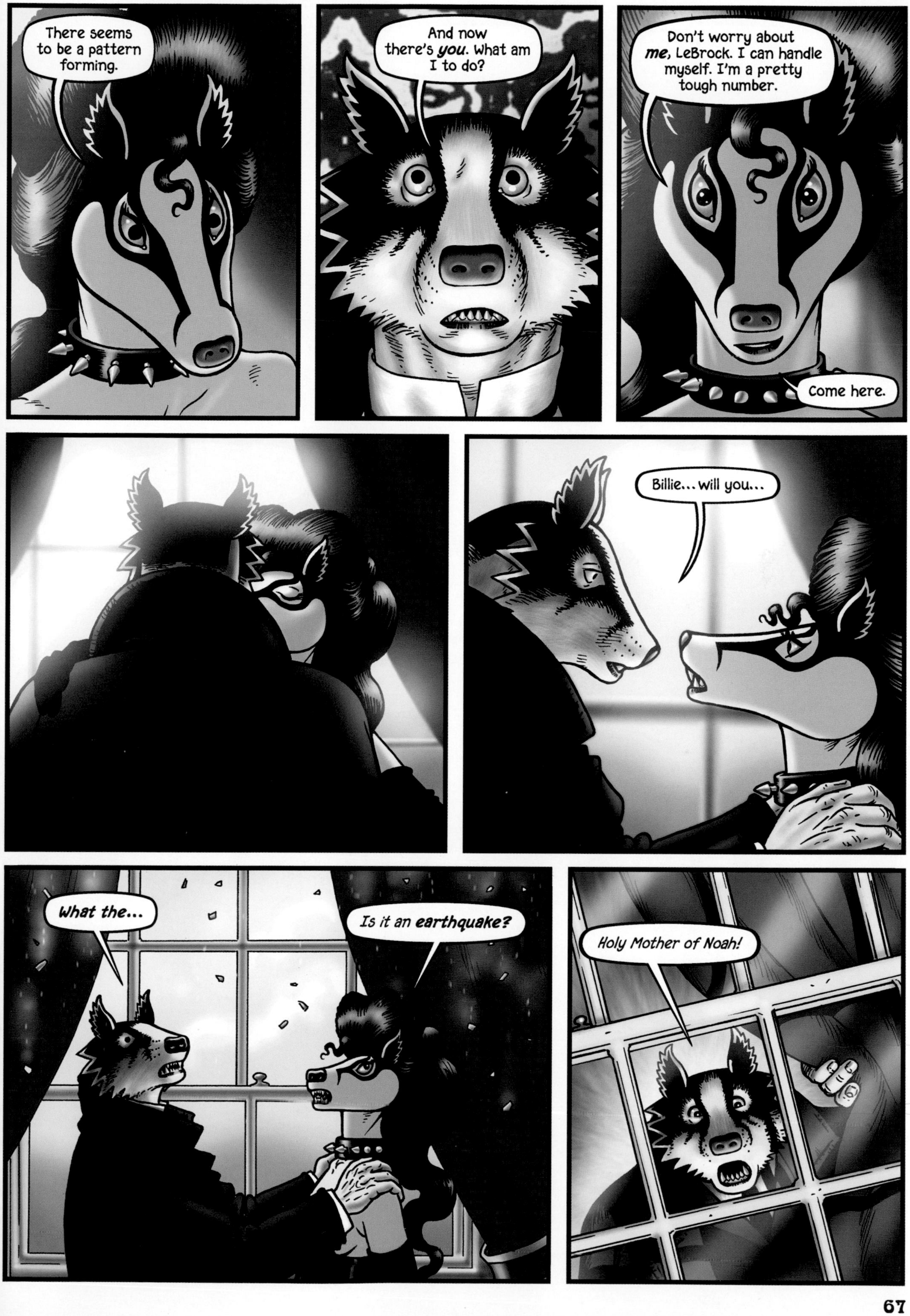
There seems to be a pattern forming.
And now there's *you*. What am I to do?
Don't worry about *me*, LeBrock. I can handle myself. I'm a pretty tough number.
Come here.
Billie... will you...
What the...
*Is it an **earthquake**?*
Holy Mother of Noah!

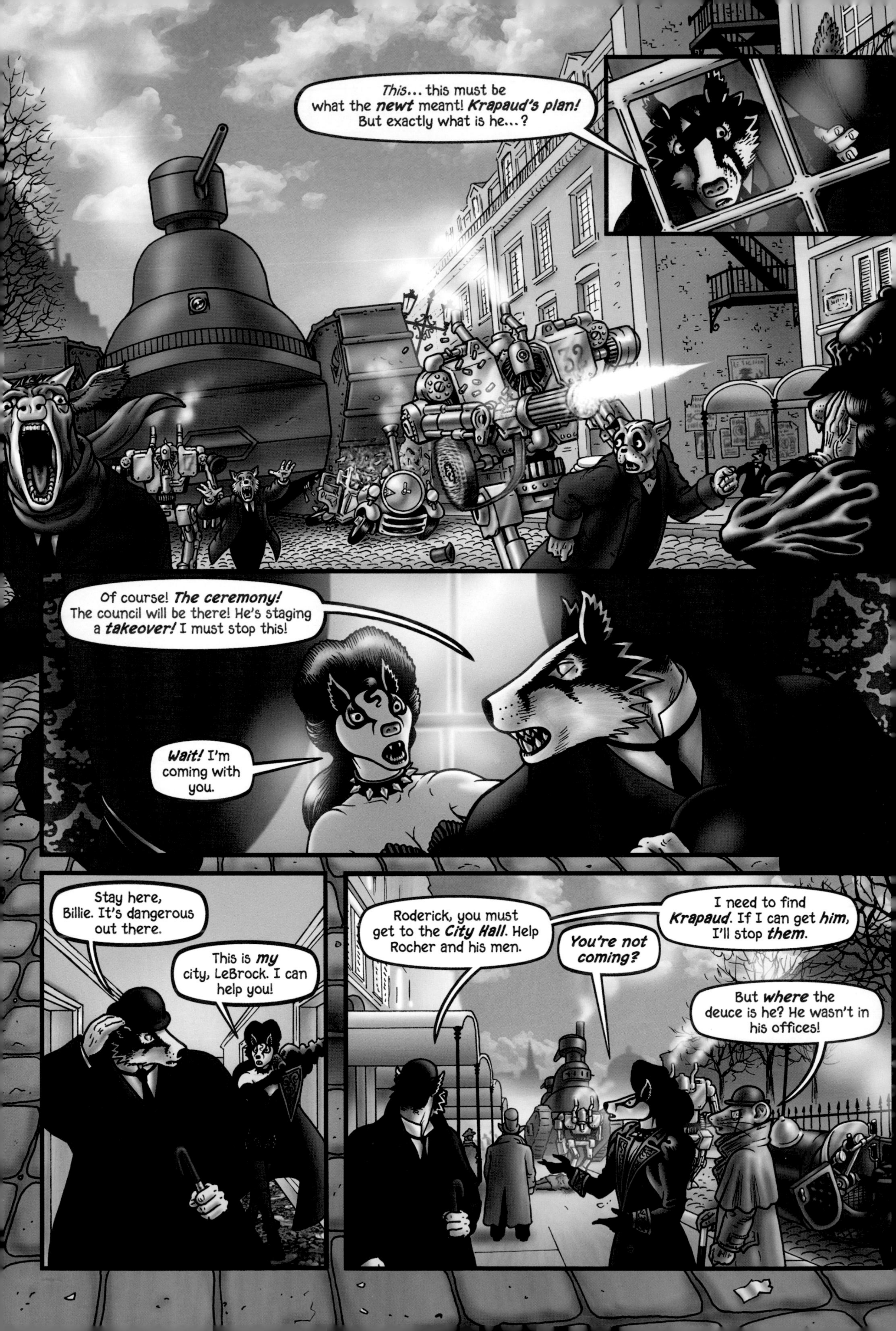

This... this must be what the ***newt*** meant! ***Krapaud's plan!*** But exactly what is he...?
Of course! ***The ceremony!*** The council will be there! He's staging a ***takeover!*** I must stop this!
Wait! I'm coming with you.
Stay here, Billie. It's dangerous out there.
This is ***my*** city, LeBrock. I can help you!
Roderick, you must get to the ***City Hall***. Help Rocher and his men.
You're not coming?
I need to find ***Krapaud***. If I can get ***him***, I'll stop ***them***.
But ***where*** the deuce is he? He wasn't in his offices!

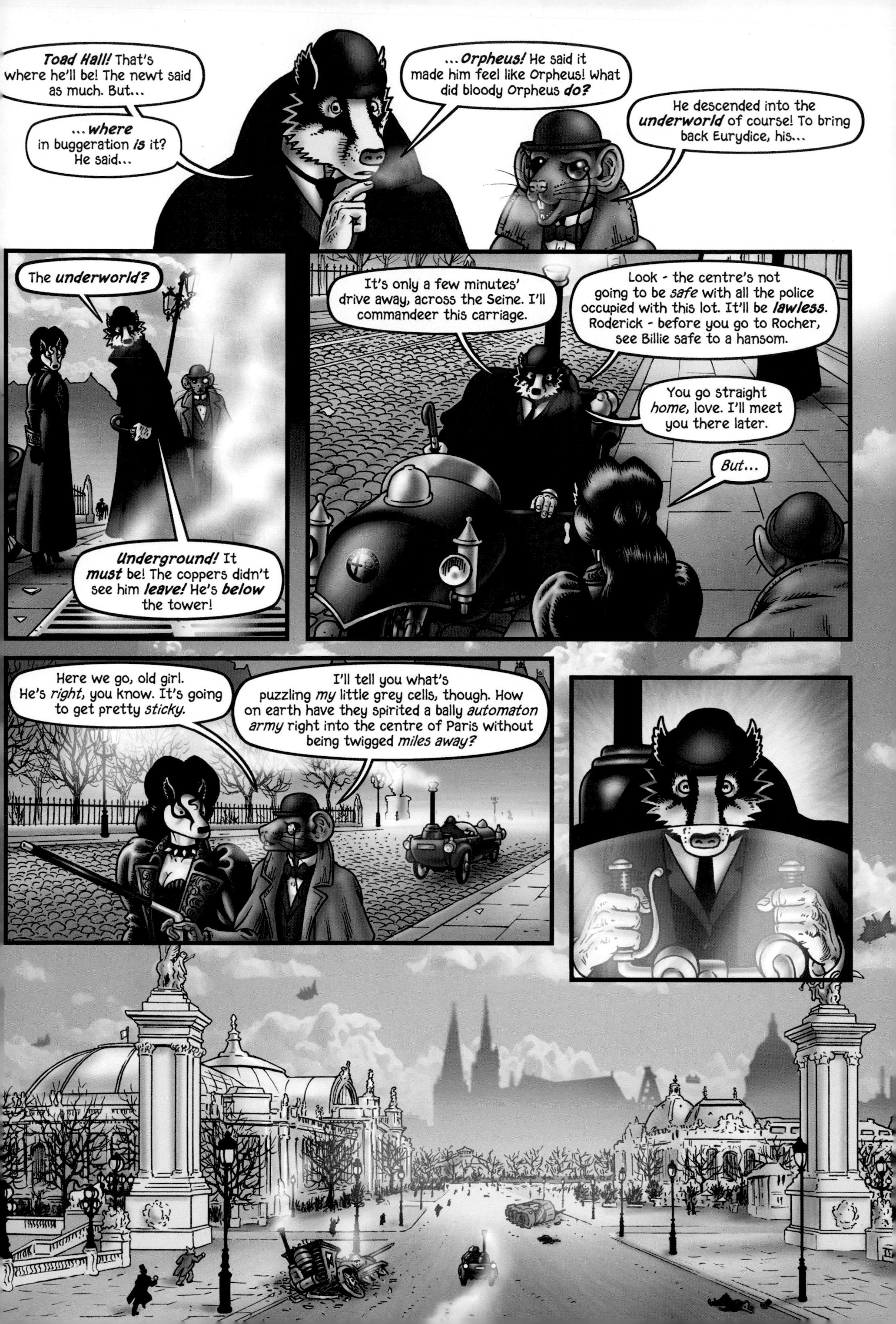
Toad Hall! That's where he'll be! The newt said as much. But...
...where in buggeration is it? He said...
...Orpheus! He said it made him feel like Orpheus! What did bloody Orpheus do?
He descended into the underworld of course! To bring back Eurydice, his...
The underworld?
Underground! It must be! The coppers didn't see him leave! He's below the tower!
It's only a few minutes' drive away, across the Seine. I'll commandeer this carriage.
Look - the centre's not going to be safe with all the police occupied with this lot. It'll be lawless. Roderick - before you go to Rocher, see Billie safe to a hansom.
You go straight home, love. I'll meet you there later.
But...
Here we go, old girl. He's right, you know. It's going to get pretty sticky.
I'll tell you what's puzzling my little grey cells, though. How on earth have they spirited a bally automaton army right into the centre of Paris without being twigged miles away?

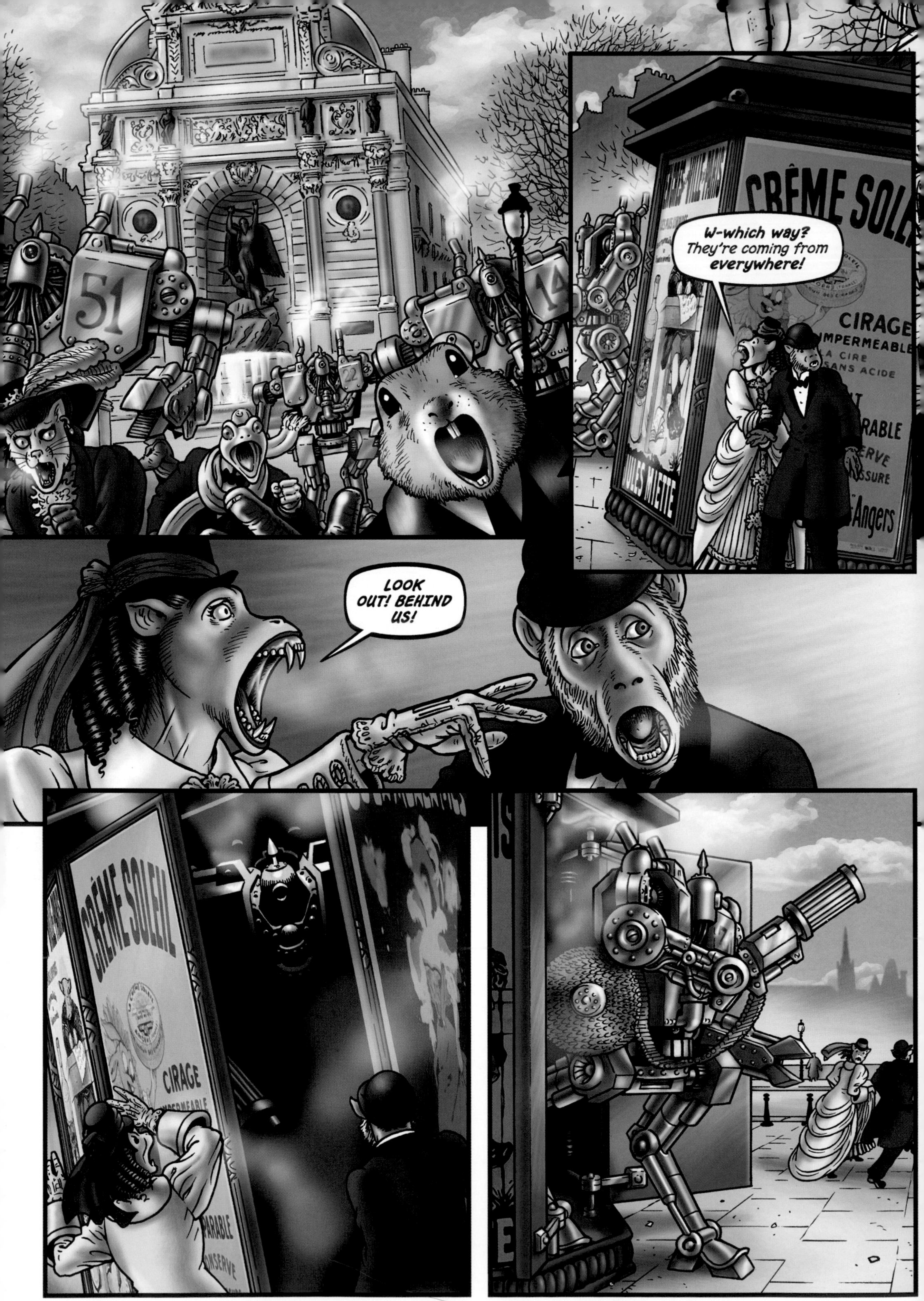
W-which way? They're coming from everywhere!
LOOK OUT! BEHIND US!
CRÊME SOLEIL
CIRAGE

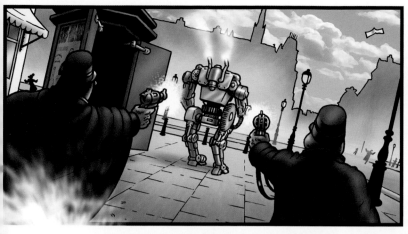

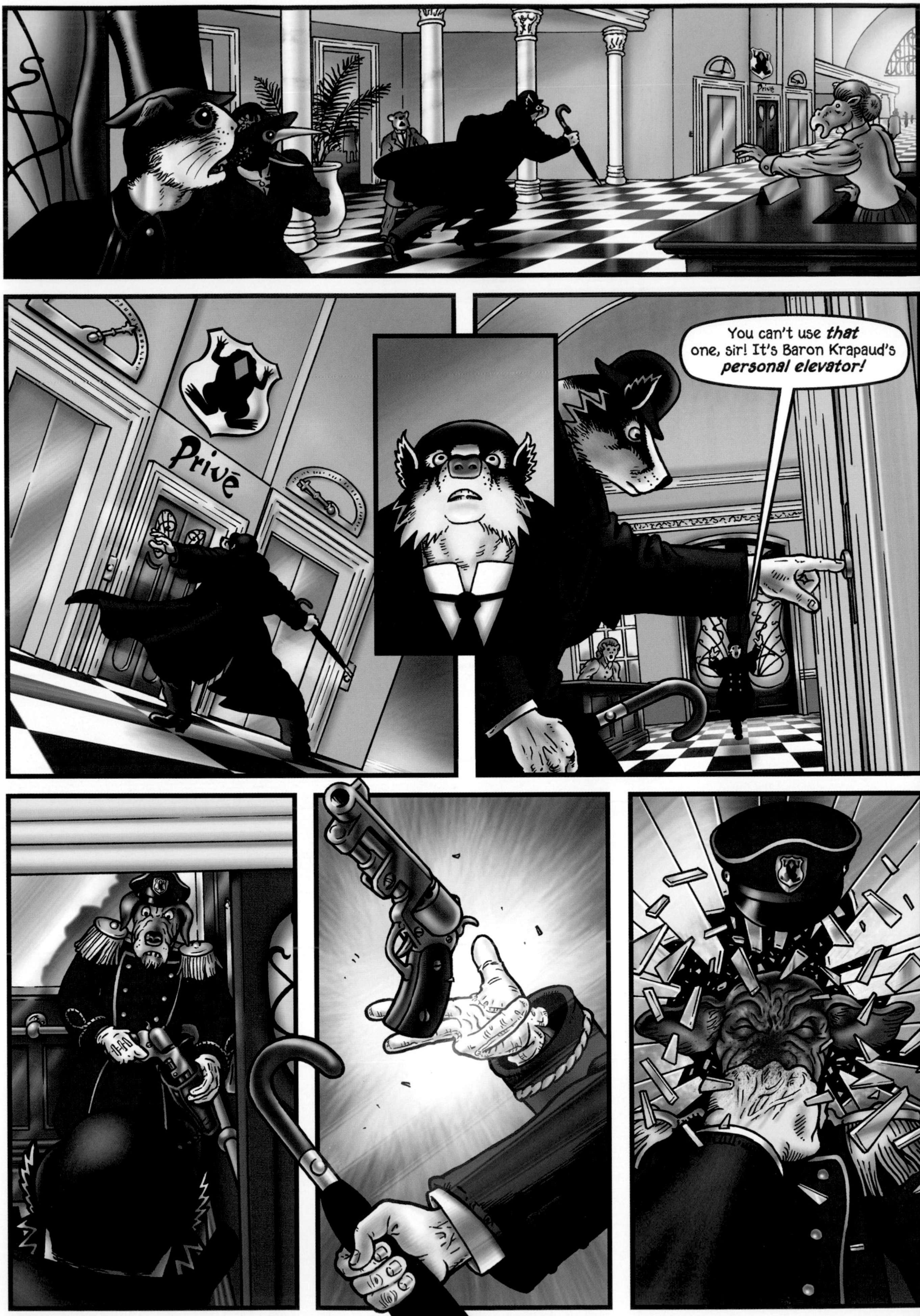
Privé
Privé
You can't use *that* one, sir! It's Baron Krapaud's *personal elevator!*

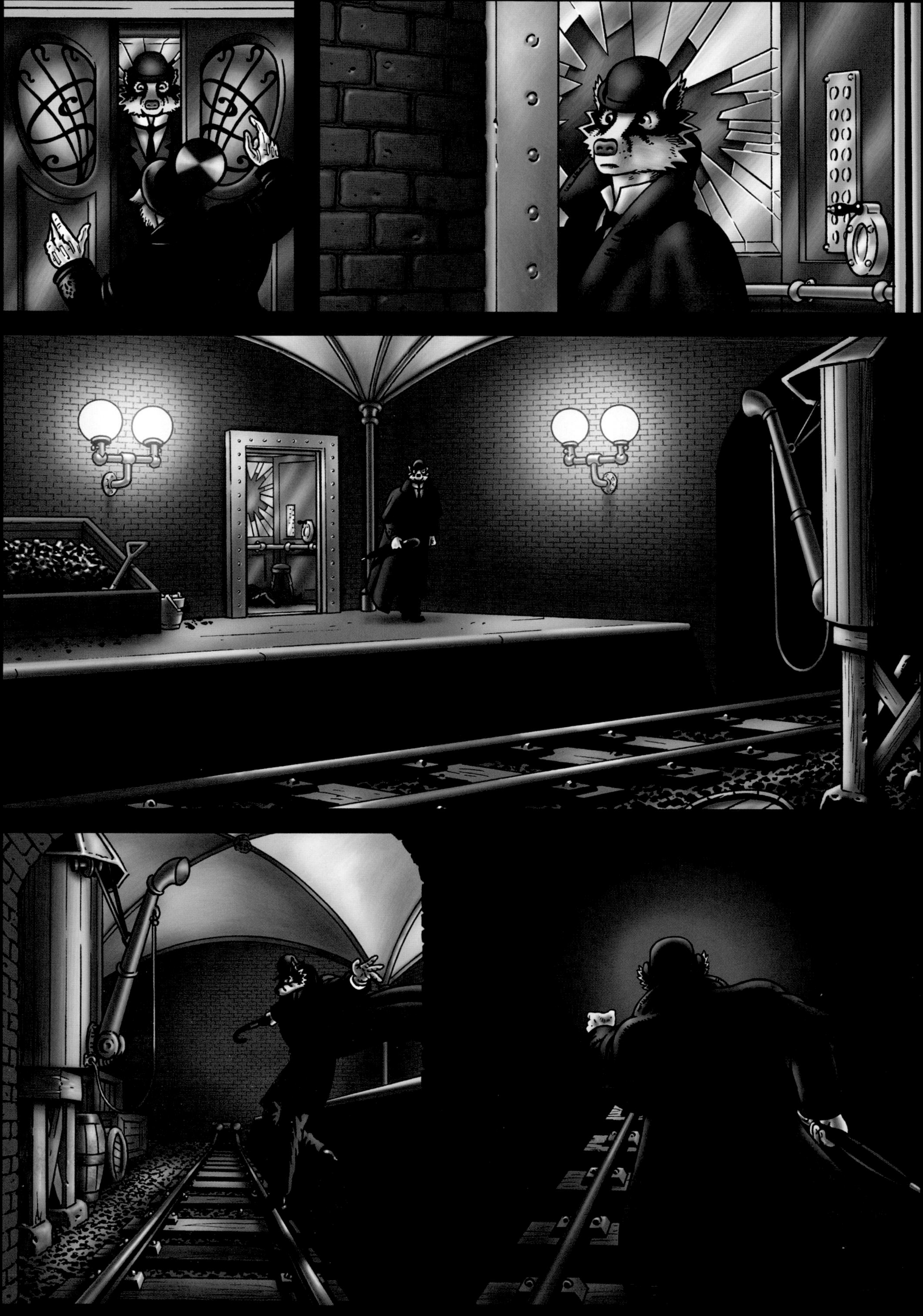

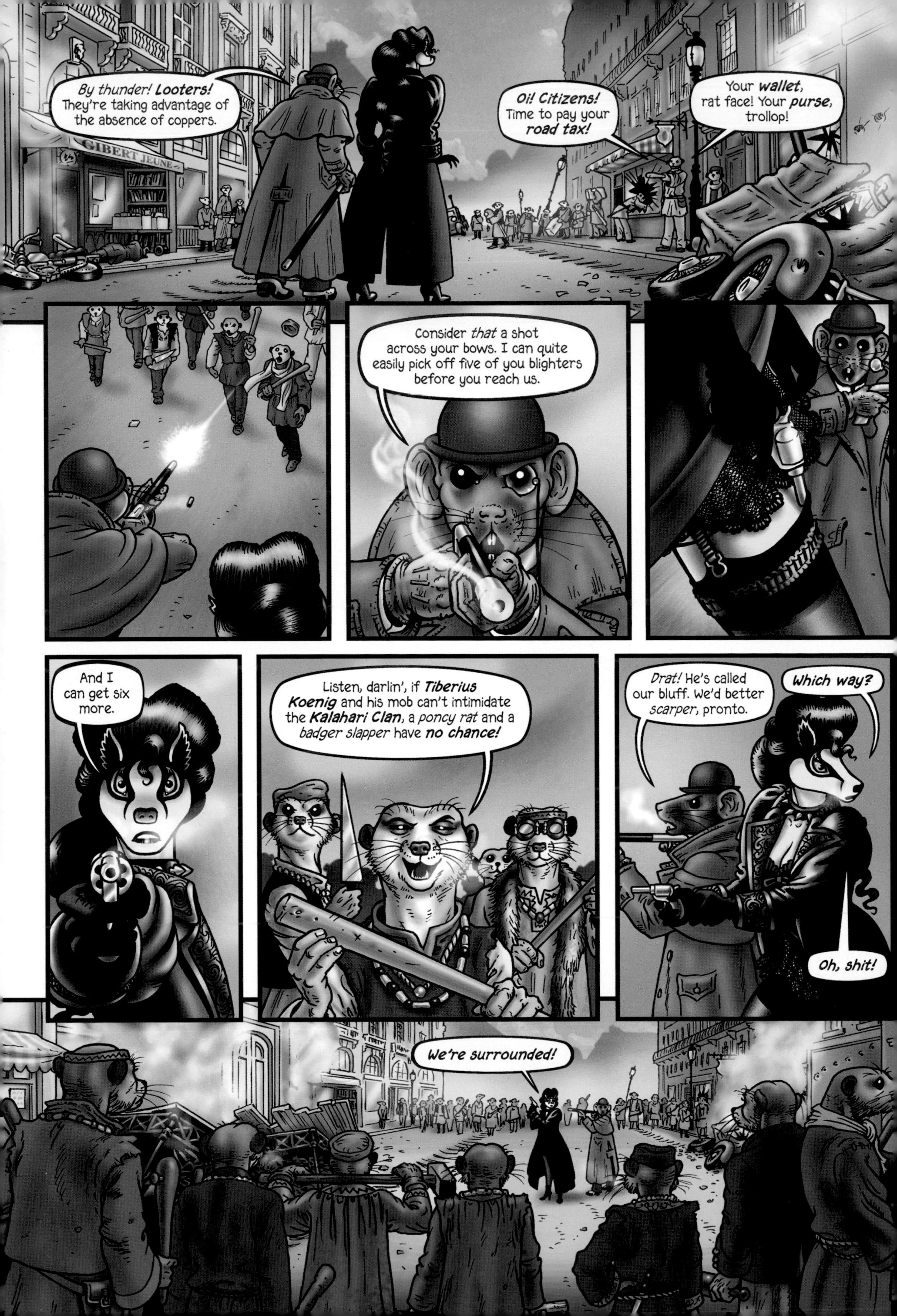
By thunder! Looters! They're taking advantage of the absence of coppers.
GIBERT JEUNE
Oi! Citizens! Time to pay your road tax!
Your wallet, rat face! Your purse, trollop!
Consider that a shot across your bows. I can quite easily pick off five of you blighters before you reach us.
And I can get six more.
Listen, darlin', if Tiberius Koenig and his mob can't intimidate the Kalahari Clan, a poncy rat and a badger slapper have no chance!
Drat! He's called our bluff. We'd better scarper, pronto.
Which way?
Oh, shit!
We're surrounded!

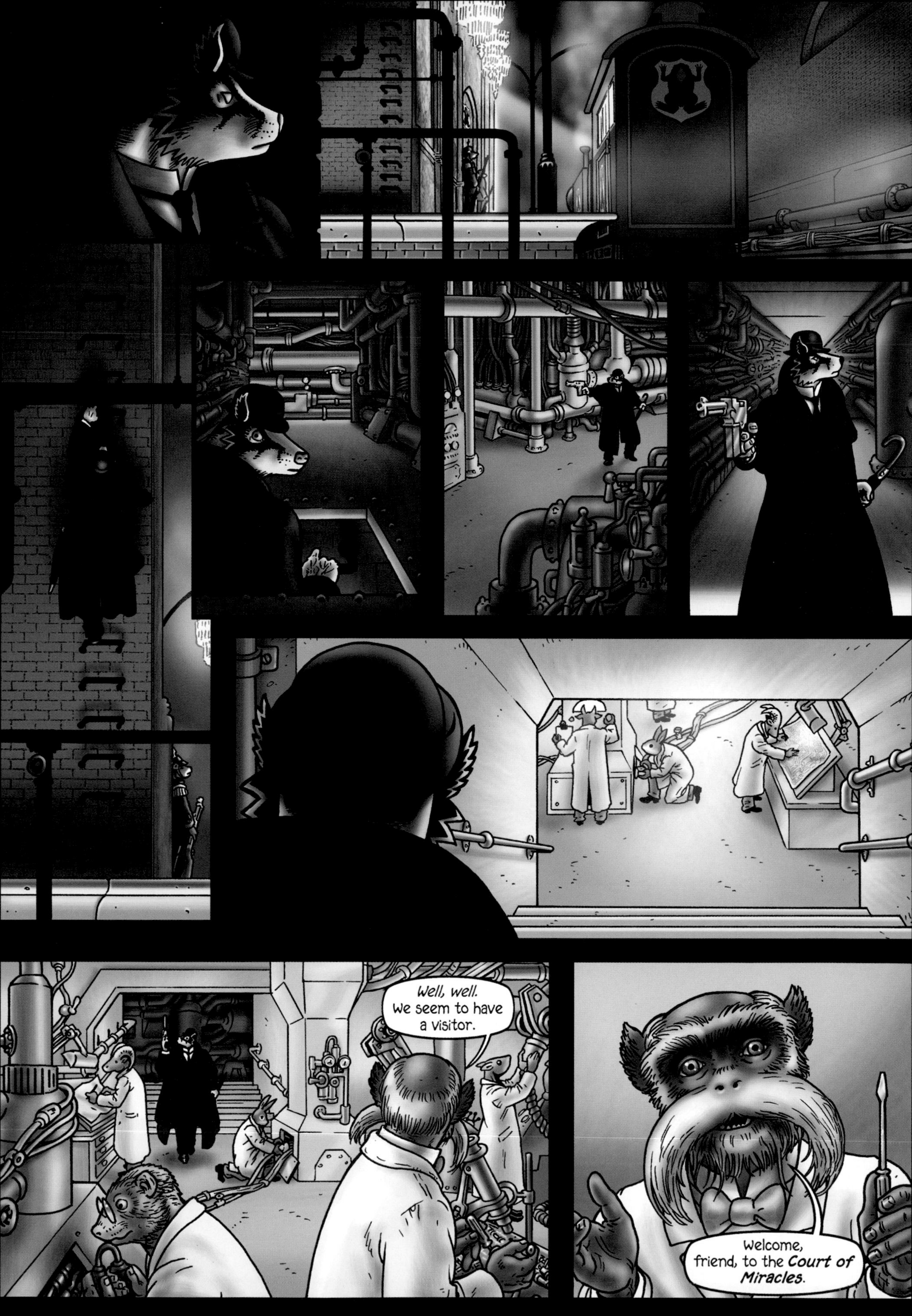
Well, well.
We seem to have
a visitor.
Welcome,
friend, to the *Court of
Miracles*.

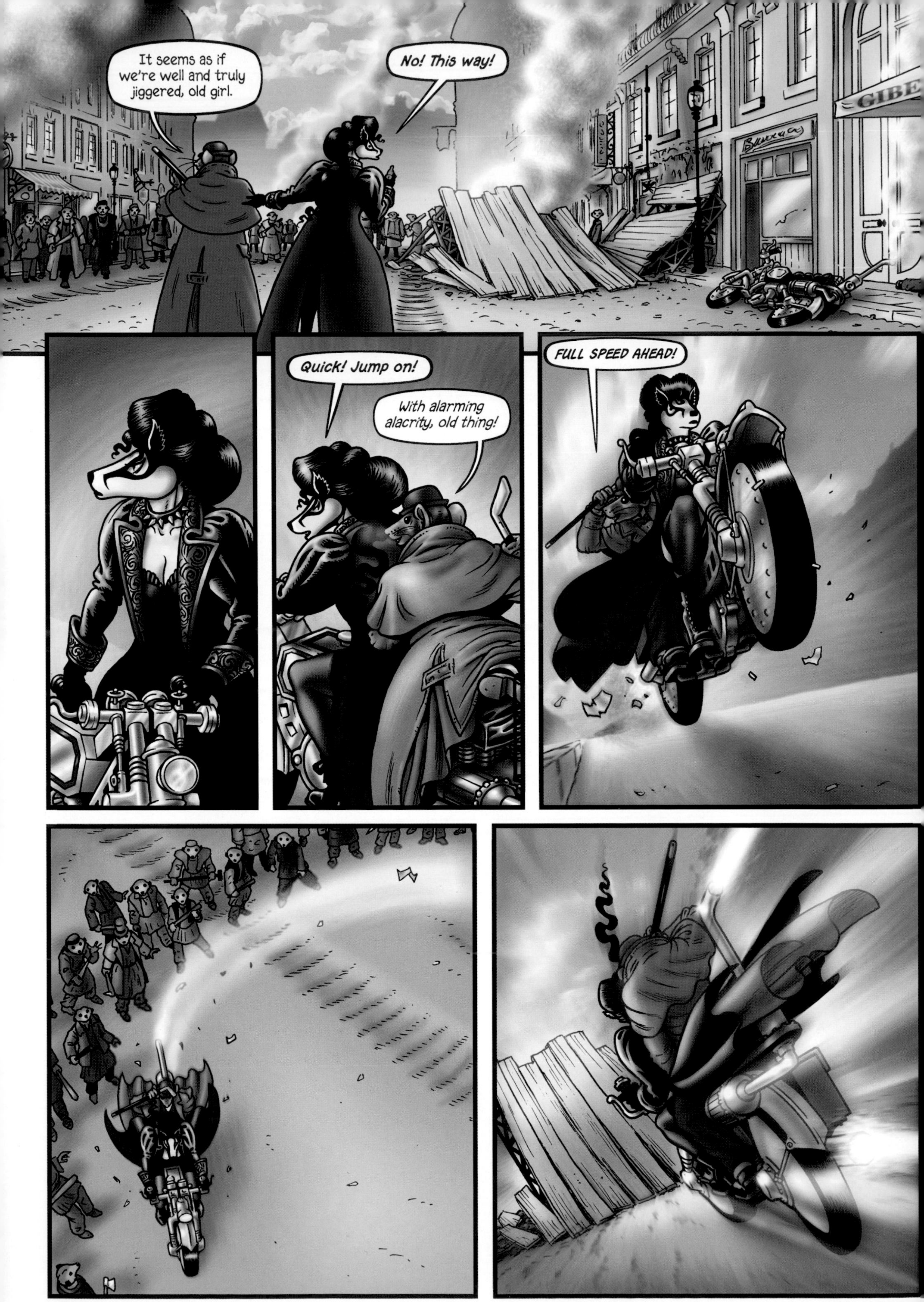
It seems as if we're well and truly jiggered, old girl.
No! This way!
GIBE
Quick! Jump on!
With alarming alacrity, old thing!
FULL SPEED AHEAD!

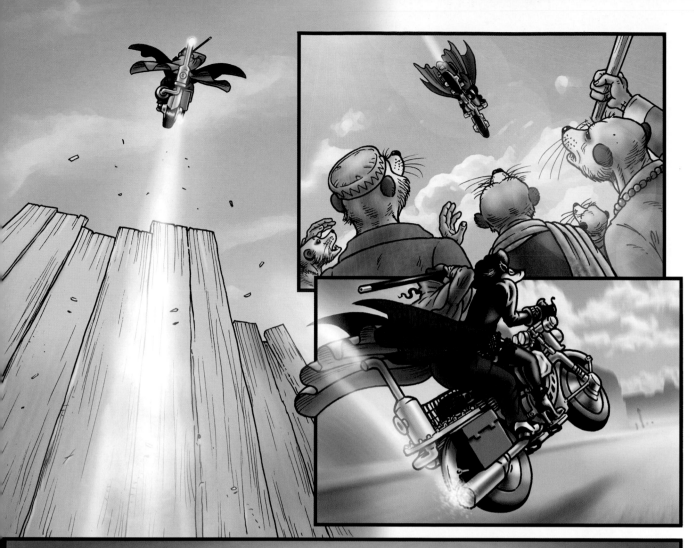

Cool!

My dear girl, you really are full of surprises!

I grew up on the streets, Roderick. I've a whole *catalogue* of *disreputable* skills.

Now, don't try and talk me out of it. I'm going to *City Hall* and *that's* that.

I don't seem to have much of a *choice*, m'dear!

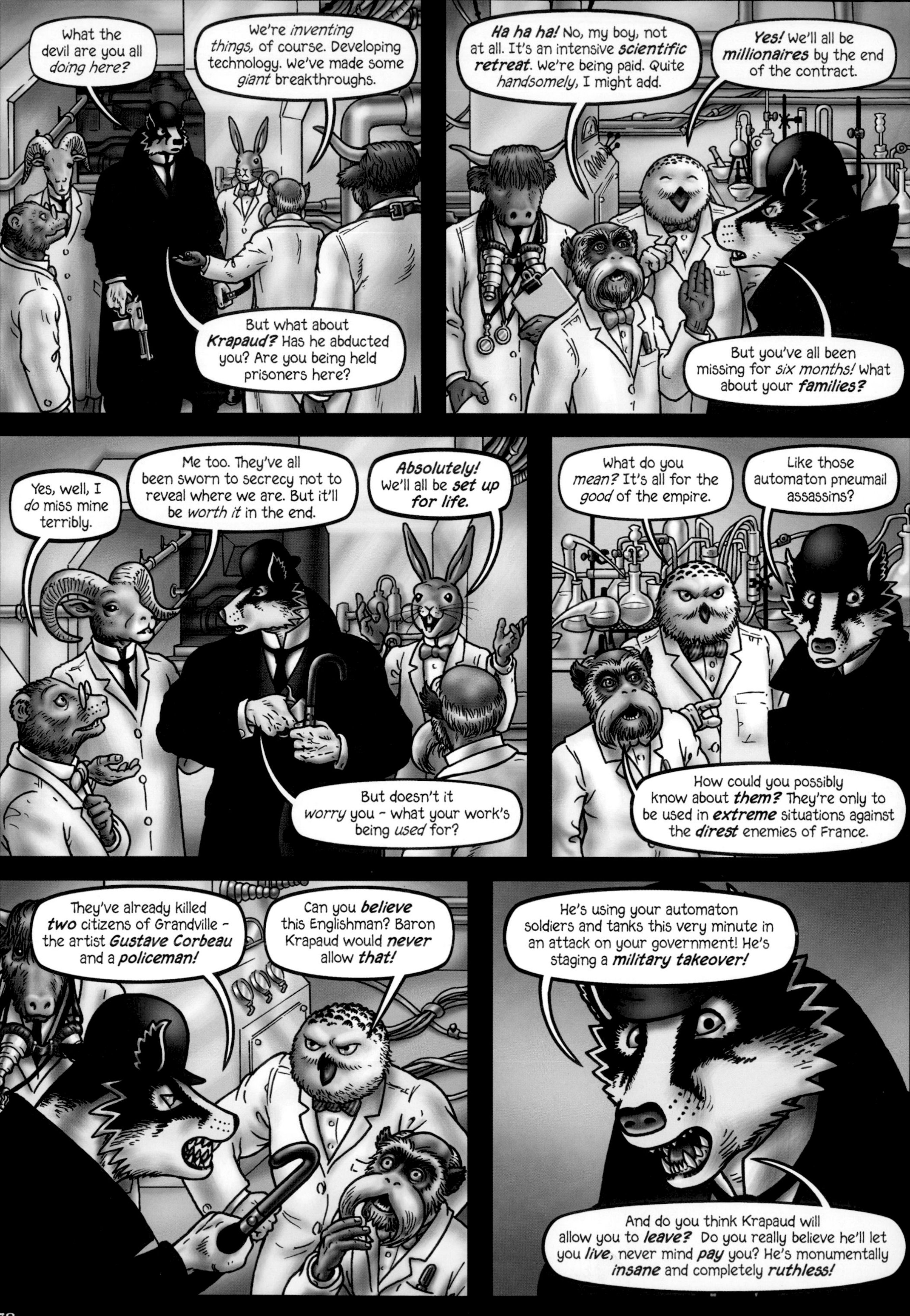
What the devil are you all *doing here?*
We're *inventing things,* of course. Developing technology. We've made some *giant* breakthroughs.
But what about ***Krapaud?*** Has he abducted you? Are you being held prisoners here?
Ha ha ha! No, my boy, not at all. It's an intensive ***scientific retreat***. We're being paid. Quite *handsomely,* I might add.
Yes! We'll all be ***millionaires*** by the end of the contract.
But you've all been missing for *six months!* What about your ***families?***
Yes, well, I *do* miss mine terribly.
Me too. They've all been sworn to secrecy not to reveal where we are. But it'll be *worth it* in the end.
Absolutely! We'll all be ***set up for life.***
But doesn't it *worry* you - what your work's being *used* for?
What do you *mean?* It's all for the *good* of the empire.
Like those automaton pneumail assassins?
How could you possibly know about ***them?*** They're only to be used in ***extreme*** situations against the ***direst*** enemies of France.
They've already killed ***two*** citizens of Grandville - the artist ***Gustave Corbeau*** and a ***policeman!***
Can you ***believe*** this Englishman? Baron Krapaud would ***never*** allow ***that!***
He's using your automaton soldiers and tanks this very minute in an attack on your government! He's staging a ***military takeover!***
And do you think Krapaud will allow you to ***leave?*** Do you really believe he'll let you ***live,*** never mind ***pay*** you? He's monumentally ***insane*** and completely ***ruthless!***

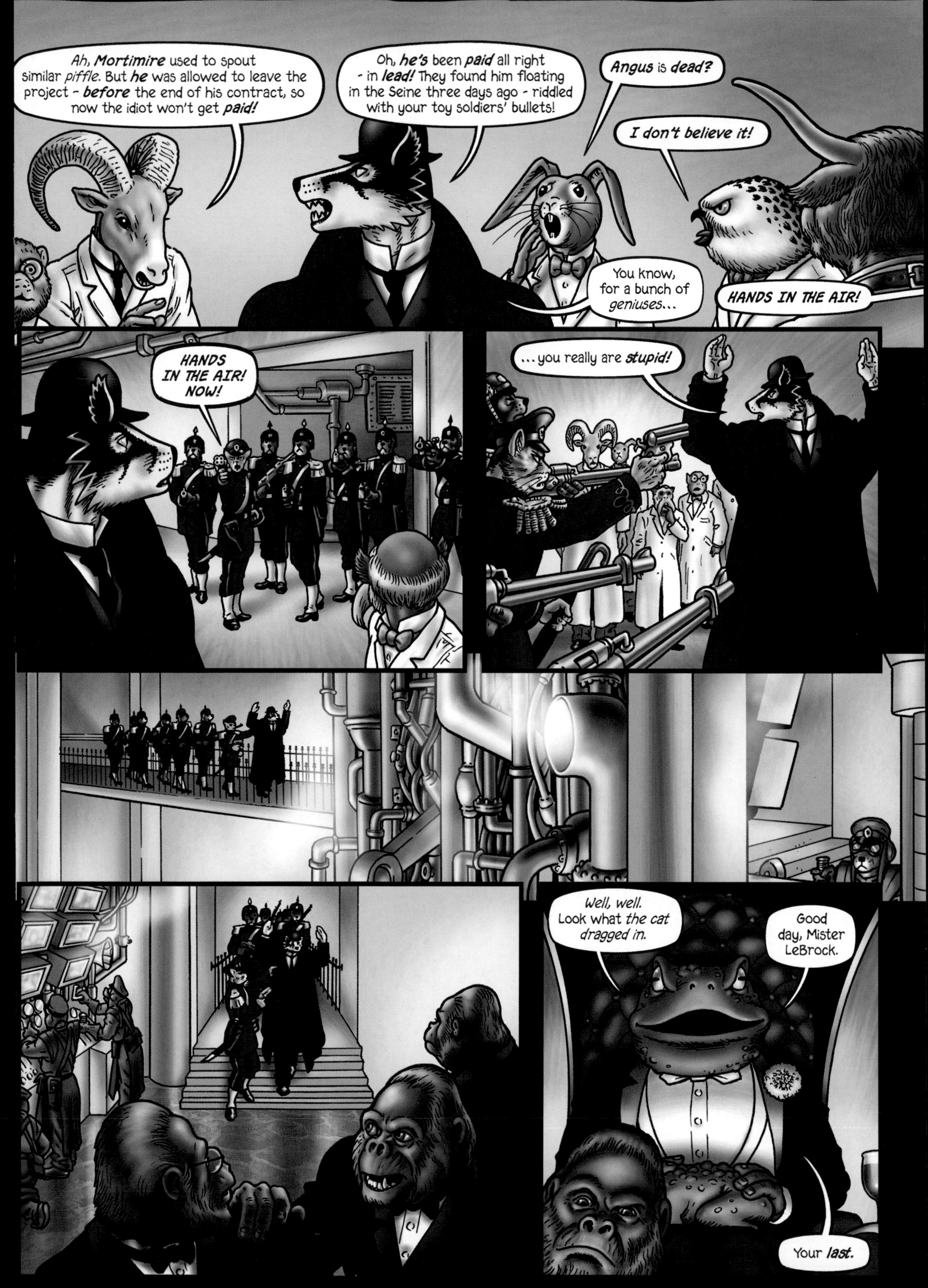
Ah, Mortimire used to spout similar piffle. But he was allowed to leave the project - before the end of his contract, so now the idiot won't get paid!
Oh, he's been paid all right - in lead! They found him floating in the Seine three days ago - riddled with your toy soldiers' bullets!
Angus is dead?
I don't believe it!
You know, for a bunch of geniuses...
HANDS IN THE AIR!
HANDS IN THE AIR! NOW!
...you really are stupid!
Well, well. Look what the cat dragged in.
Good day, Mister LeBrock.
Your last.

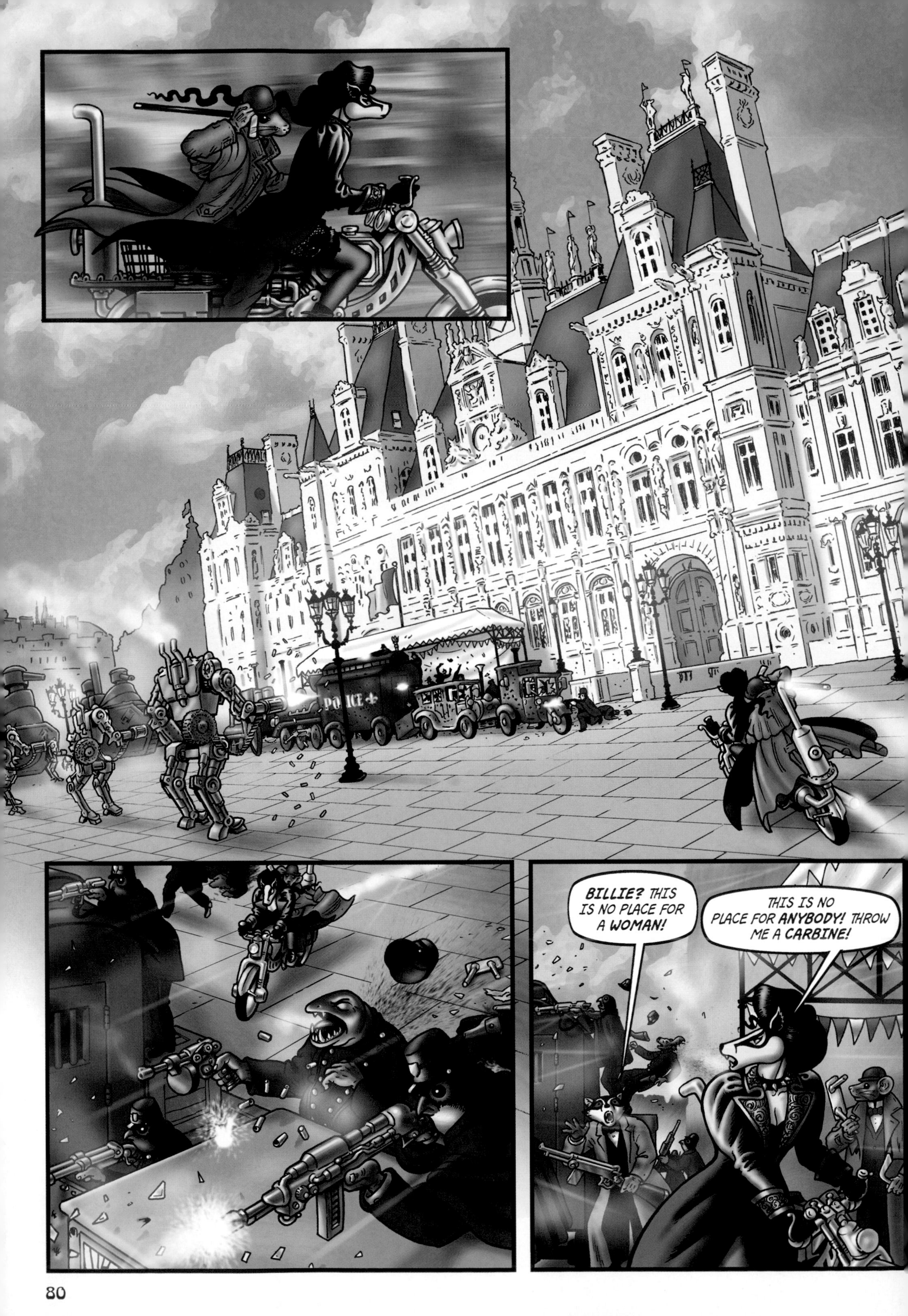
POLICE
BILLIE? THIS IS NO PLACE FOR A WOMAN!
THIS IS NO PLACE FOR ANYBODY! THROW ME A CARBINE!

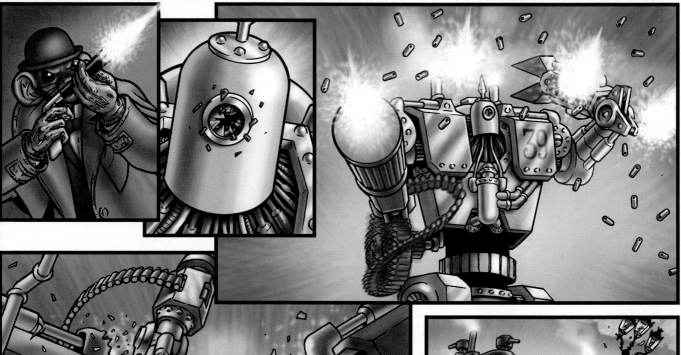
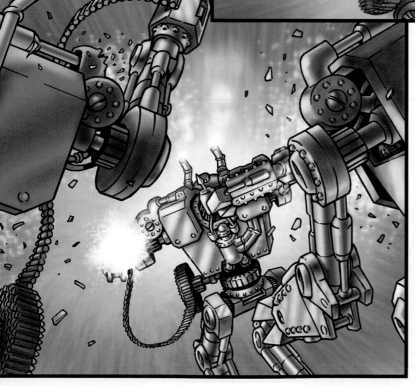

THAT'S THEIR ACHILLES' HEEL, CHAPS! AIM FOR THEIR EYES!

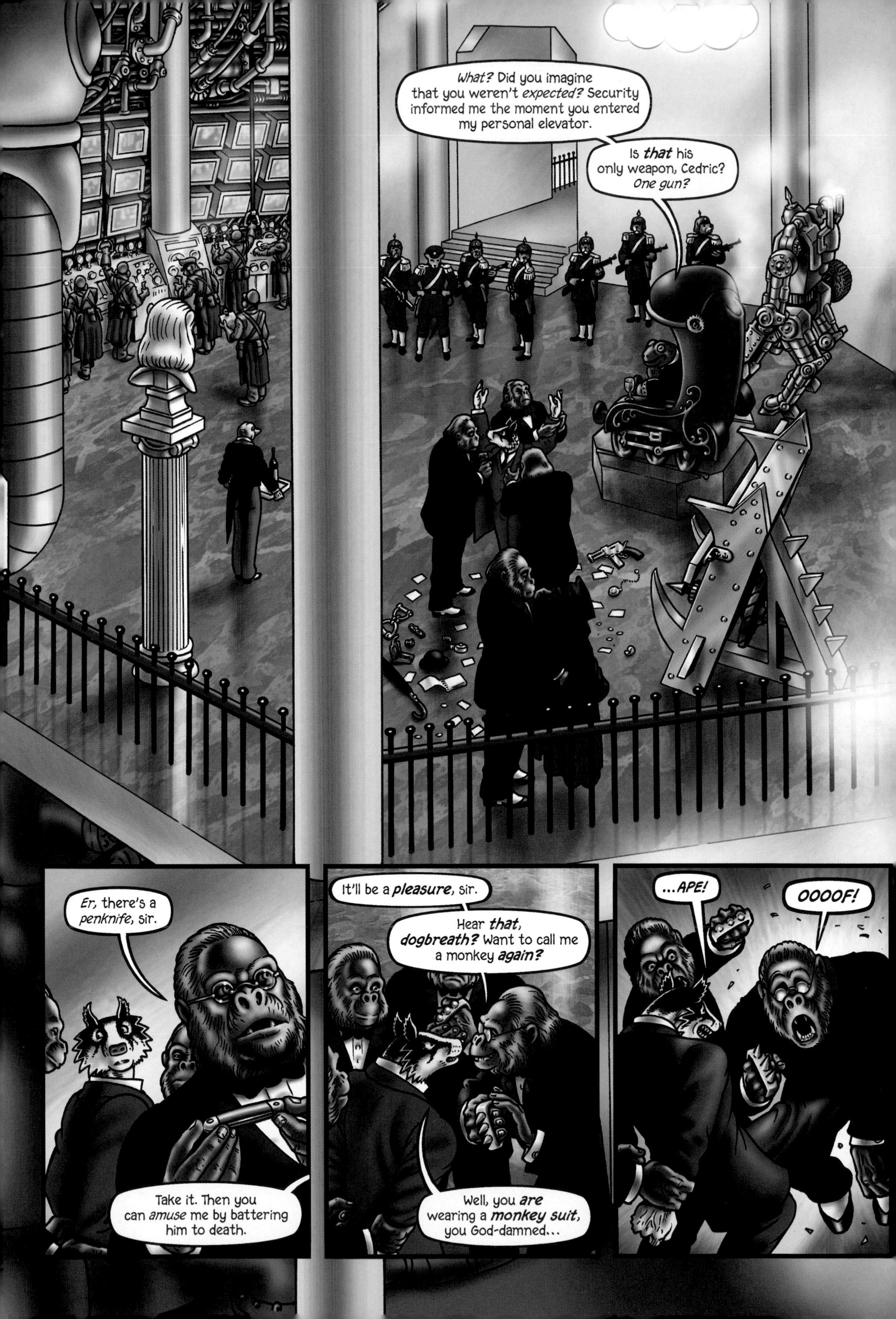

What? Did you imagine that you weren't *expected?* Security informed me the moment you entered my personal elevator.
Is ***that*** his only weapon, Cedric? *One gun?*
Er, there's a *penknife*, sir.
Take it. Then you can *amuse* me by battering him to death.
It'll be a ***pleasure***, sir.
Hear ***that***, ***dogbreath?*** Want to call me a monkey ***again?***
Well, you ***are*** wearing a ***monkey suit***, you God-damned...
...*APE!*
OOOOF!

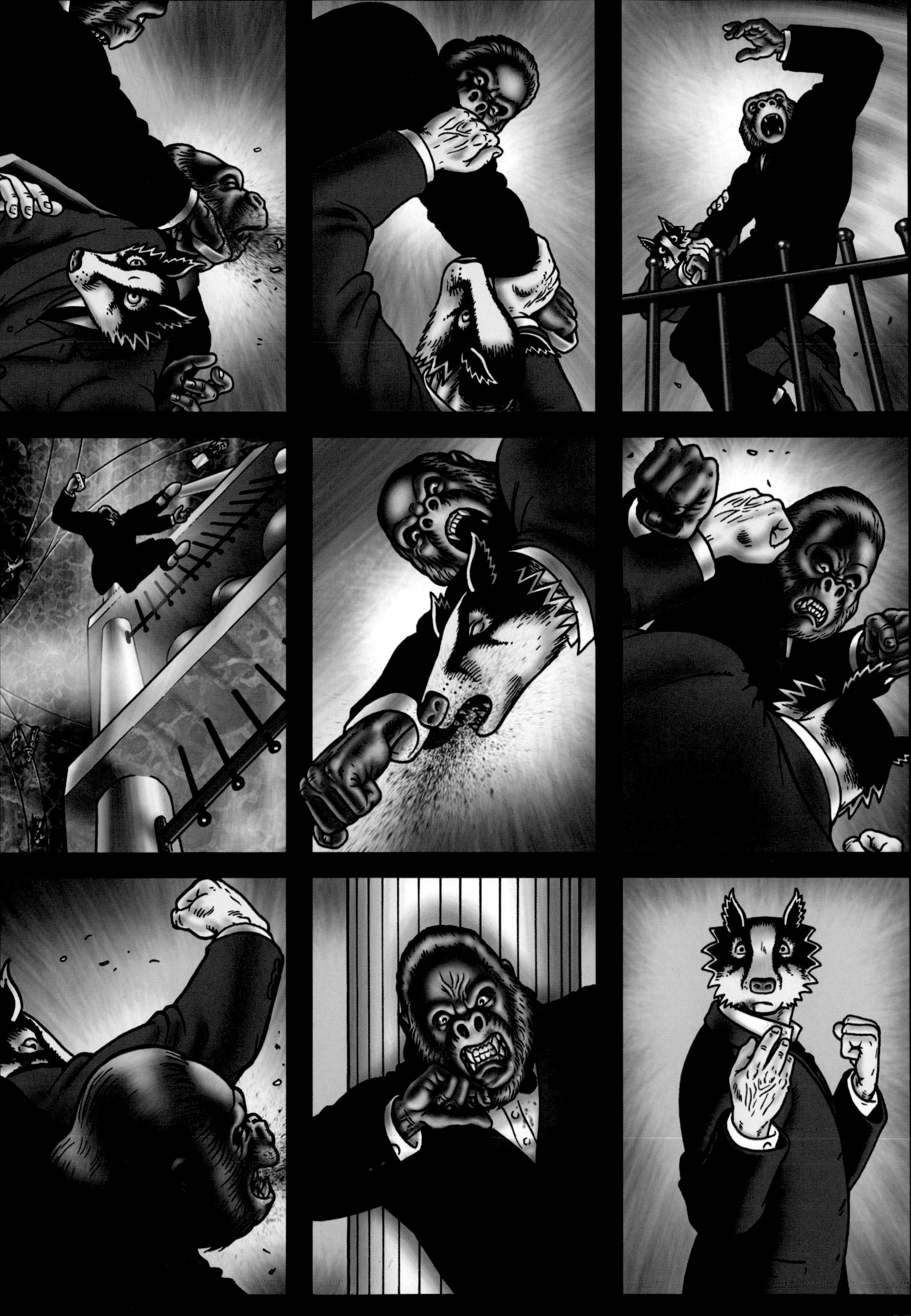

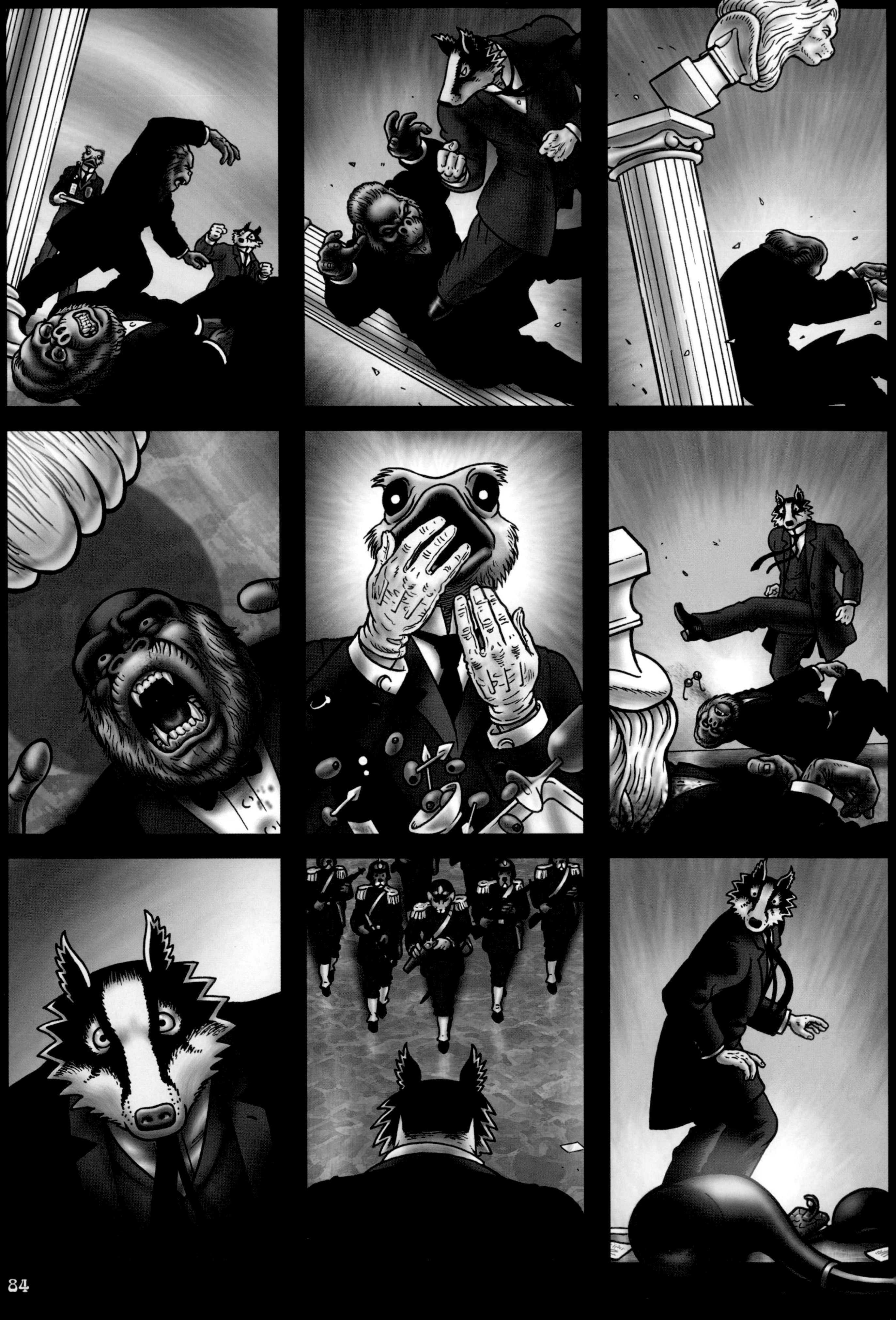

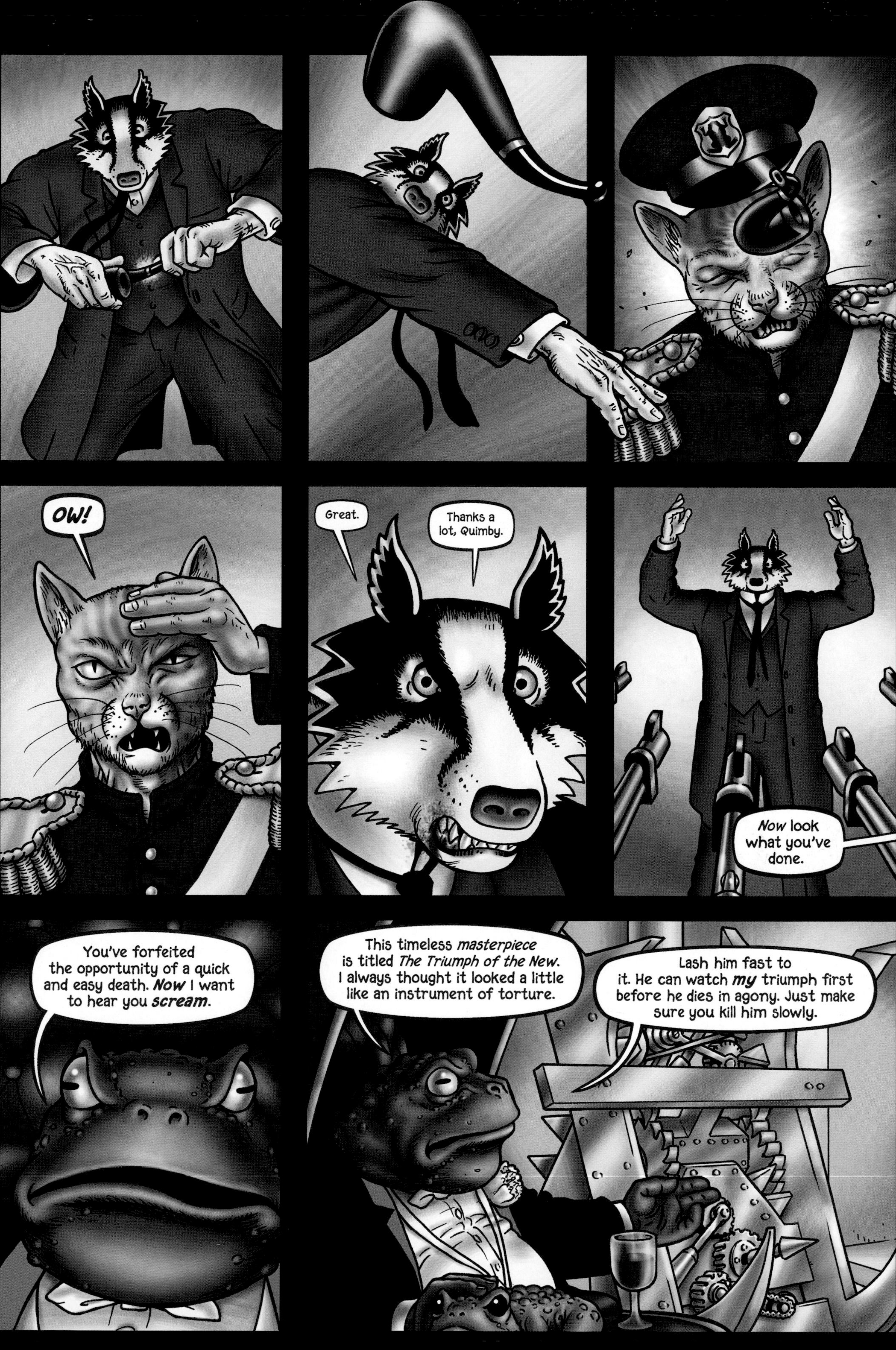
OW!
Great.
Thanks a lot, Quimby.
Now look what you've done.
You've forfeited the opportunity of a quick and easy death. ***Now*** I want to hear you ***scream***.
This timeless *masterpiece* is titled *The Triumph of the New*. I always thought it looked a little like an instrument of torture.
Lash him fast to it. He can watch ***my*** triumph first before he dies in agony. Just make sure you kill him slowly.

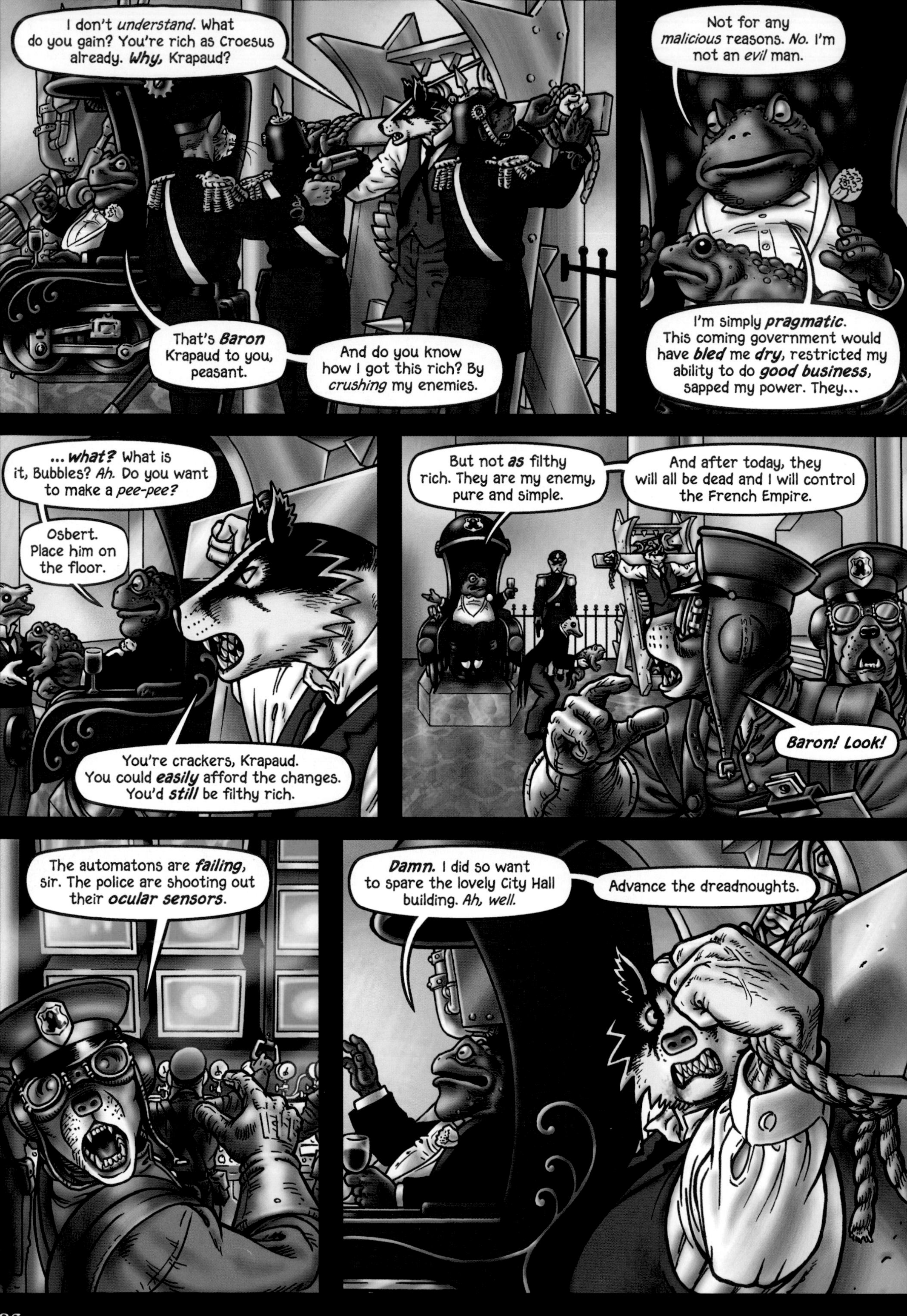
I don't *understand*. What do you gain? You're rich as Croesus already. ***Why,*** Krapaud?
That's ***Baron*** Krapaud to you, peasant.
And do you know how I got this rich? By *crushing* my enemies.
Not for any *malicious* reasons. *No.* I'm not an *evil* man.
I'm simply ***pragmatic***. This coming government would have ***bled*** me ***dry***, restricted my ability to do ***good business***, sapped my power. They...
...what? What is it, Bubbles? *Ah.* Do you want to make a *pee-pee?*
Osbert. Place him on the floor.
You're crackers, Krapaud. You could ***easily*** afford the changes. You'd ***still*** be filthy rich.
But not ***as*** filthy rich. They are my enemy, pure and simple.
And after today, they will all be dead and I will control the French Empire.
Baron! Look!
The automatons are ***failing***, sir. The police are shooting out their ***ocular sensors***.
Damn. I did so want to spare the lovely City Hall building. *Ah, well.*
Advance the dreadnoughts.

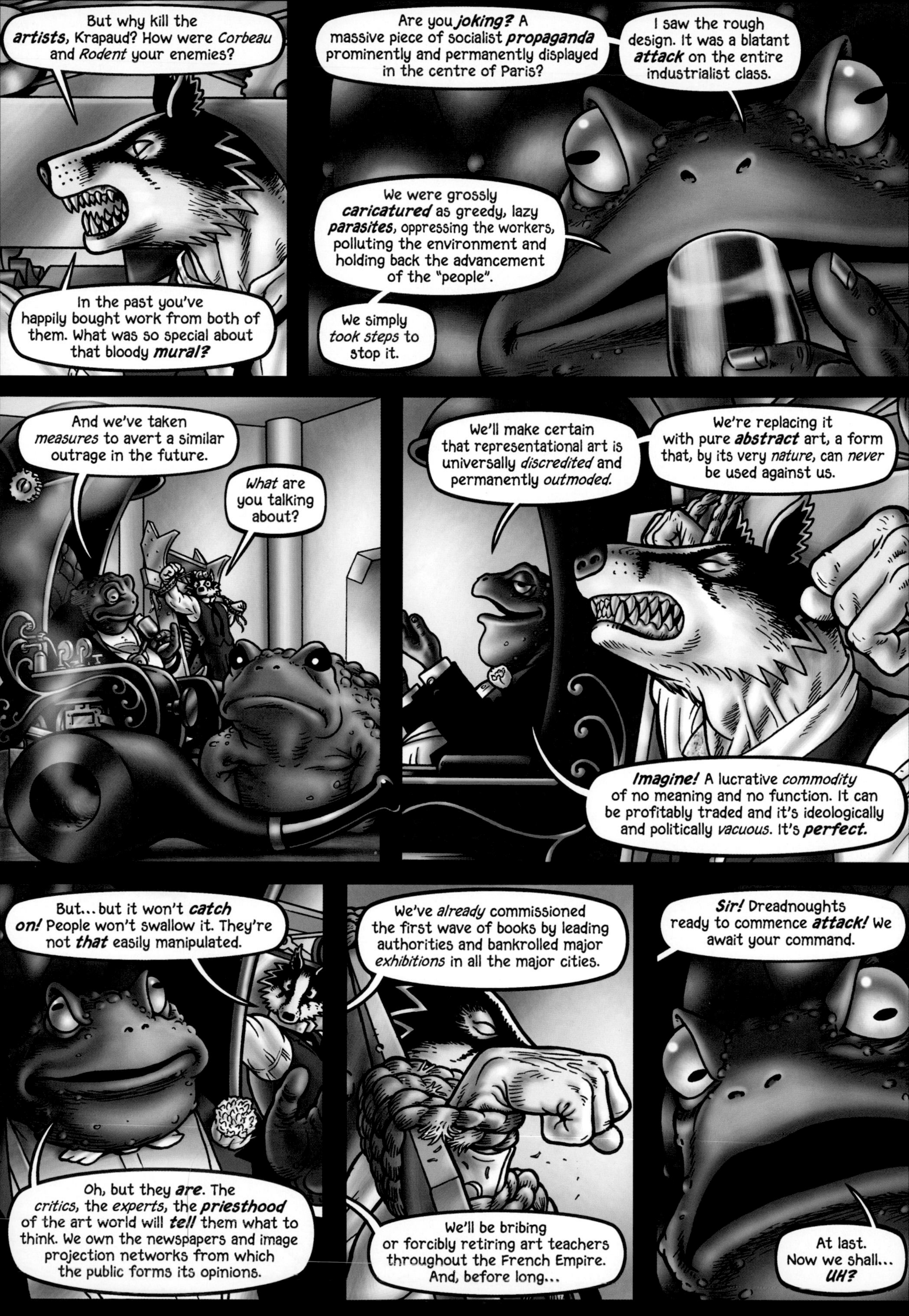
But why kill the artists, Krapaud? How were Corbeau and Rodent your enemies?
In the past you've happily bought work from both of them. What was so special about that bloody mural?
Are you joking? A massive piece of socialist propaganda prominently and permanently displayed in the centre of Paris?
I saw the rough design. It was a blatant attack on the entire industrialist class.
We were grossly caricatured as greedy, lazy parasites, oppressing the workers, polluting the environment and holding back the advancement of the "people".
We simply took steps to stop it.
And we've taken measures to avert a similar outrage in the future.
What are you talking about?
We'll make certain that representational art is universally discredited and permanently outmoded.
We're replacing it with pure abstract art, a form that, by its very nature, can never be used against us.
Imagine! A lucrative commodity of no meaning and no function. It can be profitably traded and it's ideologically and politically vacuous. It's perfect.
But... but it won't catch on! People won't swallow it. They're not that easily manipulated.
Oh, but they are. The critics, the experts, the priesthood of the art world will tell them what to think. We own the newspapers and image projection networks from which the public forms its opinions.
We've already commissioned the first wave of books by leading authorities and bankrolled major exhibitions in all the major cities.
We'll be bribing or forcibly retiring art teachers throughout the French Empire. And, before long...
Sir! Dreadnoughts ready to commence attack! We await your command.
At last. Now we shall... UH?

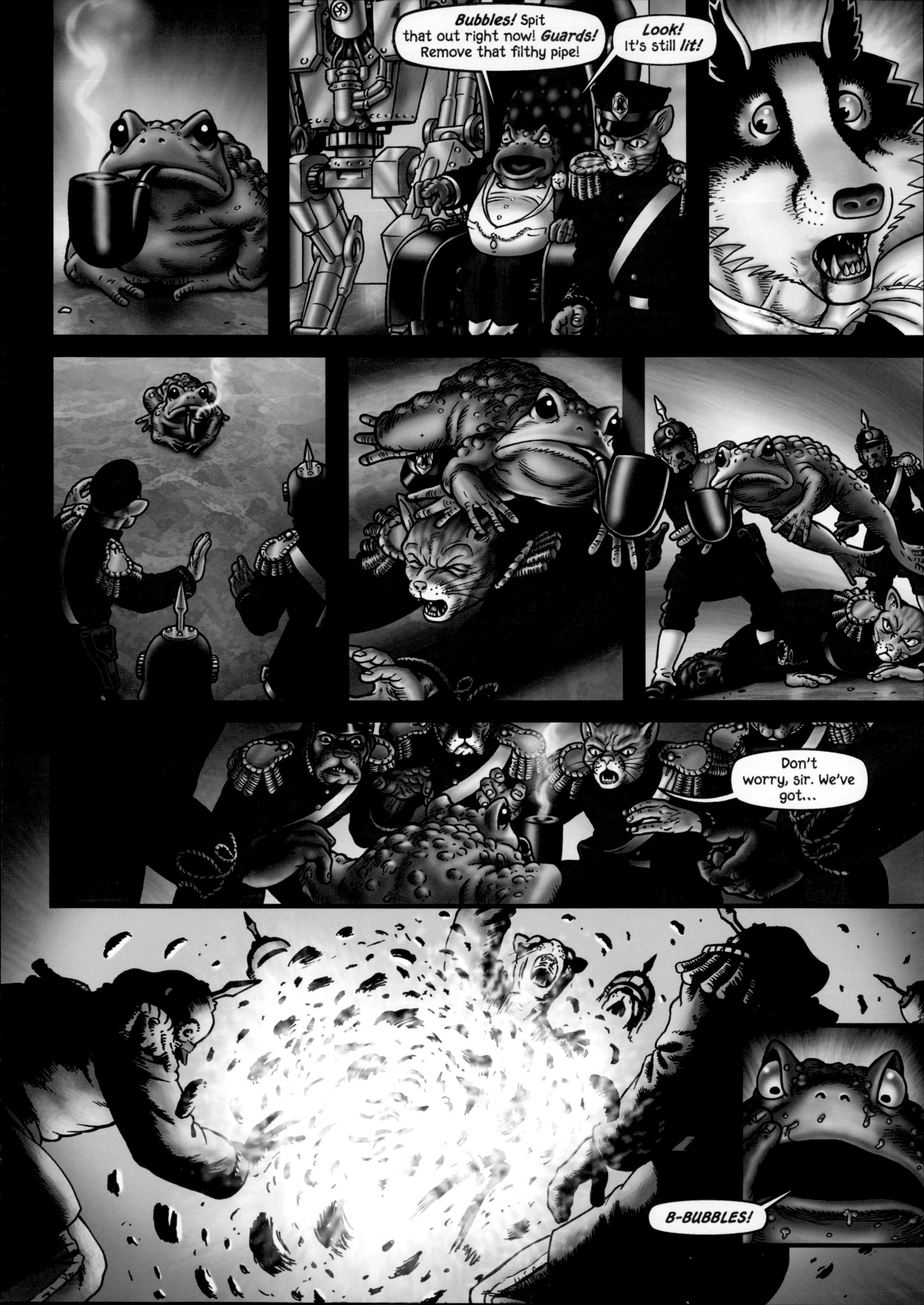

Bubbles! Spit that out right now! Guards! Remove that filthy pipe!
Look! It's still lit!
Don't worry, sir. We've got...
B-BUBBLES!

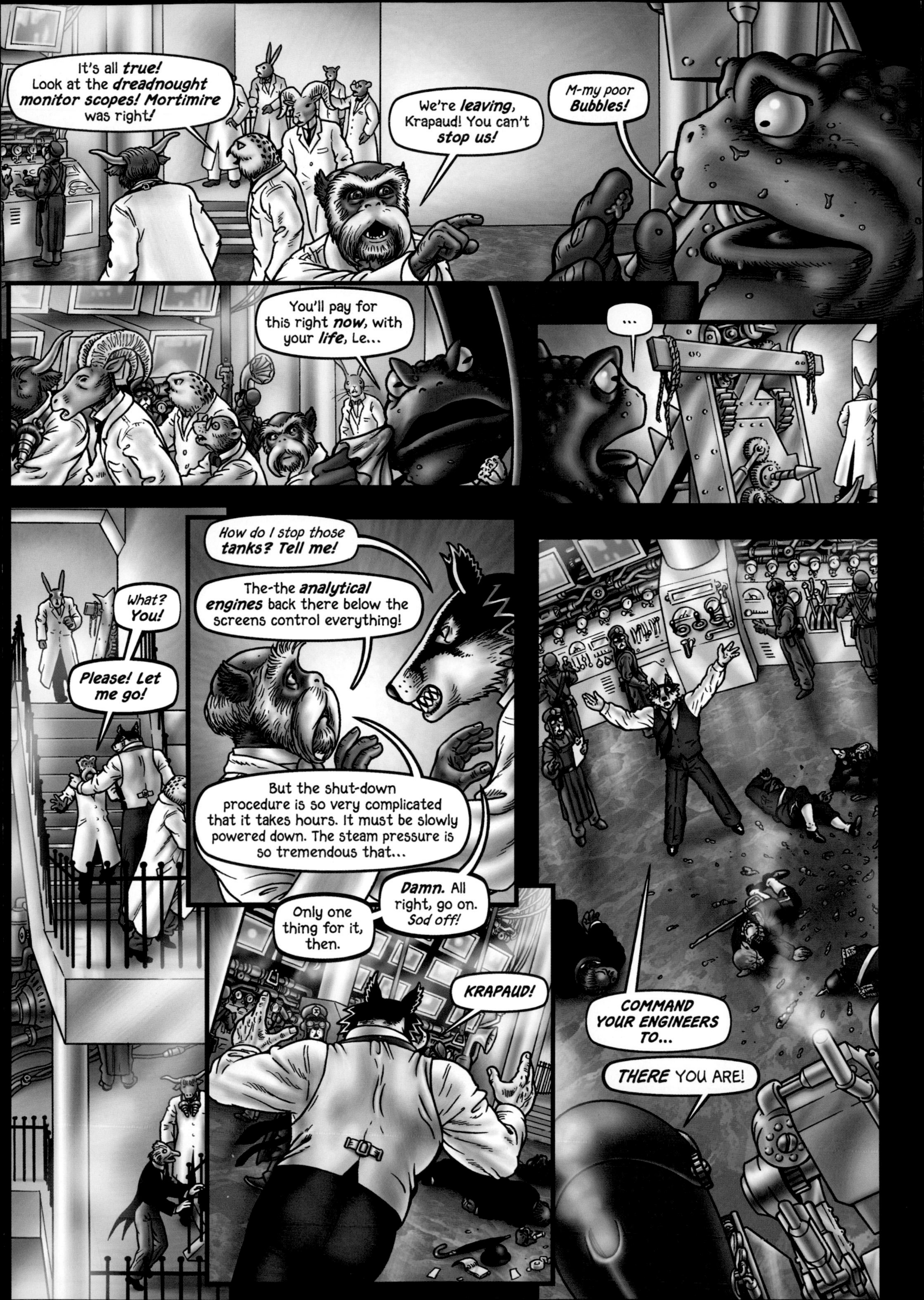
It's all *true!* Look at the *dreadnought monitor scopes! Mortimire* was right*!*
We're *leaving,* Krapaud! You can't *stop us!*
M-my poor ***Bubbles!***
You'll pay for this right *now,* with your *life,* Le...
...
What? ***You!***
Please! Let me go!
How do I stop those ***tanks? Tell me!***
The-the *analytical engines* back there below the screens control everything!
But the shut-down procedure is so very complicated that it takes hours. It must be slowly powered down. The steam pressure is so tremendous that...
Damn. All right, go on. *Sod off!*
Only one thing for it, then.
KRAPAUD!
COMMAND YOUR ENGINEERS TO...
THERE YOU ARE!

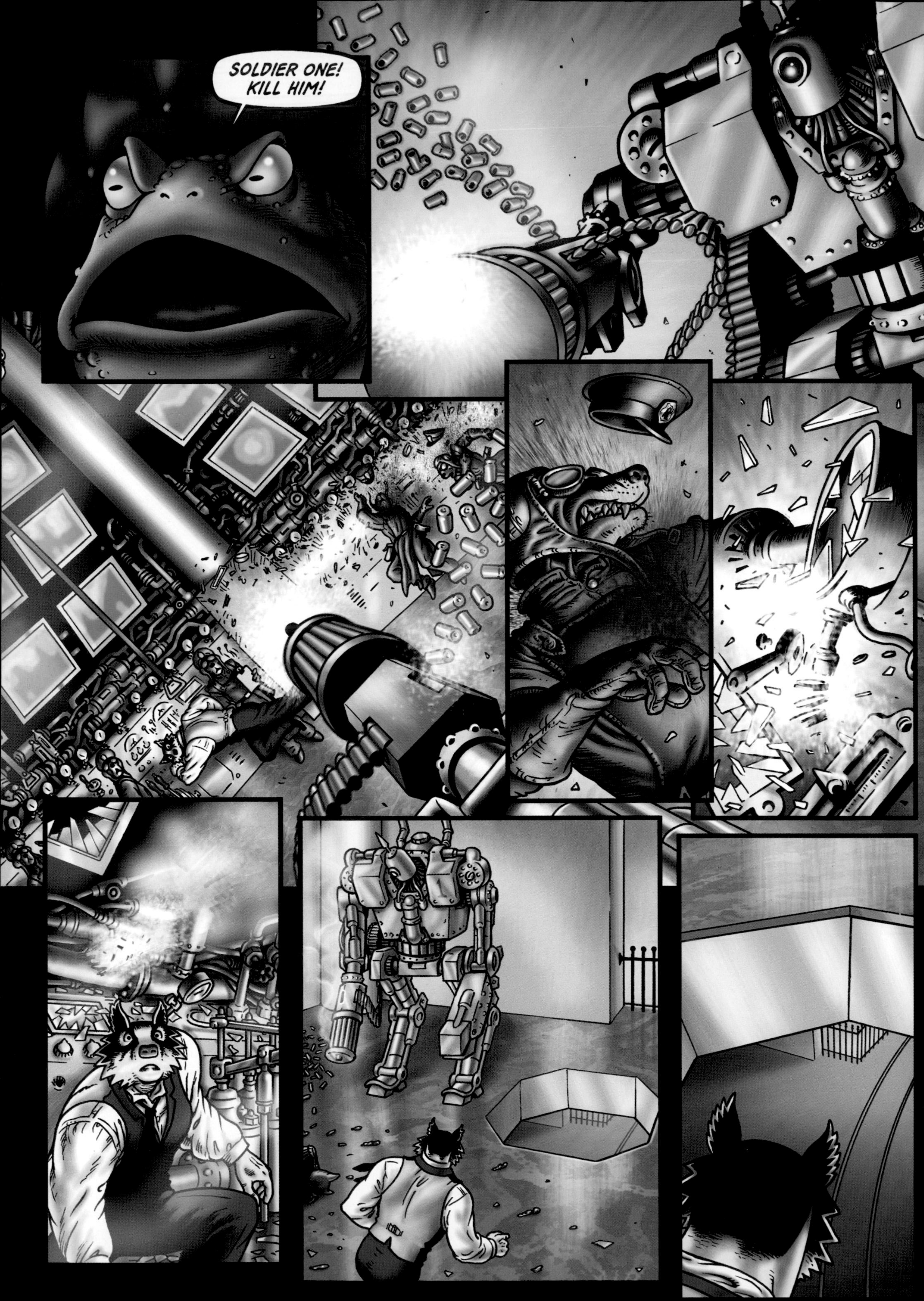
SOLDIER ONE! KILL HIM!

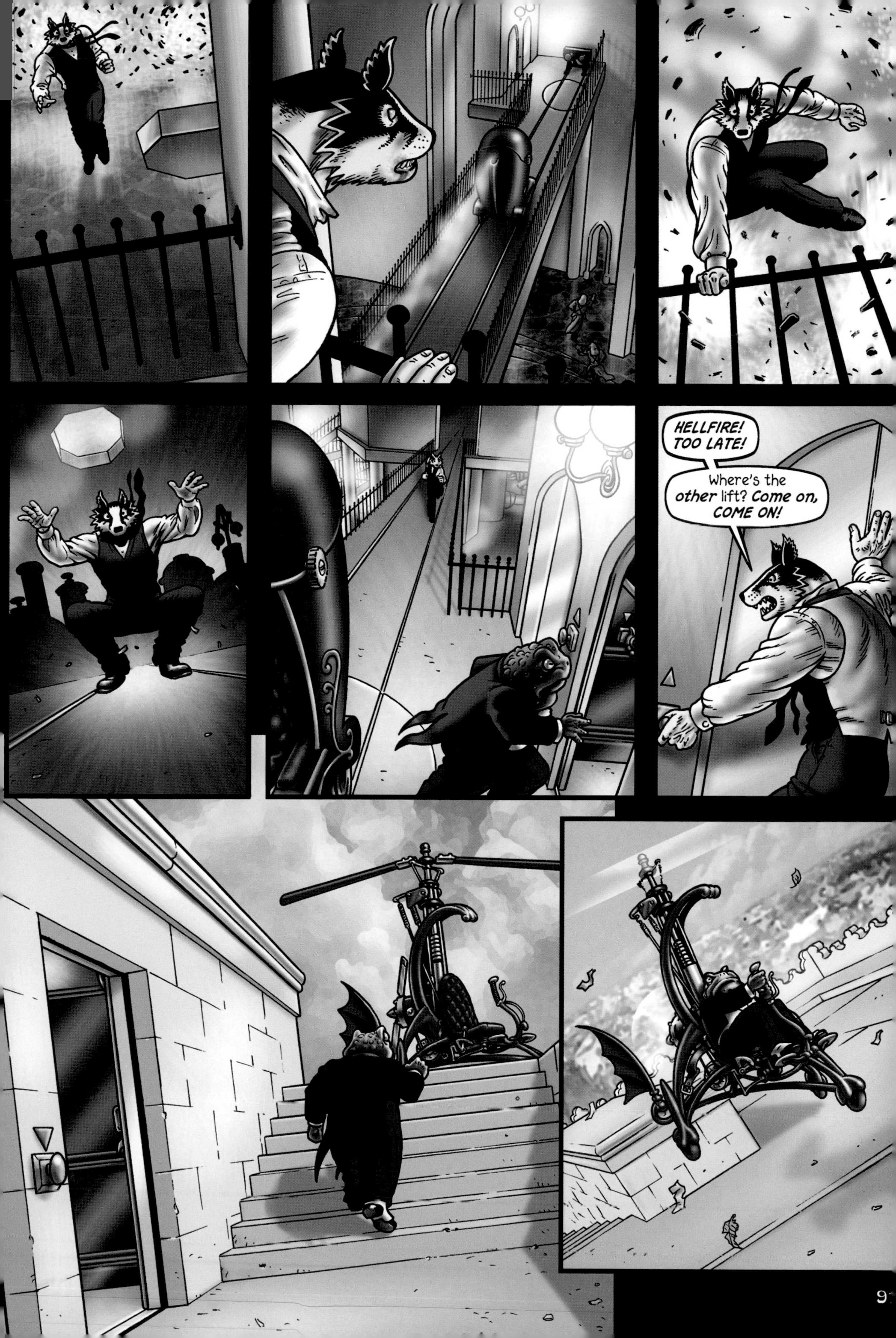
HELLFIRE! TOO LATE!
Where's the other lift? Come on, COME ON!

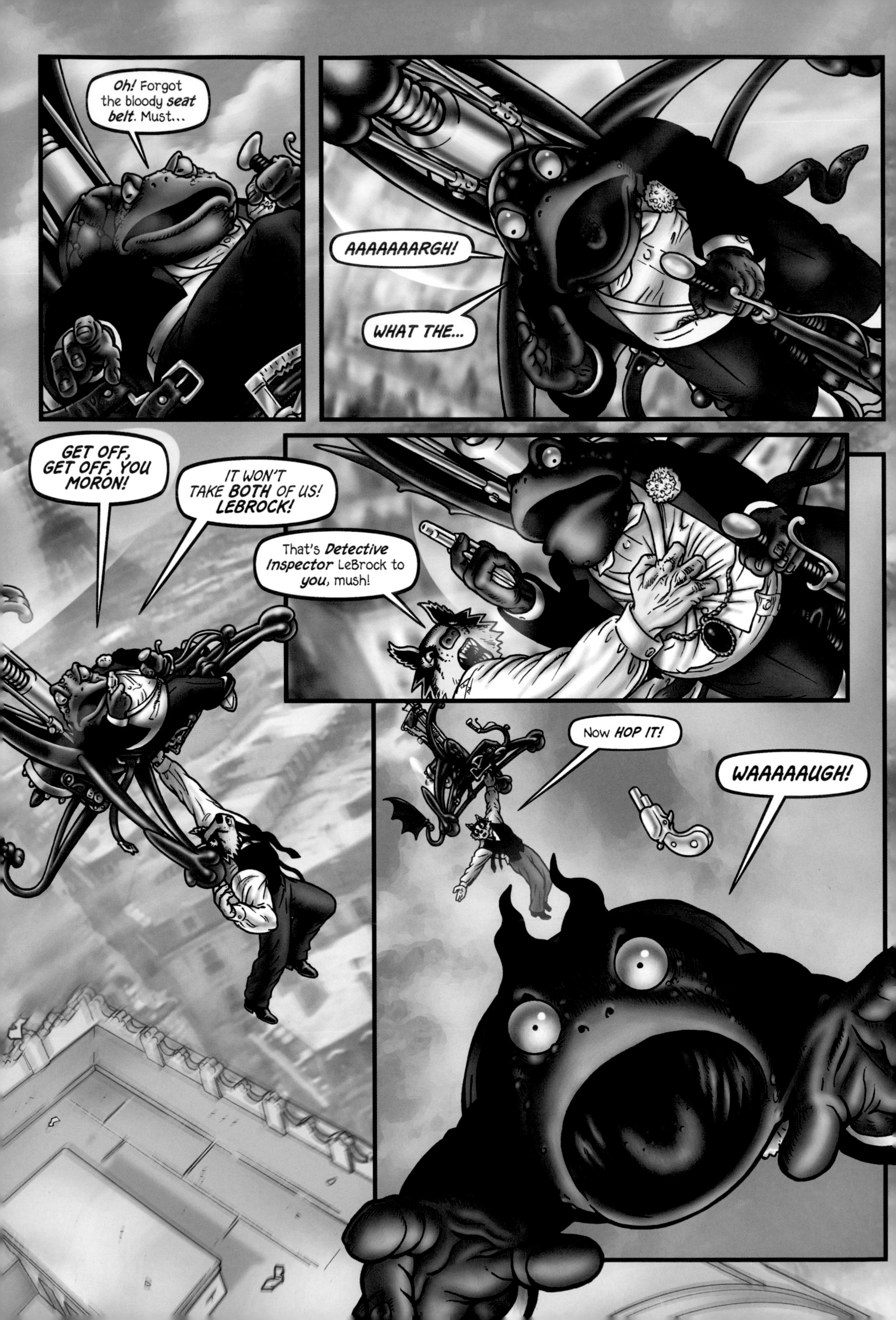
Oh! Forgot the bloody ***seat belt***. Must...
AAAAAAARGH!
WHAT THE...
GET OFF, GET OFF, YOU MORON!
IT WON'T TAKE **BOTH** OF US! **LEBROCK!**
That's ***Detective Inspector*** LeBrock to ***you***, mush!
Now ***HOP IT!***
WAAAAAUGH!

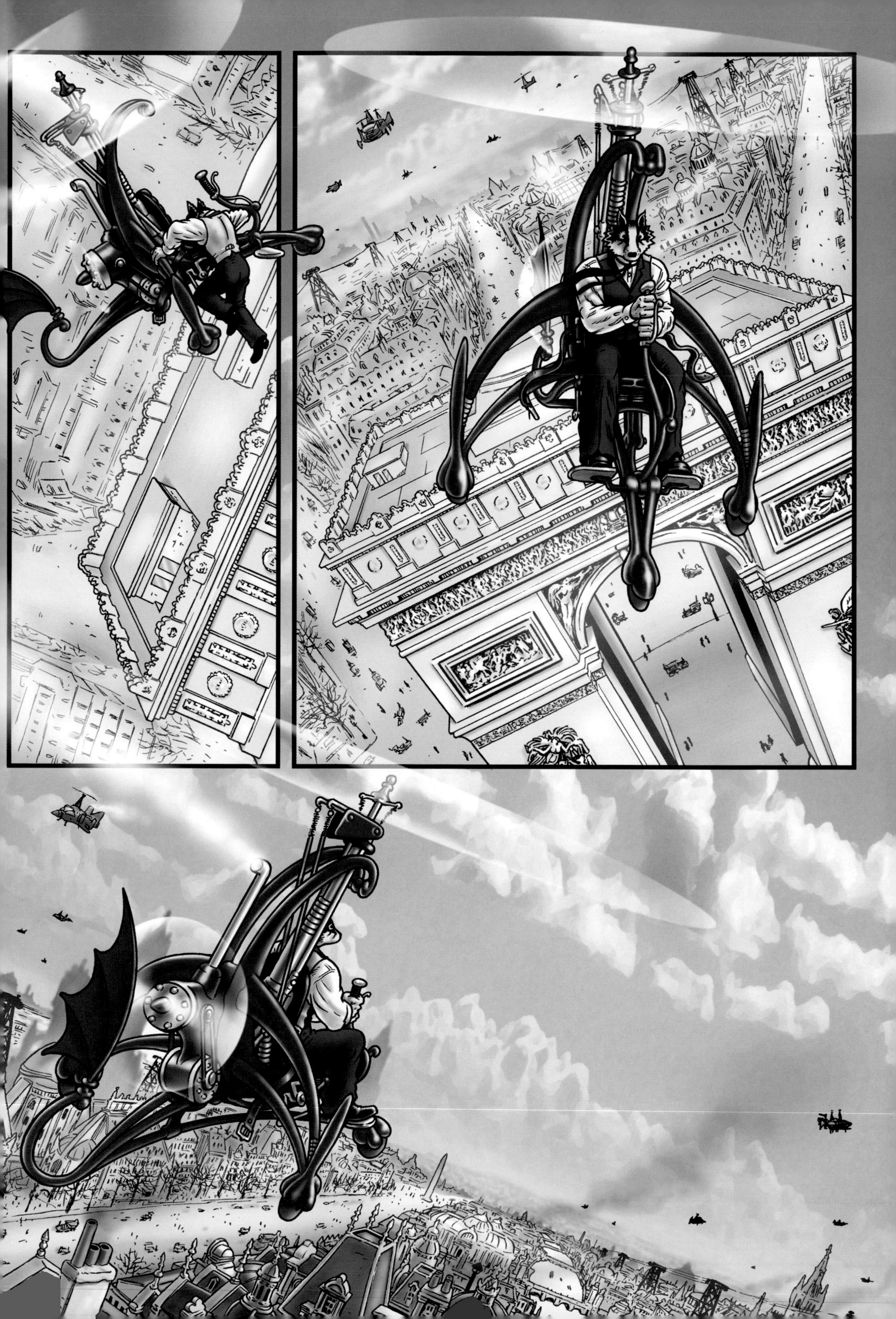

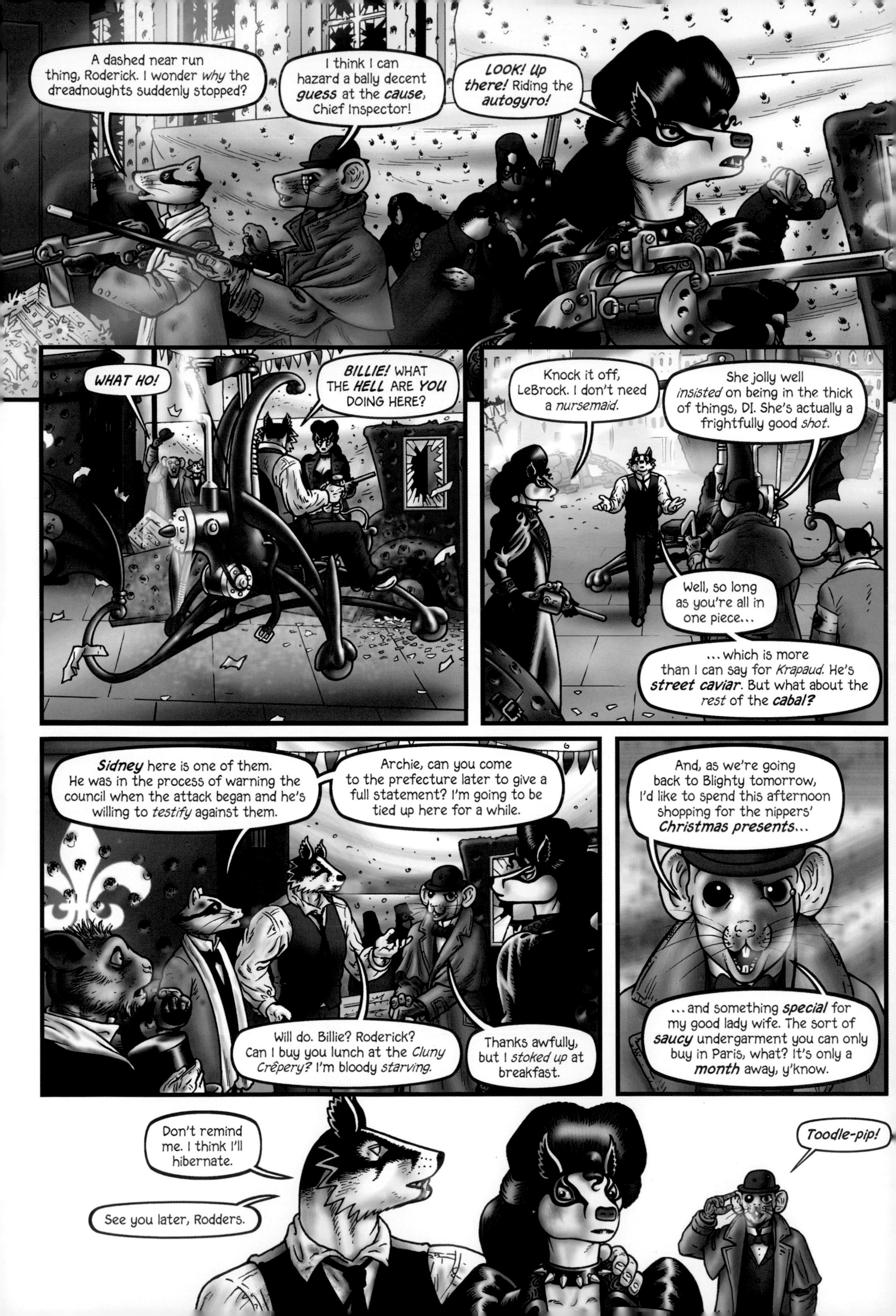

A dashed near run thing, Roderick. I wonder *why* the dreadnoughts suddenly stopped?
I think I can hazard a bally decent **guess** at the **cause**, Chief Inspector!
LOOK! Up there! Riding the ***autogyro!***
WHAT HO!
BILLIE! WHAT THE ***HELL*** ARE ***YOU*** DOING HERE?
Knock it off, LeBrock. I don't need a *nursemaid*.
She jolly well *insisted* on being in the thick of things, DI. She's actually a frightfully good *shot*.
Well, so long as you're all in one piece...
...which is more than I can say for *Krapaud*. He's ***street caviar***. But what about the *rest* of the ***cabal?***
Sidney here is one of them. He was in the process of warning the council when the attack began and he's willing to *testify* against them.
Archie, can you come to the prefecture later to give a full statement? I'm going to be tied up here for a while.
Will do. Billie? Roderick? Can I buy you lunch at the *Cluny Crêpery*? I'm bloody *starving*.
Thanks awfully, but I *stoked up* at breakfast.
And, as we're going back to Blighty tomorrow, I'd like to spend this afternoon shopping for the nippers' ***Christmas presents***...
...and something ***special*** for my good lady wife. The sort of ***saucy*** undergarment you can only buy in Paris, what? It's only a ***month*** away, y'know.
Don't remind me. I think I'll hibernate.
See you later, Rodders.
Toodle-pip!

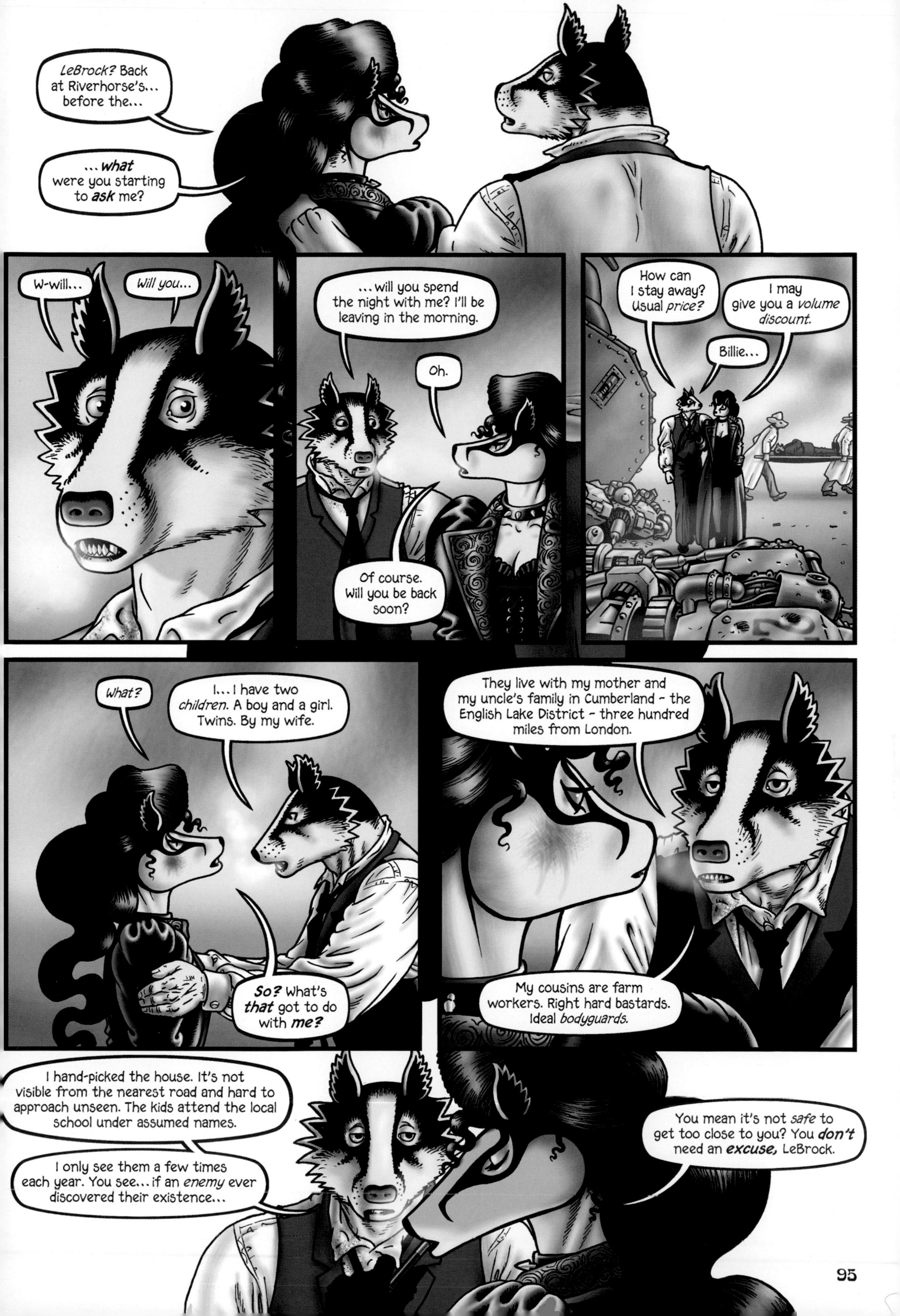

LeBrock? Back at Riverhorse's... before the...
...***what*** were you starting to ***ask*** me?
W-will...
Will you...
...will you spend the night with me? I'll be leaving in the morning.
Oh.
Of course. Will you be back soon?
How can I stay away? Usual *price?*
I may give you a *volume discount.*
Billie...
What?
I... I have two *children.* A boy and a girl. Twins. By my wife.
So? What's ***that*** got to do with ***me?***
They live with my mother and my uncle's family in Cumberland - the English Lake District - three hundred miles from London.
My cousins are farm workers. Right hard bastards. Ideal *bodyguards.*
I hand-picked the house. It's not visible from the nearest road and hard to approach unseen. The kids attend the local school under assumed names.
I only see them a few times each year. You see... if an *enemy* ever discovered their existence...
You mean it's not *safe* to get too close to you? You ***don't*** need an ***excuse,*** LeBrock.

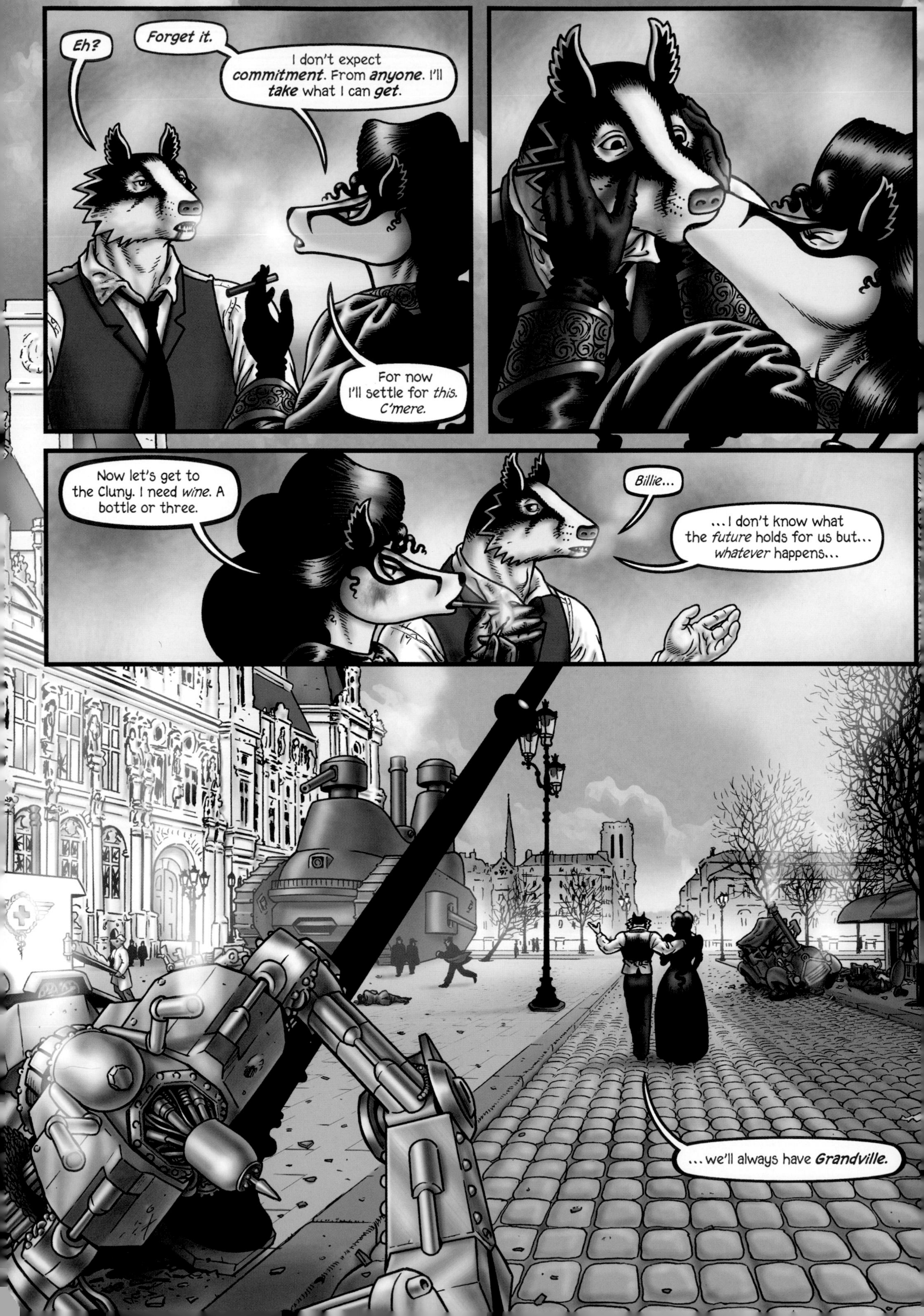
Eh?
Forget it.
I don't expect **commitment**. From **anyone**. I'll ***take*** what I can ***get***.
For now I'll settle for *this.* *C'mere.*
Now let's get to the Cluny. I need *wine.* A bottle or three.
Billie...
...I don't know what the *future* holds for us but... *whatever* happens...
...we'll always have ***Grandville.***

Grandville
Bête Noire

Fin

publication design
BRYAN TALBOT

publisher
MIKE RICHARDSON

editor
CHRIS WARNER

GRANDVILLE™ BÊTE NOIRE

Dark Horse Books®
10956 S.E. Main Street
Milwaukie OR 97222

DarkHorse.com

To find a comics shop in your area, call the Comic Shop Locator Service toll-free at 1-888-266-4226

First edition: December 2012
ISBN 978-1-59582-890-3

10 9 8 7 6 5 4 3 2 1
Printed at 1010 Printing International, Ltd., Guangdong Province, China

Afterword

The question that writers are most often asked is "Where do you get your ideas?" Ideas, of course, come from everywhere: everything that you hear and see, everything you read or experience. It's very rarely that I can point to a specific event or piece of information as a source of inspiration. *Grandville* is a notable exception. It came to me in a sort of creative rush while looking through a collection of the work of the early nineteenth-century French illustrator Jean Ignace Isidore Gérard, who drew under the nom de plume "J. J. Grandville." Even though I'd had this book for years, it only then suddenly occurred to me that "Grandville" could be a nickname for Paris in an alternative reality in which it was the largest city in the world, the hub of a globe-spanning French empire populated by talking animals. The story practically wrote itself in the following week. Gérard's forte was the depiction of clothed animals behaving like people, illustrations of anthropomorphic characters satirizing contemporary mores of French society.

Grandville Bête Noire is, of course, a partial pastiche of the James Bond stories, with Toad from Kenneth Grahame's *The Wind in the Willows* in the role of Bond villain. I loved the book as a child but always hated the utterly selfish, egotistical, obsessive spoilt brat that was Toad. Roderick also partly comes from this book, being almost a mixture of Ratty, P. G. Wodehouse's Bertie Wooster, and Dorothy L. Sayers' Lord Peter Wimsey. Badger is the most capable character in the story and certainly one of the reasons that I chose one of that estimable species as *Grandville*'s protagonist.

Art history is a theme of and an inspiration for *Bête Noire*. Au Lapin Agile, run by the jovial Father Freddy, was the Montmartre lair of many an artist during La Belle Époque and it survives to this day. The punch-up at the Louvre between mainstream and radical artists is not that far removed from the brawl at the Théâtre des Champs-Elysées in 1923 during the Paris debut of George Antheil (as depicted in *Dotter of Her Father's Eyes*) and involved Marcel Duchamp, Man Ray, Picasso, and others, including an assortment of surrealists.

But what inspired the preposterous notion that millionaires would suppress figurative art and actively promote abstract expressionism for their own nefarious ends?

In 1933, art patron Nelson Rockefeller commissioned Mexican artist Diego Rivera to design a large mural for Rockefeller Center in New York City. Despite Rivera having made no secret of his pro-Communist sympathies, Rockefeller was taken aback by the prominent inclusion in the painting of the late Soviet leader Vladimir Lenin in a design that openly pitted socialist ideology against capitalism. Rivera refused to change the piece, resulting in orders to cease work on the project. In 1934, the mural was hammered into rubble in what was described by Rivera as "cultural vandalism." Thereafter, Nelson Rockefeller actively promoted abstract expressionism, a form that can carry no overt political message.

For two decades during the Cold War, abstract art was seen as a cultural weapon against the Soviet Union. The CIA spent millions of dollars promoting and staging international exhibitions of what Nelson Rockefeller had called "Free Enterprise Painting." In the propaganda war, works by the likes of Jackson Pollock, Mark Rothko, and Robert Motherwell were supposed proof of the intellectual freedom and cultural power of the USA, despite abstract art being deeply unpopular with the vast majority of American citizens. The CIA influenced newspapers, magazines, and art institutions, covertly funding publications that utilized art critics supportive of the movement. Using the analogy of the world as a jukebox, it was said that when the CIA pressed a button it could hear what it wanted playing all over the world. A conspiracy theory for decades, the CIA funding of abstract impressionism is now a matter of public record.

Bryan Talbot
Shropshire, June 2012

Other books by Bryan Talbot

Brainstorm!
The Adventures of Luther Arkwright
Heart of Empire
The Tale of One Bad Rat
Alice in Sunderland
The Art of Bryan Talbot
The Naked Artist (Prose)
Grandville
Grandville Mon Amour

Metronome
(Writing as Veronique Tanaka)

Cherubs!
(With Mark Stafford)

Nemesis the Warlock Vols 1 & 2
(With Pat Mills)

Sandman: Fables and Reflections
(With Neil Gaiman, Stan Woch & Mark Buckingham)

The Dead Boy Detectives and
the Secret of Immortality
(With Ed Brubaker & Steve Leialoha)

Dotter of Her Father's Eyes
(With Mary M Talbot)

www.bryan-talbot.com

Eisner and Eagle award winner Bryan Talbot has produced underground and alternative comics, notably *Brainstorm!*, and science-fiction and superhero stories, such as *Judge Dredd*, *Nemesis the Warlock*, *Teknophage*, *The Nazz*, and *Batman: Legends of the Dark Knight*. He's worked on DC Vertigo titles, including *Hellblazer*, *The Sandman*, *The Dreaming*, and *Fables*, and has written and drawn the graphic novels for which he is best known, including *The Adventures of Luther Arkwright*, *Heart of Empire*, *The Tale of One Bad Rat*, and *Alice in Sunderland*. He is published in over fifteen countries and is a frequent guest at international comic festivals. He was awarded an honorary Doctorate in Arts by Sunderland University in 2009 and a Doctorate in Letters by Northumbria University in 2012.

Illustration by JJ Grandville